C A R L Y L E

CARLYLE IN 1846

CARLYLE

⋙ ⋙ ⋘ ⋘

---

by EMERY NEFF

NEW YORK / RUSSELL & RUSSELL

TO

ASHLEY H. THORNDIKE

who opened my mind

to Carlyle

CONTENTS

꠹꠹ ꠸꠸

PREFACE

꧁ ꧂

IN interpreting the life and writings of Thomas Carlyle in the setting of his time, I have incurred debts to a host of biographers and scholars, from James Anthony Froude to Mr. David Alec Wilson and Mr. Isaac Dyer, many of whom I have the pleasure of naming in the appended notes and bibliography. I owe more, perhaps, than I can fully realize to the fresh and original point of view of my colleague and former teacher, Professor Ashley H. Thorndike, to whom this book is admiringly dedicated. My researches in Great Britain were generously facilitated by Professor and Mrs. John A. Carlyle, who entertained me at Craigenputtock, by Dr. Henry W. Meikle, who opened the rich resources of the National Library of Scotland, by Mr. Alexander Ormiston Curle, Director of the Royal Scottish Museum, by Mr. A. J. B. Wace, Deputy Keeper of the Victoria and Albert Museum, by the officials of the Reading Room of the British Museum, and by the late Mrs. Isabella Strong, of the Carlyle House, Chelsea. In the United States I have received the equally generous assistance of Miss Belle da Costa Greene, who permitted me to consult unpublished letters of the Carlyle family in the Pierpont Morgan Library, of Mr. Roger Howson, Librarian of Columbia University, of various officials of the New York Public Library, to whose courtesy I am indebted for the frontispiece, and of Professor George Nesbitt of Hamilton College and other former students, who have given me the benefit of their investi-

9

gations in Victorian periodicals. In the revision of the manuscript I have received valuable aid and advice from Professor Robert Morss Lovett of the University of Chicago, and from Mr. Elling Aannestad. I have had the advantage, in all matters, of the constantly available scholarship and taste of my wife, Wanda Fraiken Neff.

For the gracious hospitality of Yaddo during the planning of this book, I welcome the opportunity to express my gratitude to Mrs. Elizabeth Ames. The quiet and detachment of the Mac-Dowell Colony for two summers, which enabled me to complete the writing, I owe to Mrs. Edward MacDowell and her staff of assistants, whose many favors it is impossible to acknowledge.

Permission to quote from *The Love Letters of Thomas Carlyle and Jane Welsh* and *New Letters of Thomas Carlyle* was courteously given by the late Alexander Carlyle.

Mr. William Maxse Meredith and Charles Scribner's Sons have kindly authorized extended quotation from a letter of George Meredith.

E. N.

Columbia University,
January 6, 1932

CARLYLE

ERRATA.

Page 44, line 5, for ' effecive ' read ' effective '

Page 130, line 24, for ' Kayldor ' read ' Kalydor '

Page 156, line 20, for ' Shilbeer ' read ' Shillibeer '

Page 176, line 25, for ' contrasts ' read ' contrast '

Page 98, line 24, for ' 882 - foot Glaister's Hill ' read ' 1300 - foot Craigenputtock Hill '

Page 150, line 34, for ' Glaister's Hill ' read ' Craigenputtock Hill '

Page 187, line 19, for ' offered to lead ' read ' considered leading '

Page 235, - 236, delete paragraph reading ' with steadier employment . . . . glass windows '

Page 257, line 29, for ' Jane ' read ' Mary '

Page 260, line 18, for ' one of his nieces ' read ' his niece '

CHAPTER I

THE SCOTCH VILLAGE

⊰⊰⊰ ⊱⊱⊱

§ 1

CARLYLE'S birthplace, Ecclefechan, lies in the western Lowlands of Scotland, close to the English border. It is sheltered by wooded hills in the dale of the bright river Annan, a country of wide prospects. From Burnswark Hill, rising steeply behind Ecclefechan, one looks to the south-west upon a great arm of the sea, Solway Firth, so shallow that low tide exposes miles of sand and mud flats. Across the Solway to the south stand distinct the mountains of English Cumberland, Skiddaw, Helvellyn, thronging peaks renowned in the verse of Wordsworth, Southey, and Coleridge. To the south-east is Yorkshire. Northward loom the Scottish mountains of Galloway, joining the Carlyle and Burns countries; and north-eastward the eye follows the Annan to its source near Moffat, where heights shut off the eastern Lowlands centring in Edinburgh and meeting the English border in the Scott country of Tweeddale.

In 1795, the year of Carlyle's birth, Ecclefechan was on the main line of communication between these areas. Twice daily mail coaches stopped to change horses; going northward from England to Moffat, where the coach-route divided toward Glasgow and toward Edinburgh, and going southward to English Carlisle, nineteen miles from Ecclefechan, and thence to Manchester and London. Another route to England was by sailing

13

vessel from the mouth of the Annan, six miles distant, around the Solway to Liverpool.

Ecclefechan was a village of some five hundred inhabitants, a centre for one of the most fertile districts of Scotland, and well known for its weekly swine markets, monthly cattle markets, and yearly fairs attracting thirsty drovers who were the chief support of its four hotels and twenty-two other "tippling houses." Its stable population, besides agricultural workers, included, in those latter days of hand labor, a great variety of artisans, and hand-loom weavers of woollen cloth. In his boyhood Carlyle sang "Blind Harry's" ballads of Wallace to cheer the weavers at their work according to the custom of centuries, but stage-coaches stopping to change horses gave him glimpses of Glasgow and Manchester manufacturers enriched by the machine industry which was to starve and then to ruin the unlucky handloomers. Agriculture was likewise on the verge of change. In the year before Carlyle's birth, peasants in the vicinity were protesting against the lingering feudal obligations of "boon work" on the landlord's fields and "thirlage" in his mills; [1] but the more prosperous had already become "farmers" with leases of twelve to twenty-one years, which gave them an interest in improved agricultural methods, and, before long, in agricultural machinery.

Ecclefechan had an unusually wide main street, through the accident of an open "burn" or creek running along it. Beside this little stream, in which ducks paddled, Thomas Carlyle was born on December 4, 1795, in a thatched stone cottage. Before he was three years old, his parents, who meanwhile had had a second son, Alexander, removed some distance to the rear, into a larger house in a walled garden. Here were born four sisters and two more brothers, of whom John, six years younger than Thomas, was to play an important part in his history. The economic position of the Carlyles was in the lower middle class, distinctly above the average for the village. But the Scotch standard of living was low; the quarters of the family of ten were crowded, especially for sleeping, and the food was potatoes, milk, and the national oatmeal, seldom varied by meat or other luxuries. Yet the household was neither slatternly nor vulgar, having rather the home-spun cleanliness and the pious dignity described by Burns in "The Cotter's Saturday Night."

The head of the house, James Carlyle, a master-mason em-ploying helpers, was a stern, self-made man of whom the children stood in awe. His own childhood had been of Spartan severity. His father, neglecting a small farm to hunt and carouse with his distant cousin, the Laird of Bridekirk, had left his boys to shift for themselves by doing odd jobs for neighbors and by hunting like Indians. The Bible, taught by the local schoolmaster, had raised James Carlyle above the rude standards of a countryside which respected the fighter, the hunter, the hard drinker, and had made him a sober, frugal, industrious artisan. The stoicism result-ing from his early privations was indurated by religion according to the Burgher sect, which proscribed cards, fiction reading, and other frivolous amusements, and pointed a straight and narrow way between Heaven and the literal flames of Hell. His humor was rare and "of a most grim Scandinavian sort." He was read in few books but the Bible. Yet when deeply moved to sorrow or anger, he had an amazing gift of picturesque speech, which his sons inherited: "he had no need of oaths; his words were sharp arrows which smote into the very heart." He taught his children to speak the truth and to abhor bad workmanship, fundamental principles in the writings of his famous son. The children admired him, but "his heart seemed as if walled in" from them. For demonstrative affection they turned to their mother, the daughter of a small farmer, as pious and frugal as her husband, but gentle and often over-fearful of their taking the risks of village play. Thomas Carlyle combined the dis-similar natures of his parents. "He's as hard as granite and soft as a rabbit," observed his puzzled father. Pity and anger, sym-pathy and intolerance, in bewildering union, were to remain at the core of his mature personality.

He led the barefoot out-of-door life of the village boy, but soon stood out from other children by his cleverness and curiosity. Fortunately, though his parents could give little to feed his mind, Ecclefechan did not have the imagination-killing lack of background of the usual American village. Burnswark Hill had been a fortified Roman station, and young Tom was sometimes called to decipher, with his school-boy Latin, inscriptions on tools and stone figures dug up on the site of the town of Blatum or Blato-Bulgum. In the years of his fame as an historian he liked to recall his first encounter with remains of an ancient civilization, a *cloaca* or sewer, "strange face-to-face vestige of the vanished æons." Annandale still rang with ballads of Border warfare, in the course of which King James V, the father of Mary Queen of Scots, had watched from Burnswark Hill the burning of English farms by his army of 10,000 men, driven before the day was over into marshes of the Solway in a crushing defeat that broke his heart. As recently as 1745 Ecclefechan had seen Prince Charlie with his Highland clansmen retreat from the final effort to restore the Scottish Stuarts to the English throne. To the north, just beyond the market centre and county town of Dumfries, rose the mountains where the Covenanters had made their last stand against the attempt of the Stuarts to force upon them the episcopal authoritarianism of the Church of England. Searching in the Dumfries graveyard for old Covenanter inscriptions, Tom chanced upon something of very different import: an inconspicuous flat stone with Robert Burns on it and the dates 1759-1796, inspiring symbol of the literary fame that might lie before a poor Scottish lad. And four miles out of Dumfries on the road to Ecclefechan he often passed the ruined tower of the Carlyles of Torthorwald, feudal barons to whom tradition traced his descent. His adoption in 1825 of their crest with griffins and the motto *Humilitate* as a seal and later as a bookplate, shows how far this sense of good blood entered into Carlyle's dreams of his future.

§ 2

POVERTY was not the terrible obstacle to the intellectual development of the ambitious poor that it was elsewhere in Europe.

For Scotland gave opportunities for cheap education unrivalled except in the young republic across the Atlantic.[2] These opportunities the Scotch owed to their religion. A Protestantism that encouraged laymen to read the Bible and opened the ministry to men of intelligence and morals, regardless of their origin, had need of universal elementary education. This, which England was not to offer until 1870, had been provided in Scotland since 1696 by legislation establishing a schoolmaster in every parish to teach reading, writing, arithmetic, and Latin for a nominal fee. As a consequence, the Scotch were the best educated peasantry in Europe. The Ecclefechan villagers, gathered in the evenings around the big sycamore opposite the Grapes Inn, delighted in discussion of theological subtleties incomprehensible to Englishmen of their station in life.

Thomas entered the Ecclefechan school at the age of five. The master proving incompetent, the promising boy from the age of six was sent trudging through a mile-long avenue of fine old beech trees to Hoddam Parish school, where he learned his three R's and Latin. Out of school hours he attracted the notice of his elders by skill in checkers and in arithmetic, the forms of intellectual distinction most readily understood in a village community. "Tom, I do not grudge thy schooling, now when thy Uncle Frank owns thee to be a better Arithmetician than himself," his father said in a burst of confidence, probably when he was transferring him at the age of eleven to Annan Academy, six miles away, where he boarded with a great-aunt.

This day school at Annan, a thriving port and market town of 2,000 inhabitants, was in advance of the contemporary English Public School in stressing algebra and geometry and making French compulsory, though otherwise it repeated much less competently the routine of Latin stimulated by the rod, and offered no Greek beyond the alphabet. Coeducation was another novelty of the Scottish secondary school. Socially, however, it gave none of the cultural advantages of the English Public Schools with their exclusiveness and high fees, for the children of the Scottish gentlefolk were educated by tutors in their homes.

Indeed the Annan pupils, using a Scottish dialect, had to be taught English to a considerable extent as a foreign tongue. Carlyle learned to speak and write correctly, but his pronunciation remained Annandale to the end of his days, as David Hume's had remained Berwickshire. He was eager for instruction in music and drawing, for which his keenness of ear and eye especially fitted him; but that was unobtainable. A desire to deserve his father's confidence by learning docilely whatever his teachers bade, even to meaningless Latin exercises against which he inwardly rebelled, did not endear him to his schoolmates. He replied to their bullying by formidable sarcasm and invective like his father's, that earned him many beatings so long as he obeyed the promise of Christian non-resistance made to his mother. But the Carlyle temper finally got the better of his pledge, and he dealt a tormenter such a blow with one of his "clogs" (wooden shoes shod with iron) that he had henceforth considerable respite from the coarseness and brutality of boys reared in the Border fighting tradition.

The uncongeniality of his school companions was relieved by access to a circulating library maintained by the Annan cooper, Maconachie, from which he had sufficient pocket money to borrow two books a week. Among these was Robertson's *Charles V,* which gave him his first conception of history. Without guidance, he devoured any reading matter that came his way: *"Roderick Random,* with great delight, a bundle of old numbers of *The Lady's Magazine,* another of the *Belfast County Almanac* sewn together," the last including a department of mathematical questions which he worked out for himself. Despite its brutality, *Roderick Random* fascinated him by its theme of a poor Scotch boy seeking his fortune in London and in the West Indies. Shakespeare he happened upon in a picturesque fashion. One market day in Annan, an Italian, crying "images," displayed plaster casts for sale. A woman in the crowd gathered about him read beneath a bust a name she pronounced "Shankspeare" and the lines beginning "The cloud-capt towers—." The schoolboy Tom listened entranced to the concluding words, "our little life is rounded with a sleep," and sought out the plays, which then were not thrust upon unwilling and ungrateful students. The existence of poetry had already come as a "revelation" when he heard a companion recite "with ecstacy" the lyrics of the contemporary poet Campbell.

This enthusiasm for Campbell was shared by his father, who discouraged, though he wisely did not forbid, the boy's reading of novels and the local poet Burns, whose life and writings had been a scandal to the godly. The subjects Campbell chose were not fictitious, but from real history, "Lochiel," "The Mariners of England," "Hohenlinden," "The Battle of the Baltic," frequently episodes in the war with France which had been going on almost without interruption since two years before Thomas Carlyle's birth. The Napoleonic Wars were the chief topic of political discussion at Ecclefechan, and were regarded with feelings not entirely unmixed. Though all were united against a possible invasion by Napoleon, there was an undercurrent of sympathy for French democracy.

The Revolution and the writings of Tom Paine had spread talk about the rights of man among the lower classes in Scotland, a feudal country that had never had free institutions. In 1792, the year before England went to war with France, Robert Burns, exciseman at Dumfries, finding a smuggling brig armed with four "carronades" aground on a shoal in the Solway, had bought these contraband cannon and sent them as a personal contribution to the cause of French liberty. At that time there were great popular demonstrations in industrial centres like Glasgow, many of whose leaders were convicted of sedition for continued agitation after England declared war. The news of the conviction of the young lawyer Muir to fourteen years' transportation to Australia for having visited France and having recommended the reading of Paine's works set Burns to composing, in white-hot defiance, "Scots Wha Hae" to a tune said to have been sung by the Annandale spearmen as they repelled the charges of the English knights at Bannockburn. Henry Dundas, Viscount Melville and Lord Advocate, profiting by the fear that the contagion of French ideas might bring a reign of terror to the British Isles, and supplied with government patronage sufficient to control the tiny group privileged to vote for Scottish members of Parliament, had made himself virtual despot of Scotland. To prevent the spread of democratic ideas, he censored the press and forbade public meetings. But the independent spirit which had resisted English aggression for centuries, and had produced the Covenanting martyrs, still smoldered in the Scottish people, ready to leap into flame if favorable occasion arose.[8] James Carlyle, although prejudiced against Paine on account of his religious views, had abundant sympathy for the privations of the working classes during those lean years of war.

But the landed aristocracy waxed fat on their monopoly of foodstuffs, and out of their profits set up new buildings which made brisk business for a master stone-mason. James Carlyle felt able to give a university education to his promising son. Tuition at Edinburgh University was small, and living expenses could be pared down. Tom could walk to Edinburgh, share a room with two students as poor as himself, send his clothing home to be washed and mended by the carrier's cart that left for Ecclefechan every two weeks, and on its return receive eggs, oatmeal, potatoes, and other farm produce to cook for his frugal meals.

Scottish tradition pointed to the ministry as the proper vocation for such a brilliant, industrious, and pious youth. He had been reared as a Burgher, a sect that in 1734 had seceded from the established Church of Scotland in order to retain democratic choice of its ministers, free from dictation by aristocratic lay patrons. His father, however, prudently stretched a point by having Tom prepare to preach in the Church of Scotland, which, supported by government funds, paid its ministers better. Having met with nothing that threw a shadow of doubt upon Christianity, James Carlyle had no misgivings as to the effects of higher education. Nor did his son realize that the French and the mathematics he had learned at Annan Academy had fitted him for a type of study unheard of in Ecclefechan. Accompanying an older boy who had already studied at the University and a man driving a cart of potatoes on which he was privileged to rest when fatigued, in November, 1809, Thomas Carlyle, lacking a month of being fourteen, set out on a walk of almost a hundred miles to Edinburgh.

CHAPTER II

BLIND ALLEYS

-»» «««-

§ I

IN 1809, Edinburgh was rivalled only by London as an intellectual centre of the British Empire. The glories of the latter half of the eighteenth century, when Scotland surpassed England in philosophy with Hume, in biography with Boswell, in poetry with Burns, in geology with Hutton, in chemistry with Black, in medicine with Hunter and Cullen, in economics with Adam Smith, and in engineering with Watt, had left an Indian summer lingering over the ancient capital. Henry MacKenzie, "the Man of Feeling," remained as a link with the past generation of literary men, Dugald Stewart with the philosophers, Playfair with the scientists, and Raeburn with the great tradition of portrait painting. The younger generation was exhibiting new powers in the poetry of Scott and the political and critical writing of the *Edinburgh Review* founded in 1802 with Francis Jeffrey as editor.

After the removal of the Scottish nobility to the Court at London following the Union with England in 1707, the legal profession, supreme in Edinburgh, imparted an intellectual tone to its social life. Lawyers, enjoying ample leisure, consorted with university professors and cultivated English visitors cut off from the Continent by the Napoleonic Wars. At dinner parties, amid hard drinking and general jollity, metaphysics, science, and political economy were topics of conversation. The influence of the

University was spread over the city by the attendance of mature
men at the lectures of celebrated professors and the mingling of
graduates in student debating societies, where they lent the weight
of their experience to free discussion of controversial topics, including religion and politics. Because of this widespread mental
activity, as well as her magnificent geographical situation, Edinburgh was soon to assert her claim to be the "Modern Athens."

Thus healthily connected with practical life, Edinburgh University offered the best educational opportunities available for a
man of Carlyle's background. It did not ask the high fees that
would have excluded him from Oxford or Cambridge, or even a
pledge of conformity with the doctrines of the Established
Church. It surpassed the English universities in the modernity
of its curriculum and the quality of its teachers.[4] Its schools of
Law and Medicine were the best in Great Britain; its undergraduate college, in which Carlyle was enrolled (1809-1813),
was unrivalled in philosophy and the sciences.

It boasted in Dugald Stewart and Thomas Brown the only
original school of British philosophy, the Common Sense school.
Brown applied to the science of the mind the methods of the
physical and natural sciences, which were in a healthy experi-
mental state at the University. While Oxford neglected science
and Cambridge stagnated in unoriginal exposition of Newtonian
mathematics, John Leslie kept abreast of the great contemporary
French mathematical physicists like Lagrange and Laplace, and
was an independent physical investigator, having invented a
differential thermometer and having won the Rumford Medal
of the British Royal Society by *An Inquiry into the Nature and
Properties of Heat* (1804). John Playfair, Professor of Natural
Philosophy (physics and chemistry), was a pioneer in the new
science of geology. His *Illustrations of the Huttonian Theory*
(1802) was a clear and bold statement of the uniformitarian
theory upon which present-day geology is based, originated by
James Hutton of Edinburgh in 1785. His colleague Robert
Jameson, Professor of Natural History (zoölogy and geology)
opposed him with the then predominant catastrophic theory,

that had the advantage of harmony with the Biblical story of the Flood and other instances of the intervening hand of God. Playfair's defence of the far-reaching implications of a continuous geological process with "no vestige of a beginning—no prospect of an end," although handicapped in popular controversy by theological odium, found hearty advocates in Edinburgh intellectual circles, which were noted for their sceptical spirit.

The results of such varied scientific research and theoretical activity were disseminated among university undergraduates by compulsory attendance on Playfair's lectures in natural philosophy, preceded by two years' mathematics under Leslie; whereas science was optional in English universities. While Oxford, Cambridge, and Dublin looked to the past, Edinburgh prepared students to think and to act in terms of the mechanical age that was rapidly arriving.

But serious obstacles lay in the way of the young Carlyle's enjoyment of these advantages. In adapting themselves to the demand for cheap popular education, the Scottish universities could not afford to employ means to make intellectual contacts thorough. Boys entered at fourteen, like Carlyle, or even earlier. To give them sufficient vacation for earning a considerable part of their expenses by tutoring or farm labor, the academic year was a scant six months, mid-November to late April. Students of a tender age, left to find their own lodgings in a city of nearly 100,000 inhabitants, lost the association with teachers and fellow students afforded by residence in an English college. The tutorial system being also too expensive, there was devised the expedient of employing a few distinguished professors to lecture to very large classes. In the period of Carlyle's attendance, classrooms were becoming greatly over-crowded by the steady growth of enrollment resulting from two causes: the increase of national wealth from machine industry, scientific farming, and commercial opportunities, and the reaction against the sceptical tendencies of the French Revolution, which was making religion more popular in Scotland than it had been since Cromwell overthrew the Presbyterian theocracy at the battle of

Dunbar. By 1822 the Church of Scotland was to look with alarm at the "enormous glut" of candidates for the ministry. As a result of these handicaps, Edinburgh could not provide genuine higher education, and gave a cheap substitute amounting to a superior form of secondary education, like that offered at present by many American universities faced with the problems of postwar overcrowding.

Carlyle found himself an inconspicuous unit in preposterously large classes.[5] Latin and even first year Greek were taught by the lecture method to groups of 150 to 200; so there was ample excuse for the inability of Professor Christianson, in a dimly-lighted classroom, to distinguish Thomas Carlyle from another Carlyle who was a miserable Latinist. Brown lectured to 194 in logic, and to 151 in moral philosophy. Only in mathematics did Carlyle find manageable groups. The enrollment, falling from 70 in his first year to 46 in his second, and 41 in his third, permitted Leslie, the only teacher with whom he came into personal contact, to recognize his ability. This circumstance decided Carlyle's specialization in mathematical studies, hitherto pursued less from temperamental inclination than environmental influence. On turning thus to the scientific side of the curriculum, he hoped to be noticed similarly by Playfair, whose recommendation would be of much weight in securing the teaching position necessary for his support during the long period of theological study that must follow graduation. The large enrollment of 131 proved no barrier, for the "quiet and philosophic" Playfair, past sixty and absorbed in experiments, lectured so dully that there were days when no one attended but Carlyle. Even then Playfair spoke to his audience of one as formally as if the hall were crowded, probably inwardly cursing the pertinacious rustic whose tactful retirement would have spared him the necessity of lecturing. It was only in signing the certificate of proficiency at the term's end that he noticed Carlyle's devotion to science by adding to the usual formula the words "I have reason to know," a delicate distinction with no humor for the aspiring youth of nineteen, but only bitter disappointment.

Carlyle's contacts with the student body of 1,500, and with the intellectual and social life of the city, were even less satisfactory. He lodged near the University in a quarter of artisans and small tradespeople, sharing a room and meals with one or two other students. His associates were, like himself, "ministerials" from humble families in the west Lowlands, in whose company he took the long walk homeward over the mountains at the beginning and end of terms. One of them gives a glimpse of him as an undergraduate: "Young Carlyle was distinguished at that time by the same peculiarities that still (1849) mark his character—sarcasm, irony, extravagance of sentiment, and a strong tendency to undervalue others, combined, however, with great kindness of heart and great simplicity of manners. His external figure, though then only about fifteen years of age, was similar to what it now is—tall, slender, awkward, not apparently very vigorous. His provincial intonation was then very remarkable, and it still remains so; his speech was copious and bizarre." Had he matched wits in a University debating society with the best Edinburgh youth and with the English who, shut off from the Continent, frequently studied at Edinburgh in the interval between public school and an English university, there might have been a wholesome mitigation of his sense of superiority and perhaps a softening of his accent. But social distinctions were sharp in those days of the Tory reaction against democracy.

The ungainly Ecclefechan youth was too shabbily dressed to join the promenade of Edinburgh society in the afternoon sun shining full upon Princes Street from over the towering Old Town crowned with its Castle. The influence of the ancient Scottish alliance with France was apparent in the free out-of-door sociability of this fashionable crowd, in the constant round of its dinner parties, and even in the kinds of pastry it consumed. The array of uniforms told of the continuance of stubborn warfare against Revolutionary France of the new era, and the determination to remain in the eighteenth-century atmosphere of Scotland's intellectual flowering. Nor was Carlyle at home on the southern extreme of the city in the restricted residence section of George

Square, with its quiet gardens and neoclassical architecture. His daily student life kept him within the bounds of the Old Town. He lodged close to bustling commercial Nicolson Street, which crossed the ravine left by the seventeenth-century draining of the South Loch, and mounted steeply past the University to meet at right angles the even busier and more crowded High Street of the mediaeval settlement.

The Old Town in its situation and architecture showed marks of long warfare against the English, in which it had been directly in the path of invasion. It occupied a sharp mile-long ridge between the sites of the old North and South Lochs, rising from Holyrood Castle on the east to a termination in the three-hundred-foot precipices of Edinburgh Castle on the west. In this narrow space surrounded by city walls had crowded a population that could be accommodated only by building into the air. On both sides of the High Street, which followed the crest of the ridge, rose ancestors of the modern apartment house, sometimes to nine or ten stories climbed by circular staircases in round, conical-roofed towers of French design. On the street level the ranks of houses were now and then pierced with gateways that led into alleys called "pends" or "wynds," descending the steep slopes on either side of the High Street and widening to the rear into "closes" surrounded with dwellings. If an invader penetrated the city walls, he found these gates shut and the line of high buildings presenting an impenetrable front.

In Carlyle's student days the city, though shorn of its walls, had still a martial air, as Volunteers drilled in preparation for a Napoleonic invasion; even his professors could be seen ranked in the college yard. At night defence was necessary against gangs of footpads, one of which broke Carlyle's hat before being frightened away. Watchmen kept an eye alert for them while making the rounds and calling the hours. For severe disturbances it was necessary to summon the city guard, one hundred and fifty strong, armed with muskets. By day there was constant hubbub from swarming beggars and the small shopkeepers who in mediaeval fashion made the High Street a narrow lane between their booths, especially about St. Giles Cathedral and the ancient fortified Tolbooth, or prison. These "Luckenbooths" made a vivid impression upon the youthful student, as did the noisy confusion of the courts in Parliament House close by, where he saw judges throned aloft and celebrated lawyers, Francis Jeffrey, Walter Scott, Henry Cockburn, pleading before them. But this was Carlyle's closest view of the legal and literary aristocracy of Edinburgh. At church he could have only crowded standing room at the rear to look over largely empty pews, paid for but not occupied by sophisticated Edinburghers, toward some polished pulpit orator, as he ornamented a moral commonplace with allusions to the beauties of nature, just coming into fashion. The stratification of society confined him to the mediaeval city, and to companions whose intellectual outlook, like his own, was in many ways that of the seventeenth century.

From these limitations, of which he was as yet only partially aware, Carlyle found one escape—through books. From the University library, despite the lack of a catalogue, the absence or indifference of the retired clergyman who held the sinecure of the librarianship, and the hostility of his ignorant Highland deputy, the earnest student succeeded in drawing many important works in eighteenth-century and contemporary philosophy, history, and belles-lettres: Locke's *Essay on the Human Understanding,* Hume's *England,* Robertson's *Scotland,* forty-five volumes of *British Essayists,* Swift, Fielding, Sterne, Scott's *Waverley* on its appearance in 1814, the new poetry of Scott, Byron, and John Wilson, and current numbers of the *Edinburgh* and *Quarterly* Reviews. He chanced upon Gottlieb Heyne's edition of Virgil, whose supply of what his classical teachers had failed to give was gratefully acknowledged when he returned triumphantly to Edinburgh University as its Lord Rector in 1866: "For the first time, I understood Virgil.... Heyne had introduced me ...into an insight of Roman life and ways of thought; had pointed out the circumstances in which these works were written, and given me their interpretation." A result of this undirected but voracious reading was a prophetic prayer to Fortune written in

1814 on a rear fly-leaf of a book of Greek prose: "Grant that with a heart of independence, unseduced by the world's smiles, and unbending to its frowns, I may attain to literary fame. And though starvation be my lot I will smile that I have not been born a king! ! !"

His student admirers, nicknaming him "Dean" or "Jonathan" from the likeness of his satiric turn to Swift's, predicted a brilliant future in letters. But science offered immediate financial rewards. He had partially earned his way through college by tutoring in mathematics during the long vacations; and in 1814, on completing the study for the M.A. degree which was a prerequisite to ordination in the Church of Scotland, he accepted a mathematical teaching post at Annan Academy. He returned to his native region with tantalizing glimpses into new realms of thought, but largely self-trained except in mathematics, untouched by civilizing social influences, and bearing resentment against the educational policy of the University.

§ 2

CARLYLE turned his back upon Edinburgh reluctantly, feeling that he was "leaving the fountain-head of knowledge and good-humour." His only consolation was that, by taking the option of six years' *in absentia* rather than four years' resident theological study, he was delaying the step of entering the ministry, concerning which he had acquired "grave prohibitive doubts." In his first year at the University the keen-witted boy had detected from the tone of their lectures the amusement of some of his professors at the simplicity which accepted the Scriptures literally. Close cultural contact with eighteenth-century France had permeated the upper classes with the sceptical spirit of Voltaire and the Encyclopaedists, among whom David Hume had been a favorite visitor. Edinburgh had made him its idol and had named the street in which he had lived St. David's in affectionate humor. Clergymen had fallen out of the highest society because they were not considered sufficiently enlightened, and deism, or even atheism, was a mark of cultivation.

The quality of his professors' incredulity is indicated by the questions which the puzzled fifteen-year-old boy asked his mother on returning to Ecclefechan for vacation: "Did God Almighty come down and make wheelbarrows in a shop? How was it known that Solomon's Song was symbolical, representing Christ and the Church?" These shocking inquiries kept the simple-hearted woman awake at night, weeping and praying for her son. He had the kindness and good sense to lock his continued doubts in his own breast, but they rankled there. On his return to Edinburgh his brother Alick (Alexander) accompanied him with cheerful conversation as far as Moffat, but when left alone to walk "all day, with no company save the great dumb monsters of mountains," he lay down at night in a roadside inn "the most miserable being under God's creation." For a long time thereafter he kept reading books on the evidences of Christianity "with the greatest desire to be convinced, but in vain"; for scientific studies deepened his insecurity. Even across the social gulf the atmosphere of intellectual Edinburgh had disturbed the course of his efforts.

These doubts would not necessarily bar him from the ministry of the Church of Scotland as it was then constituted. Since the second quarter of the eighteenth century, the governing classes had been endeavoring to liberalize theology and raise the cultural level of the clergy. The first means employed had been encroachment upon the ancient right of congregations to choose their own ministers, by the patron, or largest landholder in the parish, who picked clergymen free from the fanaticism of the masses. This drove from the National Church those who feared innovations in theology; the first seceding body dividing in 1737 into Burghers, in whose fold Carlyle had been reared, and Anti-Burghers. The second step was legislation in 1782, raising the educational qualifications for clergymen to those which Carlyle was now trying to fulfill. In 1784 "patronage" was formally recognized by the General Assembly of the Church as the regular means of selecting clergymen. Patrons filled pulpits with "moderate" clergymen, who preached simple morality and little or no dogma, and were chiefly distinguished from the laity by hostility to theatre-going and Sabbath-breaking.

Thus Carlyle, shocked by the moral laxity of the intellectually emancipated in Edinburgh, considered whether there might not still be a place for him as a member of the majority party of Moderates, since his theological laxity might be a recommendation in the eyes of an aristocratic patron. Accordingly, he attended the General Assembly in May, 1814, to study the tricks of the best pulpit orators, and coming up from Annan at Christmas time delivered a "trial discourse" on the uses of affliction sufficiently imitative of the "moderate" manner to win the decided approval of his Divinity Hall professors. His next task was to write in Latin an "exegesis" on the question "Is a Natural Religion Possible?"—that is, does the world give evidence of the existence of God independent of Scriptural revelation? In preparation he felt it intellectually honest to read what the arch-enemy of orthodoxy, David Hume, had to say on the topic; with the result that Hume's formidable reasoning shook his belief in the Divine government of the world. Not even this blow was decisive, for the Church offered the surest road to respectability and financial security. In one mood, he tried to persuade his friend Robert Mitchell, who had lent him Hume's *Essays,* to reconsider his decision to abandon candidacy for the ministry, using the surprisingly snobbish argument that the "prevalence of infidelity" was "on the decline," because its recent spread among discontented weavers and artisans had made it no longer a mark of superiority to the vulgar herd.

Carlyle's conscientious scruples outweighed this momentary temptation; but there were still to be considered the financial needs of his family and his discontent with the social status of teaching. The schoolmaster, like his female counterpart the governess, was on the uncertain borderline of respectability. Carlyle might have insinuated himself, through the parents of his pupils, into the group of professional men and successful tradesfolk who comprised the "gentility" among the two thousand inhabitants of the thriving port and market town of Annan. But his difficult combination of pride and shyness forbade this, and incidentally shut him from the society of the refined young women whom he admired from afar. He was too fastidious to dally with village sweethearts. As at the University, books were the chief solace of the severe and ambitious young Scotchman; in his seclusion the habit of self-analysis induced by Dugald Stewart's metaphysics sometimes made him acutely miserable. His only intellectual stimulus came through Mitchell, who was living in the nearby hamlet of Ruthwell as assistant to the remarkable clergyman Henry Duncan, discoverer of the Ruthwell Cross with its runic inscriptions and editor of the *Dumfries Weekly Courier*. Otherwise, he kept closely to his family, now established at Mainhill farm, two miles from Ecclefechan.

The close of the Napoleonic Wars in 1815 was followed immediately by widespread hard times. Building was at a standstill, and James Carlyle, who had married late, was obliged at the age of fifty-seven to seek a new occupation for the support of a large family of young children. He decided upon farming, protected by the newly enacted Corn Laws prohibiting the importation of grain until the domestic price exceeded the war-time level of eighty shillings a quarter (eight bushels). Land rents had gone up some seventy percent during the war, and James Carlyle's resources were strained to the utmost to lease at about a hundred pounds a wet clayey farm, requiring two hundred and fifty or three hundred additional pounds to stock. He must also hire help in rush seasons, for his third son John, aged fourteen, was becoming a student like Tom, leaving at home only Alick, aged eighteen, and Jamie, aged ten, besides the four girls under twelve and their mother. He also needed agricultural machinery, a novelty in farming. The Scotch inventions of the all-iron plow and the threshing machine were in general use in the Lowlands, and some progressive farmers were even driving their threshing machines by the steam engine, also a Scottish invention. This mechanization of agriculture was spreading from

Scotland to the northern counties of England, but was unknown elsewhere in the world.[6] Use of a steam engine was out of the question for James Carlyle, and he had to be content with a flail and other primitive implements until Thomas sent him a contribution of twenty pounds toward a threshing machine in 1817.

During these early years at Mainhill, Thomas was generous with financial aid and spent most of his summers in the crowded three-room cottage, the usual dwelling of the small farmer in those days. He gave physical assistance in emergencies, though he probably never did a full day's work in the fields, and also the benefit of his observation of agricultural methods in the rich Lothians about Edinburgh, then the most advanced in the world. He shared his family's belief that their landlord, General Sharpe, and landlords everywhere, were asking too much rent while they gorged on the profits of the monopoly created by the Corn Laws, which kept the price of foodstuffs exorbitantly high. The reading of Lord Chesterfield's *Letters* had, he wrote to Mitchell, "a result highly unfavorable to those feelings of prostration before high birth and weight of purse, which (many tell us) is so eminently the duty of all men to cultivate. Indeed this is not the first time I have noticed in my mind a considerable tendency to undervalue the great ones of this world. Conscious that this sentiment proceeds in a considerable degree from my situation in life, I sometimes endeavor to check it; but after all it requires little observation to teach us that the Noble of Political Society and the Noble of Nature are different persons, in nine cases out of ten."

In 1816 came a welcome change of scene, with ten pounds increase in salary. The public academy of Kircaldy, a commercial town near Edinburgh somewhat larger than Annan, had been steadily losing pupils to a private school in charge of a brilliant Edinburgh University graduate, Edward Irving. Some parents, however, thought Irving flogged too much, so the Town Council endeavored to meet his competition by discharging their schoolmaster and offering the position to Carlyle, who had the reputation of getting work from pupils without use of the rod.

Carlyle had met Irving, a native of Annan, casually several times during the past eight years, but he was astonished when the rival schoolmaster called, on rumor of the offer, to assure him hearty welcome in Kircaldy.

Irving was the first friend Carlyle had on terms of equality. He was three years older, and had seen more of the world. Despite a glaring squint, he was decidedly handsome. His broad frame of six feet-three dominated Carlyle's five feet-eleven; but Carlyle's head, massive as if hewed from granite, with assertive Border jaw and piercing blue eyes set under projecting brows, redressed the balance against Irving's slighter, conventionally regular features. The son of a successful tanner, one of the magistrates of Annan, Irving was saved from sensitiveness as to his temporary occupation of schoolmaster. On Carlyle's arrival he introduced him at the Kircaldy manse, where he was the accepted lover of the clergyman's daughter, and at other middle-class homes. But Kircaldy found it impossible to put Carlyle at his ease. Isolation had made him taciturn, even gruff, except when consciousness of superior abilities broke out in moments of blunt, sometimes arrogant, self-assertion. Well-meaning patronizers found his sarcasm like an adder in their path. With the genial Irving, however, he was at ease, sharing in his boisterous humor, his long walks, and his well-stocked library, greatly appreciated by a poor scholar who could seldom buy a book. A ferry ride across the Forth brought them to Edinburgh, with its intellectual stimulations. Irving introduced his companion to the writings of his favorite contemporary author, Coleridge, and to the seventeenth-century divines, philosophers, and dramatists whom Coleridge recommended as models of style. Irving's sermons, on occasions of filling his prospective father-in-law's pulpit, had a seventeenth-century flavor, to the disconcertment of the solid burghers, who relished it no more than they did his demands of an immediate and literal following of the admonitions of the Bible, even to turning the other cheek. Once a pew banged open and there issued forth Beveridge, the baker, with "face and eyes all in wrath" to vanish "with a slam" out the church door. Which went to explain why Irving had had no call to a charge since securing his license to preach in 1815.

Carlyle did not tell the devout Irving what delayed his own ministerial preparation. But Hume's logic was so deep in his mind that he did not cross to Edinburgh for his third trial discourse in the Christmas of 1816. Wavering, he returned to reenroll in March, 1817. Finding the registering professor too busy to see him, he accepted the omen, and ceased to think longer of the pulpit. Two weeks later he wrote Mitchell of his joy in being delivered from a church that was chiefly a "State-engine," requiring subserviency to wealthy patrons, and never venturing to let its "'true religion' descend unsupported into the arena, and try its hand at mauling the heresies which oppose it. On the contrary, every 'true religion' is propped and bolstered, and the hands of its rivals tied up; till by nursing and fattening it has become a bloated monster that human nature can no longer look upon—and men rise up and knock its brains out." He had even greater contempt for the ignorance and cant among the Dissenting sects. In the previous year he had given Mitchell a sardonic sketch of "Brother Saffery of Salibury," a solicitor of money for the Baptist Mission: "His brow was knit together very gloomily —and his voice (naturally a deep-toned bass) was compressed into an inharmonious whine,—all denoting profound humility and passive obedience. He spoke of the designs of Providence and the projects of the Devil with great *sang-froid.*"

The decision to abandon the ministry was soon put to a severe test by the celebrated Dr. Thomas Chalmers, leader of the new and rising Evangelical party in the State Church. This party was endeavoring to undo the work of Moderatism by reviving election of ministers by their congregations, and with it the popular theology of Judgment, Heaven, and Hell according to a verbally inspired Bible. Evangelicism was distinguished from the Burgher and other Dissenting sects by its emotional rather than argumentative quality; by the novel fervor with which it preached the familiar gospel of salvation. Chalmers had been a Moderate, but in 1811 death of relatives and a long, severe illness prepared

the way for his conversion, by the English Evangelical layman
Wilberforce's *Practical View of Christianity,* to an exceedingly
low estimate of human reason and a correspondingly high valu-
ation of faith. His *Astronomical Discourses* (1817), written to
prove that the insignificance of the earth in the universe was no
argument against the truth of revealed religion, had electrified
the Scotch religious world. The propertied classes flocked to hear
the preacher who had re-discovered the secret of making attractive
the worn doctrine enjoining the poor to submit to the powers of
this world and look to another for their reward.

Among the curious who made a pilgrimage in 1817 to
Chalmers' church in Dunfermline were the two schoolmasters
from Kircaldy. Carlyle felt the sermon "piercingly pathetic—no
preacher ever went so into one's heart"; but his mind, fortified
by a knowledge of astronomy at least equal to Chalmers', was
detached and critical. It was forming the judgment of Chalmers
which, written many years later on the basis of personal acquaintance and frequent contact, stands as an excellent historical summary of the characteristic weaknesses of Evangelicism: "He was
a man of essentially little culture, of narrow sphere, all his life;
such an intellect professing to be educated, yet so ill *read,* so
ignorant in all that lay beyond the horizon in place or in time,
I have almost nowhere met with." His sermons "were usually
the triumphant on-rush of *one* idea with its satellites and supporters." At the time he wrote to Mitchell concerning Chalmers'
Discourses: "It seems strange, when his own side of the question
is so very evident, that he should deal so largely in denunciations
against his adversaries. It is very certain that the unhappy sceptic
cannot believe one jot the better, though he were brayed in a
mortar."

Evangelicism could not recall Carlyle's decision, for his belief
in the very foundations of Christianity had been shattered. *The
Decline and Fall of the Roman Empire,* borrowed in 1818 from
the unsuspecting Irving, gave the final blow. Gibbon's "winged
sarcasms, so quiet and yet so conclusively transpiercing and killing dead," destroyed the last vestige of his faith in miracles, mak-

ing him clearly see that "Christianity was not true." The struggle against temptations to acquiesce in orthodoxy had been long and hard. The mature Carlyle, writing *The Life of John Sterling* as a sort of apology for his own, singled out religion as the central problem of the age, the touchstone of a man's sincerity or insincerity.

The way for Carlyle's acceptance of Gibbon's banishment of the miraculous had been prepared by physical science, with its creed of invariable natural law. In 1815, just after his "exegesis" on natural religion had confronted him with the probing analysis of Hume, Carlyle had brought back from Edinburgh the *Principia* of Newton. As Wordsworth in an analogous situation had "Turn'd towards mathematics, And their clear and solid evidence" [7] so the young teacher in Annan, "after wandering in the thick darkness of metaphysics" thought he beheld "the fair face of truth" in mathematical physics. Prepared by diligent study of the Newtonian calculus, he attempted, soon after reading Gibbon, Lagrange's *Mécanique Analytique,* which unified by the principle of virtual velocities a whole system of mathematical truths, giving to analytic mechanics the appearance of logical perfection that led Sir William Hamilton to call it "a kind of scientific poem." Though the difficult new calculus of variations made this "nearly a sealed book" to Carlyle, the more lucid and popular *Exposition du Système du Monde* of Laplace aroused his enthusiasm by demonstrating, from the agreement of its astronomical observations with Lagrange's pure mathematics, that the irregularities of celestial bodies, which seemed to Newton to require occasional intervention of the Deity, had definitely predictable periods that equalized each other. With the nebular hypothesis suggested in one of Laplace's footnotes, Carlyle in 1818 found spread before him the perfect symmetry of the world-machine, possibly not requiring a creating, and certainly not an intervening, God. Thenceforward for seventeen years he was to watch with mixed emotions the result of an opposite course from his own: the spectacular career of his friend Irving, who was to put the literal interpretation of the Bible to the test of action in the nineteenth-century world.

§ 3

AT the age of twenty-two, Carlyle was faced with the choice of another profession. Teaching, the makeshift support of his theological studies, had always seemed an unappreciated struggle with dullards, for whom "donkeys" was his favorite epithet. Although he managed at Kircaldy to refrain from much whipping, while teaching a motley array of subjects, mathematics, English, Latin, and French, his sarcasms and scowls had reduced his pupils to twelve in the autumn of 1818. There was a secret and more potent reason for discontent. At last, he had attracted a young woman who fulfilled the dreams of a man conscious that his way lay apart from his environment. Margaret Gordon, a former pupil of Irving, had the comeliness and grace which the usual suitor sighed after, and also the wit and talent prized more highly by the exceptional man. She, in turn, appreciated what lay beneath his unprepossessing exterior. But romantic reveries had been disturbed by her prudent aunt, who was trying to arrange a mercenary marriage for a girl who was "poorish," though "proud and well-bred." Margaret could be won only by money and a more respectable occupation. So love whetted more sharply the restless ambition of the Kircaldy dominie.

In plain sight across the waters of the Forth lay Edinburgh with its opportunities, where Scott was at the height of his fame as a man of letters, Jeffrey as a lawyer and critic. Irving, dissatisfied on his own account by three years' waiting for a pulpit, urged Carlyle to accompany him thither and exploit literary talents which he considered worthy of the columns of the *Edinburgh Review*. New periodicals were springing up as a consequence of the success of the audaciously brilliant *Blackwood's Magazine,* founded in 1817, and the vogue of Scott continued to reveal possibilities of money as well as fame in literature. Carlyle found it "curious to observe the importance which the writings of Walter Scott have conferred on everything pertaining to the Border. . . . Not a beldame, in the Merse, can plant her cabbages —nor a tinker solder his kettle, but it must be forthwith communicated to the public in *Blackwood's* or the *Scots Magazine*." But scorn was converted into the fashionable passion for the picturesque when Irving took him in 1817 on a walking tour through the "Lady of the Lake" country, where Loch Katrine gave him his "first taste of the beautiful in scenery." The following summer Irving pointed out a more pleasant though less direct route from Kircaldy to Ecclefechan by way of St. Mary's Loch and the Yarrow country, whose charms, famed in Scotch balladry, had recently been sung by Wordsworth.

Returning by the same route, Carlyle described it in his first literary effort, which disappointingly was not accepted by an Edinburgh magazine. Although he prudently assured Mitchell that "to live by authorship was never my intention," he admitted that "writing for booksellers" might be one means of livelihood while looking about for a profession. Besides, with seventy pounds (about $850)* left from his savings after sending his hard-pressed father fifteen, he calculated that by strict frugality he could pass two winters in Edinburgh, even if authorship and tutoring yielded nothing. The risky step was not opposed at Mainhill. Alick thought "a man is best judge of his own case himself," and his mother, who had taught herself to write in order to communicate with Tom at the University, added a postcript in an extremely vertical hand: "I was happy to hear of

* Such estimates of the purchasing power of English money in Carlyle's day in terms of American currency of the present time (1931) make no pretense of scientific accuracy. The comparison involves too many variables and rests upon too incomplete a statistical basis, to be stated with mathematical rigor in the present state of knowledge. On the other hand, English money is unfamiliar to most Americans. Furthermore, the exchange value of the pound, especially in the present period of instability, may mislead some readers into greatly underestimating its real value in the early nineteenth century. Hence the writer, in a biography in which finances play an important part, has in a few cases ventured rough calculations.

your heroic spirit like Paul....I am rather uneasy until I hear
of your settlement." [8]

Carlyle followed Irving's example by resigning his Kircaldy
post in November, 1819. Irving could afford decent Edinburgh
lodgings, but the cost of city life obliged his friend to tolerate
"a paltry ill-cooked morsel" and a noisy room infested with
"vermin of various sorts" until February, when three hours' daily
tutoring gave him confidence that his little capital would not be
dissipated too rapidly. Science and law seemed the most eligible
callings, though there was serious objection to both. His favorite
teacher Leslie, who had been a tutor in Virginia, advised him to
learn the new technique of civil engineering, in great demand in
America; but Carlyle shrank from emigration. Law, the highest
of Scottish professions, was more attractive because its practice
was traditionally combined with literary pursuits, as in the recent
cases of Scott and Jeffrey. But on consulting the advocate J. A.
Henderson, to whom the Reverend Henry Duncan of Ruthwell
had given him a letter of introduction, Carlyle discovered that
the high fee of two hundred pounds was required for entrance
to the bar after completion of study, and that legal practice came
slowly without wealthy and influential connections.

While weighing law against science, he was diligent in
seeking literary connections. Duncan had also provided him with
introductions to the bookseller Waugh, who was projecting a
periodical, and to David Brewster, editor of the *Edinburgh Encyclopaedia* and co-editor of the *Edinburgh Philosophic Journal,*
which had an international circulation among scientists. Waugh
promised employment, but was not sure when his *New Edinburgh Review* would be launched. Brewster did not mention the
encyclopaedia, but, interested in his scientific training, gave him
an article in the autograph French of the celebrated Swedish
chemist Berzelius to translate for the *Philosophical Journal.*
Brewster also invited him to a meeting of the Royal Society,
where he listened to a discussion in geology, especially interesting
because during this winter he was attending Jameson's lectures
in natural history. Thorough in everything, Carlyle attempted

to get to the bottom of the Jameson-Playfair disagreement in geological theory by reading Werner, Jameson's teacher and chief authority, in the original German.

His interest in German literature had been awakened by the reading of Madame de Staël's *De L'Allemagne* in 1817, but the language was as little known in Scotland as French was familiar. It was with considerable difficulty that Carlyle discovered a tutor in Robert Jardine, an Annandale youth who had studied at Göttingen. Importation of books presented another problem, solved by his friend Provost Swan of Kircaldy, who had business relations with German ports. When tutoring was over in May, 1819, he left Edinburgh with his profession undecided, taking to read at Mainhill a bundle of books, of which three reflect his varied interests of the moment: a history of Frederick the Great in German, *America and her Resources* by an Anglican clergyman who had emigrated, and Rousseau's *Confessions.*

Brightened by dreams of Margaret Gordon, summer passed rapidly at Mainhill. His mother, who had been greatly disquieted by his abandoning a ministerial career, was reassured by his attendance at Holy Fair. He lounged about in the open air, reading widely from Southey's poetry to physics and mineralogy. With Jardine in the neighborhood, German lessons continued once a week. He plowed through Klopstock's overrated *Messiah* and arrived at the more spirited pages of Lessing and Goethe. But uncongeniality with Annandalesmen made him not reluctant to return to Edinburgh. "The people here are mostly peasants," he wrote to John Ferguson, a companion of the winter, "and display the usual sentiments and habits. Those in other stations are scarcely more refined. Their want of commerce tends to keep them ignorant and unenterprising; while smuggling and moss-trooping have left but too deep traces in their minds. With regard to our gentry—a stranger only would call it petulance to say that their principles and pursuits are often little different from those vouchsafed to cattle and each beast."

September pleasantly reunited him for a few days in Annan

with Irving, who had mysteriously dropped out of sight during the summer. Irving had an amazing tale to tell. In despair of a pulpit in Scotland, he had conceived the fantastic design of becoming a self-appointed missionary to Persia in the style of the Apostles, casting himself on God's Providence without money or guidance. But soon after Carlyle's departure the minister of St. George's, Edinburgh, had asked him to preach in his pulpit before the famous Doctor Chalmers, now at Glasgow and needing an assistant. Irving delivered his best sermon, but time brought no decision from Chalmers. Finally, in a caprice of desolation, he took at random the first boat he found leaving Greenoch, the port of Glasgow. This landed him in Belfast, where he was mistaken for a notable criminal and clapped into jail. An appeal to the Presbyterian minister effected his release. He then wandered aimlessly on foot for several weeks among peasants' huts in the north of Ireland, and returned to Scotland ragged and penniless. There he found a letter waiting, with the news that Chalmers wanted him after all. Excited by this reward of his faith, which opened possibilities of unhampered Evangelical preaching, he urged upon Carlyle a like confidence in his ultimate success as a writer. But Carlyle thought law a securer support, and November found him assaulting this citadel of Edinburgh respectability.

He arrived in a mood of gloomy foreboding induced by a stage-coach ride in continuous rain through the direct route from Moffat, which seemed "the most mournful in Europe, rugged without being elevated; barren, stormy, and covered, at least in winter, with an ever-brooding darkness." He found the city humming with talk of hard times and the "Manchester Massacre." In late August industrial unemployment had caused an assembly of 60,000 men and women in St. Peter's Fields, near Manchester, to agitate for the repeal of the Corn Laws and a reform of Parliament to give the masses a voice in government. Mounted volunteer yeomanry, composed of local manufacturers and their connections, had dispersed the meeting brutally, killing eleven and wounding several hundred.[9]

News of this outrage united the Scotch and English masses against the Tory government in London, which in the "panic fear of change" induced by the French Revolution had congratulated the yeomanry upon their efficiency. Glasgow industrial workers, called "Radicals" because of their advocacy of radical reform of Parliament, went on a sympathetic strike for a week, and middle-class Whigs excoriated the policy of the Government in the *Edinburgh Review*. The event in St. Peter's Fields gained the name of Peterloo from those who thought it wiped out the nation's gratitude to the Tories for Waterloo. Hostile public sentiment only stimulated the repressive policy of the "Savage Parliament," which in December passed the notorious Six Acts, abrogating the traditional liberties of the Englishman almost to the extent of Scotch despotism. Popular assemblies were made impossible in unincorporated centres of great population like Birmingham and Manchester, and a tax of fivepence on all periodicals, designed to prevent the spread of radical propaganda, in effect kept all kinds of knowledge from the poor. Carlyle could not afford to buy a newspaper, which cost sixpence or more, though at a bookseller's shop he eagerly scanned the Edinburgh Whig *Scotsman* and a Manchester journal. Irving wrote him of terrible suffering from unemployment at Glasgow. Industrial depression and political oppression, affecting Scotland and England simultaneously, united with his reading of German in breaking down the Scottish provinciality of Carlyle's interests.

Edinburgh, not a seat of machine industry, felt the depression more slowly, but a winter of exceptional severity for a city that in the latitude of Labrador stood exposed to winds from sea and mountains increased the sufferings of the poor. "Nobody who lived in 1819 and 1820 can have forgotten the frightful condition of large portions of the population," wrote the well-to-do Edinburgh lawyer Cockburn in his *Memorials* many years later, "it was the most horrid period since 1793." Carlyle, rooming in the home of a tailor, was in intimate touch with these sufferings, and bitterly resented the callousness of the governing landlords.

In terror lest the Glasgow Radicals march upon Edinburgh,

the Tories revived the Volunteers from the propertied classes that had been organized against French invasion. Even the humane and sensible Walter Scott feared "the secret and steady silence about their plans" maintained by the Radicals, indicated that "although without anything like effecive arms or useful discipline, without money and without a commisariat" they might still "according to their favourite toast, have blood and plunder." In the second week in December the Volunteers occupied Edinburgh Castle and barracks while the regular troops were despatched to Glasgow on the rumor of an uprising that did not materialize. Carlyle watched a detachment depart, while onlookers in the Nicolson Street district gave a strange farewell groan or shout which he interpreted as "May the Devil go with *you,* ye peculiarly contemptible and dead to the distresses of your fellow-creatures." Sympathetic Whigs like Cockburn had been obliged to join the Volunteers in order to escape charges of disloyalty; but Carlyle, on being told by a young lawyer of his acquaintance that he should be bearing a musket, said "Hm, yes; but I haven't yet quite settled on which side," words the startled loyalist took as a joke. He wrote frankly to his clever brother John, who at eighteen was becoming his most intimate correspondent: "When I meet one of these heroic personages, with his buff belts, his cartouche-box and weapons of war, obstructing the progress of his Majesty's subjects along the streets, I can scarce suppress a bitter smile at the selfishness and stupidity of men. In fact 'steel pills,' though a very natural, are a very ineffectual remedy for a decayed 'constitution.' "

Irving, whose duty was to take the Gospel into "the noisome recesses of this overgrown city" of Glasgow, soon found the horse-pistol with which he had armed himself a needless precaution. He assured Carlyle that the dreaded Radicals were patient and deserving, and that an uprising was "vastly improbable." In disobedience to his superior Chalmers he distributed a small legacy among the unemployed at the rate of a pound a day until it was exhausted. "What on earth is for them?" he wrote in late December; "God and my Savior enable me to lift their hearts above a world that has deserted them, though they live in its plenty and labour in its toiling service, and fix them upon a world which, my dear Carlyle, I wish you and I had the inheritance in." No longer sharing this belief in another world, Carlyle confessed to his brother Alick a certain pity for the contrivers of the Cato Street conspiracy to murder George IV's ministers at dinner in late February, 1820: "It is a horrid piece of business... but ... if the King and his ministers do not adopt a set of measures entirely different from those which they have followed hitherto, it is greatly to be dreaded that more formidable and better concerted resistance will ensue."

The social situation affected his attitude toward the law. He had begun study with characteristic thoroughness on enrolling in the Scots law class of Professor Hume, nephew of the philosopher. Finding the lectures delivered "in a voice scarcely audible," he had recourse to "four ponderous quartos of notes" taken down in shorthand by a former student, and put them in proper background by studying Scotch history and Acts of Parliament and a *Historical View of the English Government* by the Glasgow Whig Millar. This solid reading did not exclude efforts for literary employment. Jeffrey failed to acknowledge or return a review of a scientific book sent off with trembling hopes to the *Edinburgh Review;* but Dr. Brewster engaged him "at frugal terms" to write short biographies for the *Edinburgh Encyclopaedia,* six of which he finished during the winter. In February he sent off ten pounds to his brother Alick on the farm, fearing that agriculture might be feeling the effect of the industrial depression; but his father assured him in early March that he was not in debt, "which is no great reason for complaint in these times."[10] Carlyle had no fear of the competition of the lawyers he heard in the courts; but continued study awoke ethical objections to the law that made him hesitate as he had hesitated in theology. Professor Hume, whose staunch Toryism had nearly involved him in a duel with Jeffrey, had written his *Commentaries* on the Scotch criminal laws in order to prove the entirely precedented character of the sedition trials of 1793-4 that had roused Burns's indignation. His clear and orderly mind had rescued decisions and procedure from chaos, but his method allowed for no readjustment to developing social conditions and ethical standards; whatever had been, even the savagery of mediaeval Privy Councils, became the eternal model of what should be. Carlyle found himself studying "formalities of customs which ought to be instantly and forever abolished," such as the tying up of the land by entails, "fatal things and worthy of all condemnation." One third of the area of Scotland could thus never be put into circulation by forced sale, no matter how heavy the debts prodigal aristocrats might have piled upon it. Even if it were possible to stomach the "shapeless mass of absurdity and chicane," there remained the usual obstacles of legal practice he had already considered; the high entrance fee and the "painful idleness" of perhaps ten years' waiting for employment. Could he hold out so long by tutoring and hack writing?

The problem of his profession, anxiety about the finances of his family, an the troubled state of the country, joined with the nervous strain of overwork in bringing on in February an especially severe attack of the dyspepsia with which insufficient and badly cooked food and continuance of country habits of diet in sedentary city life had been afflicting him with increasing frequency during the last two years. From the accompanying mood of despair Alick endeavored to rouse him by writing in his stiff copy-book hand after a hard day's work in the fields: "Were it not presumption in me in forming an estimate of your abilities I think were they known your productions would not disgrace the pages of any review—you cannot think I flatter, no you are convinced I never knew the word." Bidding him "not to fear the frowns of fortune," he pointed to David Hume and "more who became ornaments to their country whose circumstances and prospects were at a time darker than yours can possibly be thought." [11]

But in March the chief motive for perseverance in the law was removed. Margaret Gordon was being packed off by her aunt to London, a better field for husbands, and her Scotch lover was allowed one brief chaperoned meeting before she left Kircaldy. After such a blow it was vain for Irving to urge him to stick to the law in order to reform it, "the spirit of the age naturally tending that way." Cockburn, Jeffrey, and a minority of Whig lawyers were indeed advocating reform of Scottish court procedure, and thoroughgoing changes both in procedure and content of English law elaborated by the philosophic Bentham were being urged before Parliament by the Scotch lawyer Brougham. But Carlyle must solve the problem of his livelihood before he could preach reform. Theology, teaching, and now law were blind alleys. At the age of twenty-four, when most of his friends were settled in their grooves, he knew not where to turn.

§ 4

ALICK, though ignorant of Margaret Gordon's influence on his brother's state, urged him to repair his "shattered and broken constitution" by coming out of "a bustling reekel old clachan (town) like Edin" [12] to the quiet of Mainhill for his translations and other literary work. In the fourth week of April he went homeward by way of Glasgow, where he was to spend a week with the sanguine "Ned" Irving. He took a steamboat, the aboriginal "Tug" which was a novelty of the previous year, down the Firth of Forth to Bo'ness, and thence travelled by canal, encountering as he approached Glasgow "a red glare that flashed up and across the skies as if the whole world was in conflagration," coming from Dixon's ironworks. He found Glasgow humming with excitement over the general strike, involving 60,000 men, which three weeks before had shut down all industry in obedience to audacious placards proclaiming a provisional government on April third.[13] The mood of the Radicals had been desperate, for labor unions were illegal by a 1799 Act of Parliament. Blood was shed in a clash between soldiers and armed workingmen in the suburb of Bonnymuir. But hunger had been too strong for the strikers, and after five days most had returned to work, leaving forty-seven of their number prisoners, charged with treason. One of these prisoners was the Ecclefechan shoemaker, William Smith, whom a business errand to Glasgow had involved in Radical agitation. In his concern over the fate of Smith, who had been sent under guard to Edinburgh Castle, and in his resentment over the unrighted wrongs of the industrial workers, Carlyle was in no mood to listen to Dr. Chalmers' argument that the truth of Christianity was demonstrated by its visible fitness for human nature: "All written in us already in sympathetic ink. Bible awakens it, and you can read." As Irving accompanied him for his first day's walk homeward on May first, he felt obliged to explain his rebellious attitude toward the constituted powers by confessing his loss of faith in Christianity. The generous Irving refused to let this confession interfere with their friendship.

The next morning he was off at four o'clock from Muirkirk, with its "pillar of furnace smoke" and by eight in the evening was in Dumfries, fifty-four miles distant—the longest walk in his life. As he trudged with gloomy thoughts, he had passed several groups leaving the manufacturing districts in search of work and food in the countryside; an old peasant he overtook said, "unless these times alter, folks will all be Radicals together." Two days after his arrival at home he wrote a long letter to his school friend James Johnstone, who was dissatisfied with Nova Scotia, where he had emigrated the previous year after similar experiences to Carlyle's with preaching and teaching. Carlyle, who had opposed his going, now as earnestly opposed his return: "Never in the history of Britain did I read of such a situation. Black inquietude, misery physical and moral, from one end of the island to the other, Radical uprisings, and armed confederations of the upper classes, and little or no expectation of better times..... None can doubt that the Agriculture must feel the pressure of those taxes which at present exclude our commerce—except at a ruinous rate—from the markets of the world." He reinforced his conclusion by sending two articles on the social situation from opposite points of view, by Jeffrey in the *Edinburgh Review* and Southey in the Tory *Quarterly*.

There were times in this summer and the following year

when pessimism as to the state of the country and his own prospects, and even the pangs of disappointed love, were obliterated by prolonged bilious attacks, a frequent misery for the rest of his life. "Alas for the dignity of man," he wrote Irving: "No strength of soul can avail you; this malady will turn that very strength against yourself; it banishes all thought from your head, all love from your heart—and doubles your wretchedness by making you discern it." He tried to forget his troubles in work —pegging away at a variety of tasks commissioned by Brewster; a review of a book on magnetism, the translation of two scientific articles for the *Philosophical Journal,* and miscellaneous short biographies for the *Encyclopaedia.* Uncongenial, badly remunerated (the *Encyclopaedia* paid him fifty pounds, possibly $600, in two years), this hackwork would barely keep him alive; but there was nothing else at hand. He wrote to Johnstone: "I believe I am too old for beginning any new profession. One leads a strange miscellaneous life at that rate: yet if it cannot be helped—"

Smiling wryly at his early dreams of literary fame, he went back for a third winter in Edinburgh with several modest practical projects for booksellers, including a translation of Schiller's *History of the Thirty Years' War.* As usual, he lodged in the Nicolson Street district, amid noise, dirt, and stenches that were notorious as the worst in the British Isles. Hawkers and beggars cried throughout the day. The streets, never cleaned, crowded with fish and vegetable stands, contained wells that were the only supply of drinking water. There was no sewage or piping system; "water caddies," announcing themselves by blasts on battered tin horns, lugged heavy casks up the staircases of the tall houses. Here Carlyle's friend and fellow-tutor, Donaldson, had died in 1818 of malignant typhus fever, a disease so common and so fatal in Carlyle's observation that he was to wonder at the commotion made over the cholera epidemic of 1831-1832.

Across the former site of the North Loch, recently transformed from an intermediate state into the Princes Street Gardens, lay the New Town, that was giving a final glory to Edinburgh. When the fall of Napoleon had opened the Continent from which they had been excluded almost continuously for twenty-two years, Edinburgh travellers found nothing to match the site of their native city, lying on elevated ground giving a view of twenty miles of sea and of ranges of mountains whose foothills began close at hand with the Salisbury Crags and the volcanic peak of Arthur's Seat. They returned to boast of their "modern Athens" and to make it more worthy of the name by careful town planning. The few and narrow approaches to the fortified mediaeval city were replaced by numerous wide avenues. North of Princes Street on the slopes toward the Forth estuary, prosperous men erected, around gardens laid out in stately circles, crescents, and squares, houses outdoing their prototypes at Bath and even in London in variety and elaboration of design, and in the superiority of gleaming white Craigleith freestone over dingy Bath stone and Bloomsbury brick. Here the correct, cool, orderly, formal spirit of eighteenth-century Britain had posthumously its most splendid architectural monument. The Old Town, despite the ancient glories of the "Royal Mile" between Holyrood and the Castle, was coming more and more to exist only to supply the wants of the New.

But as Carlyle walked over the old North Bridge to tutor in the New Town, he was in no mood to enjoy its architectural splendors. He saw the injustice and hypocrisy upon which they were reared: injustice of gentry living idly upon rack-rents and preserved by entails from the natural results of their folly, injustice of political functionaries and soldiers, the tools of oppression; humbug of lawyers and fashionable clergy whose tricks he knew well, humbug of professors who did little real teaching. Yet in the New Town lived the literary and intellectual groups with whom he believed his talents entitled him to associate. "Edinburgh, with all its drawbacks, is the scene for me," he wrote to his brother John, now teaching at Annan Academy. "In the country I am like an alien, a stranger and pilgrim from a far distant land."

In Glasgow, where he visited Irving again at Christmas, he found a society likewise founded on injustice, and indulging in less cultivated pleasures. Strategically situated on a navigable river close to the sea and to extensive coal and iron deposits, Glasgow was a centre of textile factories, foundries, and shipping, and boasted the largest chemical works in the world. It was ruled by a busy middle class of manufacturers and merchants, who employed a well-paid body of skilled workmen and a swarming proletariat of unskilled labor, chiefly Irish immigrants and Highlanders driven from agriculture by the heads of their clans to make room for sheep-farming. While these unskilled workers crowded into "wynds" and "closes" that outdid even the Old Town of Edinburgh in squalor and destitution, Carlyle saw their newly rich employers "shovelling their beef over by the pound, and swilling wine without measure, declaiming on politics or religion, joking and jeering and flowing and swaggering along with all their heart." Here a new society had grown up outside the feudal molds that still held Edinburgh. Glasgow was bustling, hearty, crude, and horrible. The feudal and industrial societies alike presented a spectacle which Carlyle was to describe ten years later in a magnificent simile: "The Gods of this lower world sit aloft on glittering thrones, less happy than Epicurus' gods, but just as ignorant, as impotent; while the boundless living Chaos of Ignorance and Hunger welters, terrific in its dark fury, under their feet." [14]

The return to lodgings in Edinburgh after the congenial and encouraging society of Irving made Carlyle especially conscious of his desperate situation: "I am alone in this cold city—alone to cut my way into the heart of its benefices by the weapons of my own small quiver." But youthful buoyancy reasserted itself, as one day in March, 1821, when he postponed the duty of preparing a biography of Necker in order to spend "the whole blessed evening reading poetry and stuff" and writing John of his walks to "Arthur's Seat, a mountain close beside us where the atmosphere is pure as a diamond, and the prospect grander than any you ever saw. The blue, majestic, everlasting ocean, with the Fife hills swelling gradually into the Grampians behind it on the north; rough crags and rude precipices at our feet ('where not a hillock rears its head unsung') with Edinburgh at their base, clustering proudly over her rugged foundations, and covering with a vapory mantle the jagged, black, venerable masses of stonework, that stretch far and wide and show like a city of fairyland."

In such moods he could declare: "I will make the doors of human society fly open before me yet, notwithstanding my petards will not burst, or make only noise when they do." He would not follow the advice given by Margaret Gordon in her farewell letter: "Genius will make you great. May virtue render you beloved! Remove the awful distance between you and ordinary men by kind and gentle manners; deal mildly with their inferiority, and be convinced that they will respect you as much and like you more. Why conceal the real goodness that flows from your heart?" Although behind his inferiors in the race of life, he did not hide from Mitchell his "pity for the innocent dolts around one; and disgust (alas!) at the thistles and furze upon which they are faring sumptuously every day." Yet plan after plan went awry, leaving only "teaching two Dandies Mathematics" and a commission to review Joanna Baillie's *Metrical Legends* for Waugh's *New Edinburgh Review,* in addition to the *Encyclopaedia* biographies.

Enforced idleness in which, as he complained to Irving, the powers of his mind were "all festering and corroding each other in the miserable strife of inward will against outward necessity," made him brood upon his physical and emotional ills and upon the wrongs of the industrious poor. The only theory of the world that satisfied his intellect was the materialism in which Edinburgh was steeped, and into which he had been plunged since he had sought in mathematics the certainty he was losing in theology. The simple, self-contained, abstract system of Newtonian physics was the ideal sought for in every department of thought; in the philosophy of Locke and Brown, the ethics of Paley, the politics of Rousseau, Paine, and the Jacobins, the philosophic history of Voltaire and Gibbon, and the political economy of the school of Adam Smith. It was reflected in the aridity of the metaphysical discussion in which Edinburgh delighted; in the cold formality of Edinburgh society. It formed a convenient creed for the rising middle class, resting on the axioms of private property and economic individualism, unqualified by obligations toward less fortunate fellow-men, which had created industrial Glasgow. All was clear, demonstrable; but selfish, cold, and comfortless. In the midst of a "liberal measure of Earthly distresses, want of practical guidance, want of sympathy, want of hope," materialism and industrialism joined to produce a waking nightmare which Carlyle was to describe unforgettably in *Sartor Resartus*: "To me the universe was all void of Life, of Purpose, of Volition, even of Hostility; it was one huge, dead, immeasurable Steam-engine, rolling on, in its vast indifference, to grind me limb from limb." At the time, he wrote, under the influence of Goethe's *Sorrows of Werther,* in probably the first of many attempts at fictionized autobiography: "My life has been a continual fever-dream, and my awakening will be in hell." [15]

CHAPTER III

THE YOUNG IDEALIST

→»→ «←

§ 1

EDWARD IRVING, coming into Edinburgh for General Assembly in May, 1821, found his friend unable to sleep or eat. For exercise and diversion, he took Carlyle on a seventeen-mile walk along the seacoast to the old county town of Hadding-ton, where he was to fill a pulpit.

As a special inducement, Irving had suggested that they seek out Gilbert Burns, brother of the poet, a land agent there. But the visit to Burns proved less interesting to Carlyle than another among the many which Irving, who had taught at Haddington for three years before going to Kircaldy, made to old friends and pupils during the week-end. After a duty call at the manse, his companion led him, near the stately town hall designed by William Adam, along a row of low stone buildings in the High Street. Through an arch flanked with classic pillars they left the street and followed a passageway to a plain, well-proportioned house in a walled garden. Here Irving paid his respects to Mrs. John Welsh, the widow of a physician, and her daughter Jane, who had been his favorite pupil.

The impressively handsome matron greeted them cordially. As he and Irving conversed with her, Carlyle was conscious of the daughter, whose large black eyes, dominating a pale, delicate face, were intent upon him. He did not know that one of his

54

Edinburgh acquaintances had described him as having "talent plenty, fine vein of satire"; an account most intriguing to a clever girl of nineteen bored with the social round of a smug provincial town after the excitement of an Edinburgh boarding-school. She had recently written to her school friend Bess Stodart: "a visit from any man of brains would be an act of mercy to us here." Her looks of sympathetic comprehension drew Carlyle out of his dyspeptic depression, and he talked easily and so brilliantly that he reminded Jane Welsh of her idolized father, lost three years before, for whom she and her mother were wearing partial mourning. He had the tact to continue to direct his conversation principally to Mrs. Welsh, and thus made himself as welcome as Irving to return. Their stay in Haddington lengthened until the Thursday following the sermon, with almost every evening spent with the Welshes. Aided by Irving's footing of intimacy, Carlyle managed to have several tête-à-têtes with Jane. On the rebound from Margaret Gordon, he fell headlong in love. He forgot dyspepsia, banished his cares and hobgoblins, and for the moment was supremely happy. The unsuspecting Mrs. Welsh, flattered by his respectful attentions, gave a standing invitation to return as if he were "going home."

The acquaintance of the young people began on a severely intellectual plane, Carlyle promising aid in the German which Miss Welsh had begun under an incompetent tutor, and lists of books to guide her into serious study. But detailed instructions from Edinburgh were accompanied by a humorous and graceful avowal of love. Jane was unprepared to respond to such impetuosity; her admiration, not her heart, was involved. There seemed even something presumptuous in Carlyle's aspiration to her hand, for Haddington's suburban relation to Edinburgh made it keenly sensitive to class distinctions. Besides, special reasons urged her to seek the mercenary marriage customary at the time. The Welshes had little income except the two hundred pound rent of the moorland farm of Craigenputtock, sixteen miles north of Dumfries, which legally was entirely Jane's. If she married a poor man who needed it as her dowry, her mother could not maintain the scale of living proper for the widow of the leading physician of the town. Even as it was, their joint income was inadequate to their social situation, which they only maintained by a showy distribution of their budget. Well-to-do suitors, deceived into thinking Jane an heiress, were in the offing. Too frequent visits of a poor tutor might scare them away.

Still, the genuine intellectual interests that her father and Irving had encouraged made her eager to retain her clever acquaintance. Haddington eyes might be avoided by meeting him in Edinburgh on visits to Bess Stodart, who kept house for her uncle Mr. Bradfute. She decided to steer an adroit middle course by dampening Carlyle's ardor, and forbidding him to see her until she came to town. Meanwhile, she apprised Miss Stodart of his existence by using him to illustrate a discussion of Rousseau's *Nouvelle Héloïse:* "Thomas Carlyle .... is something liker to St. Preux than George Craig is to Wolmar. He has *his* talents, *his* vast and cultivated mind, *his* vivid imagination, *his* independence of soul, *his* high-souled principles of honor. But then— Ah, these *buts!* St. Preux never kicked the fire-irons, nor made puddings in his teacup. Want of Elegance! Want of Elegance, Rousseau says, is a defect which no woman can overlook." Jane was in Edinburgh for five or six weeks in mid-summer, and her tutor in German called frequently in conservative George Square. Mr. Bradfute sent no warning hints to Mrs. Welsh, for he was a bookseller and appreciated Carlyle's mind. The young people were free to join the fashionable promenade on Princes Street, where Carlyle said: "How many things are here which I do not want." Jane retorted frankly: "How many things are here which I cannot get." These remarks measured the difference between them.

Carlyle was convinced, partly by observation and partly by the blind optimism of love, that Jane had potentialities of rising above the commonplace worldliness which surrounded her. She was barely twenty and he twenty-six: he would mold her plastic character to the outlines of his own. He prescribed solid reading in history with the aid of maps, encouraged her admiration of unconventional writers like Rousseau and Byron, and pressed the merits of Goethe and Schiller on her attention, much to the horror of Irving, who reiterated his protest that the "German school" held "something poisonous to all that in this country has been named virtue." Perhaps suspecting Carlyle's designs, he added a warning as to Jane's character: "she contemplates the inferiority of others rather from the point of ridicule and contempt than that of commiseration and relief; and by doing so she not only leaves objects in distress and loses the luxury of doing good, but she contracts in her own mind a degree of coldness and bitterness which suits ill with my conception of female character and a female's position in society." He remembered bitterly his own mistake in exposing her in childhood to Virgil and other Latin classics, that had made her "a sort of Pagan." This only confirmed Carlyle's belief that he had found in Jane a kindred soul, set apart from the common order of humanity and scornful of vulgar prejudices. No longer feeling alone, he began to confront his difficulties with hopeful energy.

Better literary employment opened in the autumn. Brewster added to his commissions of short biographies a translation of Legendre's *Eléments de Géométrie*. The *New Edinburgh Review*, pleased by the success of his criticism of Joanna Bailie, offered twenty-five guineas (about $300) for an article on Goethe's *Faust*. Carlyle's reputation as a mathematical tutor had spread. He was encouraged to look about for quieter lodgings and to promise John to finance his study of medicine. He wrote cheerfully to Mainhill: "I have set faithfully to work, and am proceeding lustily; not in the whimpering, feeble, hobbling style I used." He outlined a sample day's strenuous schedule, including three hours' teaching and four hours' translation of Legendre, to be followed soon by evenings of original composition. To this creative work he was being urged by Jane Welsh, whose presence in George Square meanwhile prevented its being attempted.

Mrs. Welsh becoming aware of Carlyle's intentions, a clandestine correspondence had to be arranged for Jane's return to Haddington. Thence she wrote at the close of the year: "O, Mr.

Carlyle, if you wish me to admire—to love you (admiration and love is to me the same feeling) use as you ought your precious time and the noble powers that God has given you...and do not laugh at fame." Aware that literature had become a means to wealth and respectability unknown to her mother's philosophy, she began to consider the possibility of a bid for her hand by a man whose talents were obviously high, though he lacked elegance. At least, he would be another string to her bow. With such a prize held out, Carlyle could not fail to attempt the "Book" she thought him capable of. Leisure for it came through the ever-vigilant kindness of Irving.

There had been another dramatic change in Irving's fortunes. Invited to be a candidate for the pulpit of the Caledonian Chapel in London, he was astonished to find that his trial sermons, in the style suspect by Moderatism and outdone in their kind by Chalmers, were attracting into the tiny house of worship of struggling Scottish exiles fashionable people like the Duke of York and Lady Guernsey, politicians like Canning, Mackintosh, and Brougham, and artists like Wilkie and Lawrence. English Evangelicism, having a common origin with Methodism, like it had hitherto been almost entirely middle-class, devoting its efforts to reaching the humble. Irving had somehow made Evangelical preaching, laughed at in John Wesley by Horace Walpole and his like, palatable to the aristocracy and intellectuals. He took charge of the Chapel early in 1822 encouraged "to make a demonstration of a higher style of Christianity, something more magnanimous, more heroical than this age affords." In the flush of continued success he prefaced his *Orations for Judgment to Come,* widely popular on their publication in 1823, with a criticism of the low aims of the English Evangelicals: "They prepare for teaching gypsies, for teaching bargemen, for teaching miners, by apprehending their way of conceiving and estimating truth; why not prepare for teaching imaginative men, and political men, and legal men, and scientific men, who bear the world in hand?" Among those attracted by the notoriety of his trial sermons was Mrs. Charles Buller, wife of a retired Anglo-Indian judge. She was so much impressed that the day after hearing him she asked his advice about the education of her sons Charles and Reginald, who were dissatisfied with Harrow. Irving suggested Edinburgh University, with private tutoring by his remarkable friend, Thomas Carlyle.

The Bullers promptly offered two hundred pounds a year (about $2500), besides the cost of board and lodging, with opportunity for writing and perhaps travel. This salary was wealth to Carlyle, who had probably never spent one quarter as much in a year. In the third week in January, 1822, the Buller boys arrived at the home of the Reverend Doctor Fleming in George Square, in sight of the Bradfute house with its pleasant associations. These pupils treated Carlyle "in another sort of manner than tutors are used to," forming a welcome contrast to "General Dixon's brats" and other early trials. Irving had warned him concerning his elder charge, Charles, aged fifteen: "You will meet a rather difficult subject: clever and acute, and not ill-informed for his age; but his tastes are all given to Boxiania, Bond Street, and pleasures gathered out of the speculations and ambitions of Harrow School." Here he had been deceived by a saturnine cast of countenance that was the result of a childhood accident, and by a pose born of repugnance to "Latin and Greek husks." When offered "expansion into... wider fields of thinking and working," the fashionable youth responded by following his earnest tutor with the abrupt gestures and flashing blue eyes homeward across the breadth of Edinburgh to his lodgings at the farthest edge of the New Town, "delighting to inquire—and argue—and be demolished." Before him lay a political and social career that would be abundantly helpful to Carlyle.

Carlyle's new lodgings were clean and quiet, at the back of a house whence he looked over fields and trees to the Fife hills beyond Kircaldy, though he could not see the wide waters of the Forth that intervened. Sea bathing on either side of the port of Leith was only a mile away, yet the busy centre of Edinburgh was even nearer in the opposite direction. In these pleasant surroundings he had been able to write his *Faust* article in two weeks, completing it before the Bullers arrived. John reported the effect of the news of the tutorship at Mainhill: "The £200 figures largely in the eyes of our father, but not so largely and exclusively, perhaps, as you would be supposed to think, considering all the bearings of his character. He seems to entertain a great deal more respect for you of late than he was wont to cherish when you were strolling about the moors."

Emboldened by the turn in his fortunes, Carlyle ventured to override Jane's prohibition to visit Haddington. Mrs. Welsh showed her hostility, and Jane was unlike herself, holding him strictly to German lessons. He left "a perfect wreck," and would have been in a worse state had he known the full reason for his cold reception. A more favored suitor, son of a distinguished engineer, was in Haddington, and Jane was disconsolate because he was sailing to Italy to study architecture. Despite his agitation, Carlyle met the crisis firmly and frankly: "You bid me write to you as a *friend*. Vain injunction! I must exhibit the true state of my feelings when I write, or else write like a shallow fool.... Forget the roughness of my exterior, if you think me sound within.... The Graces cannot live under a sky so gloomy and tempestuous as mine; I lament their absence, since you lament it; but there is no remedy. If Nature had meant me for a courtly person, she would have made me richer and more impudent."

Jane did not break off correspondence, but succeeded after considerable difficulty in directing it into literary channels. At Carlyle's suggestion they began to write verses in friendly emulation. With a poor ear for rhythm and melody, Carlyle wrote persistently and fruitlessly in metre for the next ten years. In preparation for the "Book" which was to win him fame and Jane, he began to fill a notebook with reflections upon thorough reading in the history of the English Civil Wars. With these labors in addition to five hours' tutoring, some final biographies for the Encyclopaedia, and the Legendre translation, that must be finished and seen through press before the end of July, he was overworking again. He noted with irony "plenty of offers from Booksellers, etc., (whose anxiety to employ me naturally

THE YOUNG IDEALIST 61

increases in inverse ratio to my want of employment)." There
was uneasiness as to his relations with Jane, whose mother had
whisked her into Edinburgh and out again without meeting him:
"Tell me when I shall see you," he complained on July 13. "Consider, I have been a 'reasonable person' for a very long period
now—about half a year as I reckon; and a few more such periods
will put us both—God knows where!" Overwork and anxiety
brought insomnia, for which he thought of laudanum until De
Quincey's *Opium Eater* gave timely warning.

In his overstrained condition the old nightmare of the machine universe, which love and brightened prospects had banished
for a while, returned to haunt his sleepless tossings and his waking hours. A voice seemed to say: "Behold, thou art fatherless,
outcast, and the Universe is mine (the Devil's)." One afternoon in
late July or early August, as he was trudging seaward with a
towel in his pocket over the hot pavements of busy Leith Walk,
he found courage to reply: "*I* am not thine, but free, and forever
hate thee." Whereupon something "rushed like a stream of fire"
over him. From that moment in 1822 he dated his spiritual manhood: "the temper of my misery was changed: not Fear or
whining Sorrow was it, but Indignation and grim, fire-eyed Defiance." [16] His whole being had revolted against materialism. He
had no intellectual means of proving it untrue, but he would die
rather than accept it. To put his defiance promptly into action, he
left Edinburgh before August 14, in order to miss the elaborate
pageant which Sir Walter Scott was preparing to greet the dissolute George IV, who incarnated those aspects of the social order
against which he was in revolt. As Carlyle departed, the Welshes
came into the city, and Jane followed the King "as if my happiness here and hereafter depended on getting a sight of him."

§ 2

IN the autumn the Buller parents came to live in India Street.
The retired judge, a shrewd kindly man suffering from the liver

complaint that was the usual legacy of India, respected Carlyle's mind and sympathized with his dyspepsia. Well-pleased with the tutoring, Buller reduced its hours to four, leaving Carlyle's mornings free for writing. Mrs. Buller, whom wealth and cosmopolitanism raised above provincial snobbery, invited him frequently to her drawing-room, where he first met the upper ranks of Edinburgh society. But he shyly avoided such contacts when he could, and was ill at ease in the luxurious house. He wrote to his mother: "Tea I now consume with urns and china and splendid apparatus all around me, yet I often turn from these grandeurs to the little 'down the house' at Mainhill, where kind affection makes amends for all deficiencies." Mainhill was brought closer by the arrival of his brother John, now twenty-one, to share the Moray Street lodgings while studying medicine. His round, good-humored face and lounging ways were a healthy antidote to strenuous solitude. And there came a delightful chatty letter from Jane, whom boredom in the society of young officers in the Highlands had made more appreciative of solid merit unadorned. He resumed zealously his efforts to give her habits of serious reading and steady mental application.

In the deliciously free mornings, he set her the example of resolute attempts at original writing. He cut decidedly adrift from science by refusing to consider what would once have been an attractive position as professor of mathematics at the Royal Military College at Sandhurst, not far from London, with two hundred pounds a year, house, garden, and two vacations of seven weeks. "Many a time," he confessed to Jane, "I have wished that, while ruining my health with their poor lean triangles and sines and tangents and fluxions and calculi, I had been writing any kind of doggerel, however weak." Despite favorable conditions, the masterpiece failed to materialize. The history of the Civil Wars was too ambitious; various plans for a novel and a tragedy were shipwrecked on his limited experience with life; the verse he produced was awkward imitation of Byron, Campbell, and Burns. He consoled himself by telling Jane: "A man must write a cart-load of trash before he can produce a handful of excellence." But he did not destroy the verses and a short story, "Cruthers and Johnson," which were to serve him well in an hour of need.

Soon came the joyful news that Mrs. Welsh, appeased by his prudent behavior, would welcome a visit to Haddington. He went there for a week-end in the middle of February, 1823, and pronounced Jane's mind "almost doubled in power and real wealth" during the year of their separation. Her plans, however, for a return visit in Edinburgh were indefinitely postponed by the renewal of Mrs. Welsh's suspicions when she saw the young people together.

Meanwhile, Carlyle was somewhat comforted by an important literary commission. Irving had been pressing his friend's project of a "picture-gallery of literary great men" upon John Taylor, the scholarly editor of the *London Magazine,* which had gained a high reputation since its founding in 1820 by the contributions of De Quincey, Lamb, and Hazlitt. Taylor now requested Carlyle to inaugurate the series by a biographical sketch of Schiller. Here was a chance to show his powers.

The time and the place were highly propitious for entry into the profession of letters. The depression of 1819-20 had been succeeded by a period of prosperity, in which the enterprise of Constable, Murray, the Ballantynes and other publishers was reaching a new middle-class reading public. For once, authors seemed scarcely numerous enough for the demand. In his *Memories of a Literary Veteran* (1850) the mediocre Scottish writer Pearse Gillies looked back regretfully to these years: "In 1822, the fortune of literary men from high to low wore *couleur de rose.* ... Strange to say, even minor authors were paid and encouraged then." At the top of the profession rewards were dazzling; Lockhart thought that in 1822 "Scott must have reckoned on clearing £30,000 at least in the course of a couple of years by the novels written in such a period." The year previous, Byron had received £2700 for the rights of the (chiefly closet) dramas *Sardanapalus, The Two Foscari,* and *Cain,* while the boom in poetry gave the uninspired craftsman Milman 500 guineas for the forgotten *Belshazzar*. For the industrious journeyman there was variety of steady, well-paid employment: in translation; in encyclopaedias, from the *Edinburgh* that had employed Carlyle to the much more generous *Brittanica,* which was issuing a supplement to its fifth edition; in the reviews with the *Edinburgh* offering twenty guineas ($250) for a "sheet" of sixteen pages; and in the magazines, with *Blackwood's* offering sixteen guineas a sheet. The *Quarterly Review* was the mainstay of Robert Southey, an encouraging example of a literary man-of-all-work able to support himself by his pen without lowering his artistic or ethical standards.

Although the chief reading public was in London, cheaper printing made Edinburgh a rival centre of the publishing trade, drawing directly on fertile Scottish talent. Edinburgh had never had a Grub Street, and in the late eighteenth century, when Scotland began to lead England in literature, "the Scotch feeling that literature was something too fine and sacred to be produced merely for money gave a better tone to the profession without in the least diminishing the pecuniary rewards." [17] The Napoleonic Wars had not left Scotland as provincial in its reading as England. There remained a lively interest in continental literatures; in French Classicism, endeared by memories of the *Vieille Alliance,* and the rival German Romanticism, which was returning to favor after a long period of Tory suspicion of the *Sturm und Drang* school. In 1817 the publisher John Blackwood had advanced three hundred pounds to Lockhart, a barrister of twenty-three who had scarcely begun his literary career, for study in Germany on condition that he translate Friederich von Schlegel's lectures on the history of literature. Since 1819 *Blackwood's Magazine* had maintained a series of *Horae Germanicae,* translations of extracts from various German writers chiefly contributed by Gillies, in addition to extended reviews of German works by Lockhart and De Quincey. Thus Carlyle found in German, which, acquired for scientific purposes, had also opened "a new heaven and new earth" of literature and philosophy, very saleable literary material.

The theme of Schiller's life was most congenial. Sprung like himself from humble parents, Schiller had found his way into literature after false starts in the Church, law, and medicine. He had revolted against a ducal patron and the false values of a decaying feudal society. He had achieved literary recognition as a result of unremitting effort without compromising his sense of truth and rectitude, and finally died a martyr to overwork imposed by his exacting artistic standards. Like Milton, he had made his life "a heroic poem." On the threshold of his own literary career, Carlyle found in Schiller a guide and an inspiration. He identified himself with his hero, and endeavored to transport himself "into his circumstances outward and inward," to "see as he saw, and feel as he felt." Notwithstanding valuable apprenticeship in biography for the *Encyclopaedia,* Carlyle wrote with extreme difficulty, for he was determined to produce the best work of which he was capable. He consoled himself for his slowness by thinking of "Rousseau lying in his bed and painfully wrenching every syllable of his *Nouvelle Héloïse* from the obscure complexities of his imagination. He composed every sentence of it, on the average, *five* times over!" The result of such hard writing was easy reading. Carlyle achieved a style at once clear and melodious, that ranged from the concise antitheses and fluid rapidity of the French Classicism with which he had spent many years, to the quiet irony, the gentle melancholy, the exalted yearning of the Romanticists. His thoroughness had burst the bounds of a magazine article. What he sent to London in late April, 1823, was the first twenty-five years of a full life, leaving Schiller, like himself, at the moment of entry into professional authorship.

June found him in the Buller summer home in the Highlands, hard at work on a translation of Goethe's *Wilhelm Meister's Apprenticeship,* for which the publishers of his *Legendre* had offered "the very handsome payment" of £180 for the first thousand copies on date of publication, and £250 for every subsequent thousand. In a household crowded with guests for the hunting season, he had the opportunity to observe the Scottish and English leisure classes at play. He accompanied Mrs. Buller to watch a chase ending with a bag of "two fauns about as large as your long-eared warlock, in value somewhere about sixpence apiece," that young Oxford men pronounced "royal sport." Of one of these youths he made an acid portrait: "Reginald has been at Oxford studying the nature of horses. Philosophy is all a hum [humbug], but the short back, and the price, and the speed— these are the points for a future parson of the English Church." The women gave an excellent opportunity to preach obliquely to Jane against the evils of an ambitious marriage: "As a fine Lady I do not see how you could get through the world on even moderate terms.... From day to day and from year to year, the problem is not how to use time, but how to waste it the least painfully: they have their dinners, their routs, they move heaven and earth to get everything arranged and enacted properly, and when the whole is done, what is it? The uneasy destruction of half a dozen hours.... It is no wonder that poor women take to opium and scandal. There is something in the life of a sturdy peasant toiling from sun to sun for a plump wife and six *eating* children." This repeated sermonizing was the echo of his disappointment in the worldliness of Margaret Gordon.

When Jane had finally succeeded in getting to Edinburgh for ten days, the excessive zeal with which Mrs. Welsh chaperoned their meetings gave him food for surmise. Its actual cause was the suit of Dr. Fyffe, who had taken over Dr. Welsh's practice, but ignorance and admiration for Jane made him believe he might have an aristocratic rival. However, the tone of her replies began to indicate that he was surpassing the unknown at long range, until in September came an unexpected confession of Jane's love: "I owe you much! feelings and sentiments that ennoble my character, that give dignity, interest, and enjoyment to my life. In return I can only love you, and *that* I do, from the bottom of my heart.... When shall the world know your worth as I do? ... I heard your *Life of Pascal* criticised. My face was crimson." She made it clear that this was not a promise to marry, for marriage must await his achieving an assured position; but it was enough to set him working with a redoubled zeal that contrasted strangely with the atmosphere of the Buller household. He thought she had refused riches for him; he must make himself worthy of the sacrifice.

He translated the *Meister* from six in the evening to the small hours of the morning, accomplishing the daily stint of ten pages necessary to cover bulky material that would print as three octavo volumes. In October this toil "like steam-machinery" was transferred to the *Schiller,* whose completion was requested without delay by the *London Magazine.* A second part went off within five weeks, leaving the usual consequences of immoderate labor, acute dyspepsia and insomnia. Consultation with an Edinburgh doctor brought him near Jane again. He wrote asking to call. Mrs. Welsh, reading her daughter's face, gave grudging consent. She made Jane promise that the correspondence should be thenceforth under her eye, but the "Lovely Damsel of Many Devices," as her admirer dubbed her, found means of evasion. At the beginning of the new year Carlyle was encouraged in his toil on the final installment of the *Schiller* by seeing the introduction to Part Two quoted approvingly in the London *Times:* "almost the first testimony to merit on my part which *could* not be warped by partiality." The Bullers, impressed by his success, offered three months' vacation on the completion of the biography in February, with the stipulation that he rejoin them in London in June. Jane was delighted at this removal to London, agreeing with Irving that contact with Coleridge and other men of genius would immediately ripen Carlyle's powers and win him recognition. He returned to the *Meister* translation with accustomed energy, finishing it early in May while on a farewell visit to Mainhill.

The consequent exhaustion produced a severe sore throat, and delayed the usual letter to Haddington. Jane's anxiety was increased by the news that their favorite author had been cut off in the midst of his powers: "For God's sake write the instant this reaches you, if you have not done it before.... Byron is dead! I was told it all at once in a roomfull of people. My God, if they had said that the sun or moon had gone out of the heavens, it could not have struck me with the idea of a more awful and dreary blank in the creation.... I have felt cold and dejected ever since.... I wish you was come." The letter was crossed in the mails by her lover's lament on the same theme. Byron's was "the noblest spirit in Europe"; he felt as if he had "lost a Brother." "I dreamed of seeing and knowing him," he added. "There is a blank in your heart and a blank in mine since this man passed away. Let us stand closer by each other." Jane responded with delight to the announcement that he was soon coming to Haddington to say goodbye before sailing for London: "Thank God! I have you again. Byron's death made me tremble for all I admire and love." Carlyle always remembered "the *gimp bonnet* she wore, and her anxious silent thoughts, and my own, mutually legible both of them, in part."

Jane was indeed holding back something—a disappointment and humiliation. She had planned the surprise of meeting her lover soon in London as the guest of Irving, who had recently married Isabella Martin, the Kircaldy minister's daughter, after an eleven-year engagement. Only two weeks before, Irving had withdrawn his invitation, saying: "My dear Isabella has succeeded in healing the wounds of my heart, but I am hardly yet in a condition to expose them." The cryptic reference was to the fact that in 1820 he had vainly asked release from his engagement in order to offer his hand elsewhere. He had discovered too late the mature fascination of his favorite little pupil, Jane Welsh. It now appeared that his wife knew who her rival had been, and wished her anywhere else than in her own household. Jane had loved other men since, and Carlyle most of all, but she trembled lest bygones arise to threaten the friendship of Irving and Carlyle. Could she count on the discretion of the frank and impetuous Irving—or the forbearance of a jealous wife?

§ 3

CARLYLE had miscalculated the schedule of the Edinburgh-London steamship service. Rather than wait idly for half a week, he took a sailing smack on June 5, 1824. Almost six days later, as the boat ended its 400 mile voyage by winding slowly "thro' the forest of masts in the Thames up to our station at Tower Wharf," the young Scot began to comprehend how much wider the world was than his experience. "The giant bustle, the coal-heavers, the ten thousand times ten thousand sounds and movements of that monstrous harbor formed the grandest object I had ever witnessed. One man seems as a drop in the ocean; you feel annihilated in the immensity of that heart of all the earth." There were few young men of his outstanding ability who had seen so little. In his voracious reading he had ranged widely in space and time, but he had approached the age of twenty-nine without having been outside tiny Scotland except for walking tours in mountainous Cumberland and a week's trip to York to consider a tutoring offer, and without having social opportunities other than contacts with the Buller household and with scientists and the less exalted order of men of letters through business relations with Leslie and Brewster. The aristocracy of Scottish authors, Scott, Jeffrey, Wilson, Lockhart, was above his sphere. Glasgow, the largest city he had seen hitherto, was only a tenth the size of London, which, with 1,227,590 inhabitants by the census of 1821, was unrivalled among the cities of the world.

Irving was ready to introduce the biographer of Schiller and the translator of *Wilhelm Meister* to the best literary society in London. He had enlisted the assistance of the wealthy banker Basil Montagu, whose connection with the Wordsworth circle, begun in the days when he was tutored at Racedown by the poet, made his wife's salon a meeting-place for authors. His dapper sons looked askance at Carlyle, approving "neither his dress, his uncouth manners, nor his dialect," but the "stately matron" their step-mother, whom experience as a governess had made sympathetic with *déclassé* intelligence, received him cordially. Mrs. Montagu and Irving soon took him on the visit to Coleridge to which he had long looked forward. He admired the poems and the profound criticism of the *Biographia Literaria,* but what he desired most from Coleridge's lips was the argument of an unpublished book that had been long in preparation, a development of the German Transcendental philosophy that promised freedom from the bondage of materialism. Since his defiance of the machine universe, Carlyle had been struggling with the technicalities of Kant and Fichte in search of its disproof. He hoped Coleridge would elucidate what he found obscure. But when he introduced the topic of Kant, the nebulous and digressive monologue of Irving's oracle left confusion worse confounded.

At fifty-one Coleridge, the most astonishing English genius of his time, ruined with opium, was in the care of Dr. Gilman. The flabby, relaxed figure shuffling irresolutely beside the tense Carlyle among the garden paths gave only fleeting glimpses of his glorious heyday which Hazlitt had recently described and lamented in *My First Acquaintance with Poets.* To the ascetic young Scot whose purpose was tempered steel, the depth of the tragedy was hidden. "His cardinal sin is that he lacks will," he wrote his brother John, "I found him unprofitable, even tedious ...a great and useless genius." But he persevered in his visits, presenting a copy of *Wilhelm Meister;* for there remained a sense of indebtedness and the ghost of an old admiration. Disappointment had not had time to ripen into the brilliant malice of the eighth chapter of *The Life of John Sterling.* He did not suspect the creative fire that smoldered in the great man's embers. Later in that very year Coleridge, whiling away an illness by reading the gift copy of Carlyle's *Meister,* found in the *Confessions of a Fair Saint* the inspiration for his *Confessions of an Inquiring Spirit,* containing germinating ideas of the Broad Church Movement. And the profound social philosophy of *The Idea of Church and State* was to appear in 1828.

At Irving's house Carlyle met on June 22 another student of German, the barrister Henry Crabb Robinson, who had met

Schiller and had read Milton's *Samson Agonistes* with Goethe at Weimar. Two weeks later Robinson found Irving and Carlyle having tea with Charles Lamb, whose *Essays of Elia* had appeared two years before. The evening passed agreeably, to Robinson's astonishment, for Lamb's "incurable levity" accorded ill with Irving's piety. In other company Lamb liked to repeat "some blasphemous anecdote he told when in the company of Mr. Irving the Scotch preacher," [18] but he had a sincere admiration for his opposite. Carlyle's dislike of Lamb apparently did not develop until they met again in 1831. With Wordsworth and Southey not in town, the Montagu salon was peopled with minor writers, of whom the gracious and gentle Procter (Barry Cornwall) was the most congenial. Procter talked of his schoolmate Byron, and gave Carlyle one of his letters, which was sent to Jane as a treasure. A greater act of Procter's kindness was three years away.

On his own account Carlyle sought out Thomas Campbell. This favorite poet of his youth proved a conceited dandy in "blue frock and trousers, eye glass, and wig," who received him coldly, apparently scenting an application for employment in the *New Monthly Magazine,* of which he was editor. "Perhaps I am hasty about Campbell," he wrote to Jane, "perhaps I am too severe. He was my earliest favorite. I hoped to have found him different." For the mass of writers in those days of brutal reviewing and calumnious literary quarrels, Carlyle had abundant contempt: "This rascal rout, this dirty rabble, destitute not only of high feeling or knowledge or intellect, but even of common honesty! The very best of them are ill-natured weaklings. They are not red-blooded men at all. They are only things for writing articles." With these gentry he would have more to do in a later and less fortunate day.

Two journalists, however, William Hazlitt and Leigh Hunt, had won his respect by bold criticism of the Government, continued in the face of personal villification by the Tory *Blackwood's* and *Quarterly*. Hunt's *Examiner* had been his favorite newspaper, and he had been delighted with his short-lived

Liberal, containing Byron's "Vision of Judgment," "of the wicked-est and cleverest turn you can imagine," ridiculing the Laureate Southey's eulogy of George III. But neither of these courageous men was to be seen. As Carlyle arrived, Hazlitt was leaving London for a honeymoon tour of France and Italy with his second wife. In January, 1825, Hazlitt found Hunt in Florence, stunned by misfortune. Three great poets had graced his life with their friendship: now Keats and Shelley were dead in Italy, Byron in Greece. The ambitious enterprise of *The Liberal* had been a failure, and he was left without means or resolution to return to England.

Carlyle, but a month younger than Keats, three years younger than Shelley, and seven years younger than Byron, did not fully realize the fatality that had befallen his generation. Possibly he had not heard of Shelley and Keats. He was left isolated between the older Romanticists, the waning of whose powers was fore-shadowed in Coleridge, and the Victorians, who had still to come to manhood. If he had been gifted with prophetic insight into the London of 1824, he would have observed strange ma-terials for the future growing up about him. Charles Dickens, just released from the slavery of pasting labels on blacking bottles in a warehouse, was enjoying the dubious advantages of the Wellington Classical and Commercial Academy. Thackeray was drawing caricatures of his schoolmates at Charterhouse, near Smithfield Market. A fond father was privately printing *Incon-dita,* verses by the twelve-year-old Robert Browning. John Ruskin, aged five, was in the prison-house of his solitary and over-stimu-lated childhood. Only in the amazing John Stuart Mill, at eighteen the chief contributor to the newly launched Radical *Westminster Review,* could Carlyle have found an approach to equality and common interest among the Londoners who were to be the intimates of his mature years.

Although London literary society failed to give the stimula-tion Irving had predicted, London publishers were most encour-aging. By his translation of *Wilhelm Meister,* a book which had dropped out of sight since its favorable greeting in the original by the *Monthly Magazine* in 1798, Carlyle had "laid the foundations of a real knowledge of Goethe in England."[19] Hitherto chiefly known as the Storm and Stress author of *Götz von Berlichingen* and *The Sorrows of the Young Werther,* Goethe now appeared in the serene detachment of his maturer years. The optimism of the inexperienced author had led Carlyle to reckon on the possibility of a sale of 3,000 copies of his *Meister* the first year, bringing him £680. Brisk early sales and favorable newspaper notices, attracting proposals of other translation, seemed to confirm his hopes of a comfortable and steady income from writing. The *Schiller* also had been so well received by readers of the *London Magazine* that its owners, the publishing house of Taylor and Hessey, were offering to put it out in book form, with a guarantee of about ninety pounds on date of publication. Before he had been a month in London, Carlyle felt secure in abandoning the anchorage of the tutorship, despite Charles Buller's "passion of sadness and anger," for the open sea of the literary profession.

Detachment from the Bullers gave him a range of movement of which his keen eye for racial and social differences took the utmost advantage. To a degree difficult to realize now, England was a foreign country to a Scot in those days of slow communication. Carlyle was impressed by the richer natural gifts of the more mellow southerly climate, supporting a much denser population, and making it more easy-going, gayer, softer in manners and speech. He exclaimed at the spaciousness and beauty of the villages near London as compared with the compact bareness of Ecclefechan and its like. But he soothed Mainhill's local pride by describing the backwardness of English agricultural methods: "The husbandry of Kent is beyond that in many counties of England, but a Scotch farmer would smile at many parts of it. They plough with five horses and two men (one ca-ing), and the plough has wheels. Many a time I have thought of Alick with his Lothian tackle and two horses setting these inefficient loiterers to the right about. Yet here they are much better than in Warwickshire, where farming may be said to be an unknown art, where the fields are sometimes of half an acre, and of all possible shapes but square, and a threshing mill is a thing nearly unheard of." In sharp contrast to these relics of "merrie England" was the efficiency and unloveliness of the new industrialism typified by Birmingham: "As a town it is pitiful enough—a mean congeries of bricks, including one or two large capitalists, some hundreds of minor ones, and, perhaps, 120,000 sooty artisans in metals and chemical produce. The streets are ill-built, ill-paved; always flimsy in their aspect—often poor, sometimes miserable." A visit through the "half-frightful scene" of the iron and coal works of this "city of Tubal Cain" showed "its attractions as well as its repulsions," for here were "the sources of British power."

Five days at Paris gave another perspective on the English scene. He met Legendre, whose *Geometry* he had translated, and attended with him a meeting of the Institute, where he saw, among other men of science, the celebrated Laplace whose discoveries had helped upset his early beliefs. Curiosity as to the French Revolution led him to seek out another Legendre, the "solid butcher" who had dared ask that Danton be heard in his own defence when Robespierre arrested him, and had played an important part in putting out the last flames of Sansculotism. The outdoor frivolity of the French formed a disagreeable contrast to the substantial, home-loving English: "The people sit and chatter and fiddle away existence as if it were a raree show, careless how it go on so they have excitement, *des sensations agréables.*" Carlyle's provinciality could never break the barrier of the Latin races. But the sights and sounds of the streets, his conversation with the Revolutionist Legendre, and a close view of the new king Charles X, brother of the unfortunate Louis XVI, were stored in his memory, to serve him well in his *History of the French Revolution,* which he was to complete almost thirteen years later without having seen France again.

On his return, London seemed more astounding than ever: "Paris scarcely occupies a quarter of the ground, and does not seem to have a twentieth part of the business!" He was fascinated by the contrast of the noise and dirt of Smithfield Market, near the centre of the city, to which cattle were still driven through the streets to be slaughtered, with "stately streets and squares, calm green recesses where nothing of this abomination is permitted to enter." "No wonder Cobbett calls the place a Wen," he wrote Alick. "It is a monstrous Wen! The thick smoke of it beclouds a space of thirty square miles; and a million of vehicles, from the dog or cuddy-barrow to the giant waggon, grind along its streets for ever. I saw a six-horse wain the other day with, I think, number 200,000 and odds upon it!" Visiting Newgate prison with the Quaker philanthropist Elizabeth Fry, he was appalled at the felons: "There they were of all climates and kinds, the Jew, the Turk, the 'Christian,' from the gray villain of sixty to the blackguard boy of *eight!* Nor was it their depravity that struck me, so much as their debasement. Most of them actually looked like *animals;* you could see no traces of a *soul* (not even of a bad one) in their gloating, callous, sensual countenances." The sight contributed to that "hearty hatred of scoundrels" which was to shock readers of his *Latter-Day Pamphlets.*

Augmenting the *Schiller* with translated excerpts from his writings and preparing it for the press prolonged Carlyle's stay in London well into 1825. John Taylor, the cultivated and generous publisher of Keats and Hazlitt, produced a beautiful volume of three hundred well proportioned pages, with ample margins and large clear print on creamy paper that, in the copy preserved in the Pierpont Morgan Library, shows no signs of age. He proposed a similar life of Voltaire, on the improved terms of one hundred pounds for the first thousand.

Carlyle's services were also in demand for translation of German tales of terror and chivalric sentiment, which were the fad of the moment. G. B. Whitaker, who had handled the English sales of the *Meister,* was saying confidentially to Connop Thirwall: "German tales are now the rage, and I wish to take advantage of the mania while it lasts." Carlyle, disliking the type of fiction wanted, found some attraction in the offer of Tait of Edinburgh to give him a free hand in the choice of materials.

With the general financial inflation keeping the book trade steadily brisk, he seemed sure of continuing to earn by his pen at least the two hundred pounds yearly it had been recently winning him. A letter from Goethe, arriving in December, was a gratifying sign of his recognition as a man of letters. Irving urged that the prospect justified his settling permanently in London; one of the Montagu circle offered patronage to the extent of paying his lodging. But the cost of living was considerably higher than at Edinburgh; his independence rejected the thought of patronage; and he was resolute that no depression in the literary market should force him to lower his standards of art and honesty.

He had adopted as his own Schiller's lofty and ascetic ideal of the profession of letters: "The end of Literature was not, in Schiller's judgment, to amuse the idle, or to recreate the busy, by showy spectacles for the imagination or quaint paradoxes and epigrammatic disquisitions for the understanding: least of all was it to gratify in any shape the selfishness of its possessors, or to minister to their malignity, their love of money or even of fame." To this Carlyle added the Hebrew Prophetic ideal remaining from his theological background: "Genius is 'the inspired gift of God'; a solemn mandate to its owner to go forth and labor in his sphere, to keep alive the 'sacred fire' among his brethren, which the heavy and polluted atmosphere of this world is forever threatening to extinguish.... 'The Artist, it is true,' says Schiller, 'is the son of his age, but pity for him if he is its pupil or even its favorite! Let some beneficent Divinity snatch him when a suckling from the breast of his mother, and, having grown to manhood, let him return, a foreign shape, into his century; not however to delight it by his presence, but terrible, like the Son of Agamemnon, to purify it! The Matter of his works he will take from the present; but their Form he will derive from a nobler time, nay from beyond all time, from the absolute unchanging unity of his nature.' "

In revulsion from the vanity of London authors, Carlyle was letting the *Schiller* appear without his name on the title-page, and was keeping steadily before him, on his letter seal and bookplate, the motto of the Carlyles of Torthorwald, *Humilitate*. Humility, though inculcated by his early religious training, was a virtue he did not take to naturally, and his diaries and letters are full of self-exhortations, in a continued confessional. "Literary fame," he wrote to Alick on February 14, 1825, "is a thing which I covet little; but I desire to be working honestly in my day and generation in this business, which has now become my trade."

Temperamental reasons also urged him away from London. Always abnormally sensitive to noise, smells, smoke, and confinement, he felt his health rapidly deteriorating in city lodgings. His splenetic remarks on London authors were indeed partly produced by his physical state. His village soul was offended by the shoddiness and dishonesty of the rapidly growing metropolis: "You are packed into paltry shells of brick houses (calculated to endure for forty years and then fall); every door that slams in the street is audible in your most secret chamber; the necessaries of life are hawked about through multitudes of hands, and reach you, frequently adulterated, always at rather more than twice their cost elsewhere; people's friends must visit them by rule and measure; and when you issue from your door, you are assailed by vast shoals of quacks, and showmen, and street sweepers, and pickpockets, and mendicants of every degree and shape, all plying in noise or silent craft their several vocations, all in their hearts like 'lions ravening for their prey.'" He confessed to Alick his homesickness for Scotland: "One hates... to be a foreigner anywhere; and this, after all that can be said about it, is the case with *every* Scotchman in this city. They live like aliens here, unrooted in the soil; without political, religious, or even much social, interest in the community, distinctly feeling every day that with them it is money only that can 'make the mare go.'" In this mood he thought of residence in the Scottish countryside, where his health had always improved, and where he could be close to his family and not too far from the book market of Edinburgh. Other men of letters had found such rural retreats practicable: "Southey and Wordsworth have retired far from the din of this monstrous city; so has Thomas Moore."

It occurred to him that at Jane's ancestral farm of Craigen-puttock, not far from Dumfries, he might unite the things closest to his heart, literary life in the country not far from his family, and marriage. Alick would do the farming, and he and Jane would be free for intellectual labors and companionship. He proposed to her: "Let us set our minds and habitudes in order, and grow under the peaceful sunshine of Nature...I will *not* degenerate into the wretched thing which calls itself an Author in our Capitals and scribbles for the sake of filthy lucre in the periodicals of the day....Explain all things to your mother, and take her serious advice respecting them."

Jane had been dreaming of a life beside him as a famous London author in a future considerably removed; she was rudely awakened by this project of immediate union with a man not yet established, on a farm that she knew to be lonely and desolate. Mrs. Welsh, alarmed by the threat to her own income, urged strongly the financial and social imprudence of such a step. Jane's reply united their objections: "I love you, I have told you so a hundred times;..but I am not *in love* with you: that is to say, my love for you is not a passion which overclouds my judgment, and absorbs all my regard for myself and others [her mother].....I conceive it a duty which every one owes to society, not to throw up that station in it which Providence has assigned him; and having this conviction I could not marry into a station inferior to my own with the approval of my judgment, *which* alone would enable me to brave the censures of my acquaintance. You and I keeping house at Craigenputtock!...Nothing but your ignorance of the place saves you from the imputation of insanity for admitting such a thought.... Think of something else, then, apply your industry to carry it into effect, use your talents to gild over the inequality of our births; and then—we will talk of marrying,...at all events I will marry no one else."

Naturally much in this was offensive to Carlyle's pride and social views, but after some deliberation he replied coolly and firmly: "The maxims you proceed by are those of common and acknowledged prudence; and I do not say that it is unwise in you to walk exclusively by them. But for me, my case is peculiar: and unless I adopt other than common maxims, I look upon my ruin as absolutely sure. In fact I cannot but perceive that the stations from which we have looked at life and formed our schemes of it are in your case and mine essentially different. You have a right to anticipate excitement and enjoyment; the highest blessing I anticipate is peace. You are bound to pay deference to the criticisms of others and expect their approbation; I to pay comparatively little deference to their criticisms and to overlook their contempt.... I am not without a certain consciousness of the gifts that are in me; but I should mistake their nature *widely,* if I calculated that they would ever guide me to wealth and preferment, or even certainly to literary fame. As yet the best of them is very immature; and if ever they should come forth in full strength, it must be to other and higher ends that they are directed." He persisted in urging that Craigenputtock afforded "the elements of real comfort" and in asking Jane "to unite our resources, not her wealth and rank merely, for these were but a small and inessential fraction of the prayer; but her judgment, her patience, prudence, her true affection, to mine." But if their views were irreconcilable, he was ready to part with kindly feelings.

"How could I *part* from the only living soul that understands me?" Jane answered hastily: "I merely wish to see you earning a *certain* income, and exercising the profession of a gentleman." Although she could not reveal the extent and motives of her mother's part in rejecting the Craigenputtock project, she confessed that she had stressed external circumstances too strongly, in order to hide the fact that her feelings were not wholly ripe for marriage. But she softened this confession with an exquisitely phrased compliment: "From the change which my sentiments have already undergone during the period of our acquaintance, I have little doubt but that in time I shall be perfectly satisfied with them.... According as my mind enlarges and my heart improves, I become capable of comprehending the goodness and greatness which are in you, and my affection for you increases.

Not many months ago, I would have said that it was impossible that I should ever be your Wife; at present, I consider this the most probable destiny for me. And in a year or so perhaps, I shall consider it the only one." Meanwhile she promised to attempt to overcome the "miserable perversion" of her ideas and feelings by her environment. Although she did not tell him so, she dated her engagement from these early days of 1825.

Even without Jane, Carlyle went on with his plan of country residence. Alick leased Hoddam Hill farm, overlooking Ecclefechan, where his brother would join him after passing through Edinburgh to procure literary employment. When March brought close the day of departure, Carlyle discovered how fond of England he had become: "I cling to the hope of often seeing it again. I have found more kindness in it than I ever found in any other district of the Earth, except the one that holds my Father's house. If stony Edinburgh be no better to me than it was, I will shake off the dust of my feet against it, and abide in it no more. My health will return, and then I shall be ready for any scene." He remembered with especial warmth Mrs. Montagu, the pious Mrs. Strachey, Mrs. Buller's sister, and Dr. Badams of Birmingham, who had tried (alas! too late) to rid him of dyspepsia by a sensible regimen of exercise and diet, without the mercury pills with which he had been taught to torture himself.

He was also leaving behind the loyal Irving in a precarious situation. The success of his preaching had caused the erection of a larger church building in a better neighborhood, with the ironic result that his fashionable hearers, deprived of the piquancy of crowding into the tiny Caledonian Chapel, had flitted off to a new sensation. Of those remaining faithful, the original Scotch congregation was outnumbered by English fanatics who were encouraging his speculations on Biblical prophecies concerning the end of the world. One day Irving had taken his friend to the Admiralty House to meet an official who had a new theory of prophecy. To Carlyle the "Honorable Something or other" had "a look of perfect politeness, perfect silliness." As they came away, he asked pointedly: "Do you really think that gentleman can throw any light to you on anything whatsoever?" Irving replied good-naturedly but gravely, "Yes, I do," having none of Carlyle's habit of judging a theory by his temperamental response to its proponents. Carlyle spent his last two weeks in London at Irving's house, where they had many happy old-time talks. At parting the giant preacher insisted on giving his formal blessing, which his friend received unresponsively, full of gloomy forebodings. Irving had been "the best man" he had seen in England, and was worthy of a better fate.

§ 4

CARLYLE found Edinburgh very ready to employ him after his late publications and acquisition of capital. Brewster pressed him to take a third share in a periodical to be printed by Tait, of which he would edit the science, Lockhart the politics, and Carlyle the literature. But since this plan would take months to mature, Carlyle meanwhile closed with Tait's proposition of a collection of German fiction to be called *German Romance,* with a hundred pounds on date of publication. During these negotiations he had many opportunities to visit Haddington. On their new footing of sincerity, he told Jane of Margaret Gordon, and she disclosed her financial situation. Disabused of his conception of her as an heiress, he persuaded her to calm her mother's fears by giving over to her the Haddington house and the income of Craigenputtock for life. Generous in her turn, Jane willed Craigenputtock to Carlyle if he outlived her mother. "My money affairs are all arranged," she said proudly. "I am as poor as yourself." She was slowly being emancipated from snobbery and materialism, and acquiring something of her lover's view of the world. In gratitude for financial security Mrs. Welsh withdrew her demand to inspect their correspondence, and gave Jane permission to visit him when he was settled in the country.

From Haddington Carlyle wrote to Crabb Robinson, who had been generous with information about Germany on several occasions in London, for advice as to the choice of fiction for translation: "My acquaintance with this branch of literature is small, for it does not stand by any means in the highest favor with me." [20] He took to Hoddam Hill forty miscellaneous borrowed books to look over, and ordered others from Germany. His final selection for the four volumes of the anthology was a compromise between popular taste and his desire to enlighten the public as to German life, character, and thought. The first two volumes met the demand for light fiction with folk material by Musaeus and Tieck (Grimm's *Fairy Tales* had been published in 1823), a fantasy by Hoffman, and the chivalric mediaevalism of Fouqué's *Aslauga's Knight.* But the third volume introduced Carlyle's new discovery, Jean Paul Richter, hitherto untranslated except in fragments, with the half-sentimental, half-humorous extravaganza of *Quintus Fixelein* and *Schmelze's Journey to Flaetz.* The final volume was of still greater solidity; the heavily didactic second part of *Wilhelm Meister* (the *Travels*), prefaced by a biographical and critical sketch of Goethe that was "the first at all adequate account of him in English." [21] This educative purpose greatly increased the difficulties of translation (the Germans themselves need a special glossary for Richter), and of procuring books. On April 25, 1826, when he had been a year at work, he made an anxious appeal to Robinson, who had translated fragments of Richter as early as 1811, for biographical data concerning him and also for volumes of his works, those ordered from Germany being long overdue. But there was compensation in the greater interest of the materials, so that this period at Hoddam Hill, May, 1825, to October, 1826, was noticeably free from his usual complaints of the hardships of literary labor.

He was again in his beloved family circle, with Alick as farmer and his mother as housekeeper, assisted by a servant and some of his younger sisters. His father and the rest of the family were close at hand at Mainhill. The house was large enough to allow him the privacy of two rooms. Quiet, fresh air, and exercise brought the hoped-for improvement in health. He had at last the detachment to reflect upon his gains in battle with society: a substantial beginning of literary success, an income that although not regular would have seemed riches three years before, improved and widened social contacts, and, best of all, the approach of victory in his wooing over all the varieties of provincial snobbery. He began to find solutions for the spiritual problems that had harassed him so long.

Goethe and Richter convinced him that the wreck of the historical evidences of Christianity need not involve Christian morality. Knowing that the true Bible was not only an ancient Hebrew book but also the world literature recording the spiritual discoveries of the best men in all ages, he could now listen tranquilly to the Hoddam Kirk bell, "strangely touching, like the departing voice of eighteen-hundred years." An emotional attachment to Christianity remained, to grow gradually less under the influence of Jane's irreligion.

German philosophy offered a way out of the prison of the mechanical universe for a mind too firmly grounded in scientific habits to accept the alternate exit of Evangelicism. Carlyle, who had laughed at "the vile show of induction" by the phrenology that had a wide vogue among educated men, including the logician Archbishop Whately, did not seize upon Kant with facile enthusiasm. In May, 1823, when he had known something of *The Critique of Pure Reason* for three years, he wrote in his Journal: "I wish I fully understood the philosophy of Kant. Is it a chapter in the history of human folly? or the brightest in the history of human wisdom? or both mixed? and in what degree?" Somewhat later, in *The Life of Schiller,* he expressed his amusement at its cumbrous technicalities: "Often a proposition of dread aspect, when resolutely grappled with, proves to be a very harmless truth, familiar to us from of old, sometimes so familiar as to be a truism." Though he needed no convincing by the famous antinomies that reason was impotent to prove the existence of God, it was only in 1825-26 that he was willing to accept the affirmations of *The Critique of Practical Reason,* and the hopeful inferences Fitchte drew from them. The slowness of this assent is interesting evidence of Carlyle's self-control, in view of his strong temperamental urge toward it.

One of the chief reasons for his disillusion with science was a keen perception of the very human fallibility of its practitioners. In 1817 he had exclaimed in youthful enthusiasm: "I wish I were an Astronomer. Is it not an interesting reflection to consider, that a little creature such as man—though his eye can see the heaven but as it were for a moment—is able to delineate the aspect which it will present when ages shall have gone by?" But this idealization of the scientist had met a rude shock in the actualities of the Royal Society at Edinburgh in 1819: "If anyone should expect to find, in George Street, an image of the first Royal Society,—when Newton was in the chair and Halley at the table,—he cannot (unless his fancy be the stronger) fail of disappointment. He will find indeed a number of clean, well-dressed (some of them able-bodied) men; but instead of witnessing the invention of fluxions or the discovery of gravitation, he may chance to learn the dimensions of a fossil stick, or hear it decided that a certain little crumb of stone is neither to be called *mesotype* nor *stilbite.*" In his maturity he was to be prejudiced against the epoch-making *Principles of Geology* of Lyell, which established the Hutton-Playfair uniformitarian theory on a rock of irrefragable evidence, by his memory of the author: "I seem to hear his uninspired voice all along, and see the clear leaden twinkle of his small bead eyes." Here are the impatience and subjectivity which explain Charles Darwin's well-known saying about Carlyle: "I never met a man with a mind so ill-adapted for scientific research."

Yet Carlyle's attitude contained something of tremendous importance on its positive side; the revolt against the limitations of the scientific temperament and outlook characteristic of the international Romantic Movement. In one of his earliest publications, the analysis of *Faust* in the *New Edinburgh Review* for April, 1822, Carlyle characterized the logical product of the eighteenth-century scientific spirit: "In many respects Mephistopheles resembles some French *philosophe* of the last century.

There is the perfection of the intellectual faculties with a total absence of the moral; the extreme of fanciful pleasantry and acute thought, with the extremes of arid selfishness and contemptuous apathy." This is the better evidence of the widespread spontaneousness of the Romantic revolt, in that Carlyle was then unacquainted with *Dichtung und Wahrheit* with its vivid account of the revulsion of Goethe and his youthful group from Holbach's *Système de la Nature*. Carlyle's temperament and his favorite literature pointed to the goal toward which Kant made the more laborious philosophical approach.

Carlyle was by no means an accurate technical interpreter of Kant, but he grasped the essential truth that he was groping for—what we to-day recognize as the biological approach to the problem of knowledge. He conceived man as a living organism, having certain thinking habits, and not a machine reproducing in miniature the functioning of the world-machine. Certain of these thinking habits had produced the amazing fabric of the Newtonian world, something logical and possible, though not in any sense ultimate or more real than the world demanded for the exercise of other mental habits, such as the moral and aesthetic. The artist and the saint, having richer, fuller natures than the scientist, and being unable to live in the world of his creation, were more to be trusted.

Putting emphasis on the adjective in the *Critique of Practical Reason,* Carlyle felt released into a universe giving unlimited scope for his dynamic energies. Goethe represented God, not as a detached mechanism, "an absentee God, sitting idle, ever since the first Sabbath, at the outside of his Universe, and *seeing* it go," but as an immanent spirit, a friend behind phenomena who gave value to human actions. Matter, in Goethean phrase, was "the living visible Garment of God." Developed in terms of this conception was the character of Fichte, "standing erect and clear, like a Cato Major among degenerate men." Carlyle recognized that Novalis was correct in calling Fichte's *Wissenschaftlehre* "to a certain extent, Applied Christianity"; it was Protestant ethics rescued from the decay of Protestant theology. The moral habits to which he had clung tenaciously during the period of his doubt thus received intellectual justification. His feeling of release may be understood by those laymen for whom Professor Eddington and Professor Whitehead have performed the same service in our later day: *"une immense espèrance a traversé la terre."* "The Universe is not dead and demoniacal, a charnel-house with spectres," was Carlyle's joyous outburst in *Sartor Resartus,* "but godlike, and my Father's!"

Carlyle had no exact word to describe the psychological change that was completed in him at Hoddam Hill; he could only suggest it by the term "conversion," misleading in its religious associations. Nor did he know that his was only one of many spiritual crises in an age of conflicting disciplines, preceded on English soil by Wordsworth's, and to be followed by those of John Mill, Newman, and many others. But he knew that its end brought release of his energies from agonized introspection to pleasant outward activity, from morbid dwelling on emotions to tonic exercise of the will, from the negative revolt of Byronism and *Sturm und Drang* toward the objectivity and practical constructiveness of the elder Goethe.

As early as March 4, 1823, he exalted Goethe above Jane's more tempestuous favorites: "He is not a mere Bacchanalian rhymester, cursing and foaming and laying about him as if he had breathed a gallon of nitrous oxide, or pouring forth his most inane philosophy and most maudlin sorrow in strains that 'split the ears of the groundlings,' but a man of true culture and universal genius, not less distinguished for the extent of his knowledge and the profoundness of his ideas and the variety of his feelings, than for the vivid and graceful energy, the inventive and deeply meditative sagacity, the skill to temper enthusiasm with judgment, which he shows in exhibiting them." *Wilhelm Meister,* tracing in its hero a conversion slightly similar to Carlyle's, had taught him that "Here or nowhere is America," that the world immediately about him afforded ample scope for his ideal activities. Literature offered a wider audience than the pulpit or the classroom, and all his habits of pedagogue and preacher could find in it an instrument for making the world a better place to live in. His published writings were to have henceforth this practical character, while the Byronic strain, subdued but never killed, kept a continual undertone of self-examination and complaint in his voluminous diaries and letters.

§ 5

WITH spiritual peace came the positive happiness of knowing that marriage would be the reward for finishing *German Romance*. Early in his residence at Hoddam Hill, accident had brought Jane closer to him. He had arranged that she correspond with Mrs. Montagu, thinking that she might have something to learn from a London *grande dame*. Almost in her first letter the experienced matron took the liberty of advising her Scotch protégée that misunderstanding after marriage would be avoided by confession of her early love for Irving. Alarmed, and guiltily remembering her silence when Margaret Gordon was mentioned, she wrote her betrothed the truth at once, enclosing Mrs. Montagu's letter: "Never were you so dear as at this moment when I am in danger of losing your affection, or, what is still more precious to me, your respect."

Carlyle forgave her readily, and invited her, since she had written from Templand, her maternal grandfather's farm not far from Dumfries, to pay the promised visit to Hoddam Hill, that they might avoid the misunderstandings of the written word. Jane came for two weeks in early September, 1825. The native courtesy and delicacy of the Carlyle family dissipated her worst fears of a plebeian alliance. In October Carlyle pleased every one at Templand except Mrs. Welsh. She broke out against him on his departure, withdrawing her consent to the match. The cause of her change of front appeared in the arrival at Templand of a more splendid suitor, Jane's cousin Captain Baillie of the Guards, "in a fine emblazoned chariot with four horses; and all glittering in jewels, from the gold pendant of his rose-colored cap, to the ruby buckle of his slippers." But this apparition of the latter days of male sartorial magnificence gave Carlyle no cause for jealousy. "Oh mercy," Jane hastened to write, "when I compare this fine gentleman to the *man* I love! ...A mere painted butterfly, fluttering over the flowery surface of the earth—...while he—my own—is like to the royal Eagle, who soars aloft thro' the regions of ether, and feasts his eyes on the glories of the sun." The day would come when this spendthrift cousin would be dependent on Carlyle's charity. Jane was being steadily converted to her lover's point of view: "Often you used to tell me, in the days of my *insanity,* that there was something better than fame, 'something more exquisite still'; then I understood not what you meant, and laughed at the notion....But it is far otherwise with me now; for now I know that the deep blessedness of two souls which live in and for each other, *is* best of all that earth and heaven can bestow."

The difficulty of getting steady rent from Craigenputtock was making Mrs. Welsh think of selling the Haddington house and coming to live permanently with her father at Templand. Hence her especial eagerness to have Jane married to the affluent Captain; hence also Jane's wish to be united with Carlyle without further delay. On his advice she met her mother's hostility with good-humored patience, even to the extent of not seeing him when he was in Edinburgh for three weeks in January, 1826. This passive resistance bore fruit in Mrs. Welsh's capitulation soon after he had returned to the country.

German Romance was completed in September, 1826.* On October 16 Thomas and Jane, who had not seen each other for a year, were married at Templand. He was thirty-one, she twenty-five. The wedding took place before breakfast, and that night they were in their new home at 21 Comley Bank, Edinburgh,

---

* In May, 1826, as the result of a quarrel with their landlord, General Sharpe, the Hoddam Hill household had removed to Scotsbrig, a two hundred and fifty acre farm on the other side of Ecclefechan. Here James Carlyle and the rest of the family joined Alick on the expiration of the twelve-year lease of Mainhill the following year. Scotsbrig remained headquarters for the family during Thomas Carlyle's lifetime.

which Mrs. Welsh had furnished for them. He would have preferred the country, but bent to Jane's wishes. She chose a house well suited to his needs, away from noise and smoke, on the edge of the New Town, looking out into open fields on three sides. Carlyle had given wise advice as to the family budget: "Wives are supported, some in peace and dignity, others in contention and disgrace, on all incomes from £14 a year to two hundred thousand; and I trusted in Jane Welsh and still trust in her for good sense enough to accommodate her wants to the needs of the man she has chosen above all others, and to live with him contented on whatever it should please Providence to allot him, keeping within their revenue, not struggling to get without it, and therefore rich." Considerations of economy and health made them decide not to give or attend the formal dinners for which Edinburgh had long been famous; they served a simple tea at their Wednesday evening "at homes."

Even with this simplicity their living in Edinburgh was threatened with insecurity from the very first. In his eagerness to marry, Carlyle had not given sufficient heed to the great financial crash that had followed the inflation and speculation of 1825, bringing into the literary world in January, 1826, the especially spectacular bankruptcies of the Edinburgh publishing house of Constable and of the printing firm of the Ballantynes, involving the Ballantynes' silent partner, Sir Walter Scott, to the extent of £130,000. Nor had he been perturbed by the failure of expectations concerning his own publications, though neither the *Meister* nor the *Schiller* had gone beyond 1,000 copies, the slow sales of the latter probably influencing the withdrawal of Taylor and Hessey's proposal of a *Life of Voltaire.* But immediately upon his settling in Edinburgh his eyes were opened to the serious collapse of the literary market. Brewster, "in blackest humor about the 'badness of the times,'" had given up the newspaper project, and complained that he could get nothing published. Tait, finding himself anticipated by the appearance of four similar collections already that year, was postponing the issue of *German Romance,* printed by the ill-omened Ballantyne and

Company, into 1827 in the hope of "better times." He was doing what he could to give an impression of sensational contents by woodcuts prefixed to each volume, such as that of a hunchback telling a knight in armor a dreadful secret that makes him mop his brow. Even the philosophic *Meister's Travels* was illustrated by a peasant with a laden donkey discovering a beautiful young woman swooning or asleep in the midst of rugged and desolate mountains.

Finding no other employment for his pen, Carlyle turned to fiction, probably because his recent translations had familiarized him with narrative. The didactic, largely autobiographical novel *Wotton Reinfred,* begun in January, 1827, is an interesting document in his development, with many vigorous detached thoughts but strikingly immature in the treatment of emotion and of social life. Feeling vaguely that he was not making satisfactory progress, he left it unfinished in May. Before this time he had discovered that he and Jane had underestimated their living expenses, including the maintenance of his brother John, who was with them while pursuing his medical studies. These were cutting alarmingly into his savings of three hundred pounds at the time of marriage. It seemed best to retire to cheaper living in the country. Mrs. Welsh was also suffering from financial embarrassment, for the tenant of Craigenputtock failed to pay rent. Thus they might kill two birds with one stone by going to live at Craigenputtock with Alick as farmer, an arrangement which had proved satisfactory at Hoddam Hill. The logic of the situation made Jane withdraw her objection. So Alick took over the lease in May with the understanding that his brother and sister-in-law join him as soon as the house could be enlarged to receive them. Thomas sent him one hundred and twenty pounds to stock the farm and promised more for building alterations, an outlay more than balancing the tardy receipt of a hundred pounds for *German Romance,* which had been published in January. Despite Tait's efforts, it was selling badly and would probably yield no more. London publishers were as unresponsive to overtures as those in Edinburgh. For ready money, since books were not in demand, recourse must be made to periodicals, which, as Irving kept pointing out, were still flourishing.

Carlyle was already in touch with the *Edinburgh Review* through a letter of introduction to Francis Jeffrey given by the generous Procter. As he had gone to call at Jeffrey's home in February, his thoughts travelled back seven years to the terrible winter when, as a dissatisfied law student, he had sent off with trembling hopes the article on *Pictet's Theory of Gravitation* which Jeffrey had neither acknowledged nor returned. Now Jeffrey received him cordially, with no embarrassing remembrance of the unlucky article, as a man whose solid literary achievement might make his pen useful to the Whigs. In 1825 Jeffrey had written to his old friend John Allen at the London Whig headquarters at Holland House: "Can you not lay your hand on some clever young man who would write for us? The original supporters of the work are getting old, and either too busy or too stupid, to go on comfortably; and here the young men are mostly Tories." Meanwhile Macaulay had appeared; but Procter knew that Jeffrey was on the look-out for other young writers. After engaging Carlyle in conversation on various topics for about an hour and watching him with his keen black eyes, the diminutive lawyer asked if he would contribute to the *Review*. Carlyle replied, with characteristic candor, that it would be well for him to glance at some of the biographical and critical introductions in *German Romance* in order to know what sort of man he would be employing. Jeffrey returned Carlyle's call, and despite Carlyle's dislike of the law and Jeffrey's suspicion of German literature, they got on admirably.

So when *Wotton Reinfred* proved intractable, Carlyle had no difficulty in obtaining a commission for a short article on Richter to appear immediately in the June number of the *Edinburgh Review*. Its sly humor, sparkling epigrams, and background of solid learning won Jeffrey's hearty approval: "I feel at once that you are a man of genius, and of original character and right heart, and shall be proud and happy to know more of you." A longer essay, surveying contemporary German literature and philosophy, was requested for the October number.

But this ready admittance into the older of the two leading periodicals, with the good payment of twenty guineas for sixteen pages, did not make Carlyle forget the insecurity of literature for a man of his ideals, of which the current depression had been a sharp reminder. On his entrance into the profession he had written sympathetically of Schiller: "Poetry he loved with the passionateness of a first affection, but he could not live by it; he honored it too highly to wish to live by it," and he had noticed approvingly the professorship of history at Jena that had placed Schiller above temptation to prostitute his talents. Now he was writing in his second article for the *Edinburgh Review*: "From the number of universities, libraries, collections of art, museums and other literary or scientific institutions of a public or private nature, we question whether the chance which a meritorious man of letters has before him, of obtaining some permanent appointment, some independent civic existence, is not a hundred to one in favor of the German, as compared to the Englishman. This is a weighty item, and indeed the weightiest of all; for it will be granted, that, for a votary of literature, the relation of entire dependence on the merchants of literature is, at best, and however liberal the terms, a highly questionable one. It tempts him daily and hourly to sink from an artist into a manufacturer; nay, so precarious, fluctuating, and in every way unsatisfactory must his civic and economic concerns become, that too many of his class cannot even obtain the praise of common honesty as manufacturers. There is, no doubt, a spirit of martyrdom... which can sustain this too; but few indeed have the spirit of martyrs; and that state of matters is safest which requires it least."

Carlyle felt in himself the capacity for martyrdom, but he hoped to avoid its exercise by finding stable employment such as he looked at longingly in Germany. During his stay in England, he had learned of a projected University of London, that would admit students without the religious tests required at Oxford and Cambridge. Its initiator was the poet Campbell, an admirer of the German universities, who had been entertained at Bonn by August von Schlegel, and was making a special trip to study the organization of the University of Berlin. Campbell's chief supporters were James Mill, Henry Brougham, and other followers of Jeremy Bentham, enthusiasts for mechanistic science and the associated Lockian philosophy, and accordingly anti-clerical. Irving soon found it necessary to resign from the committee of founders because he suspected that the majority intended the new institution not only to admit Dissenters like himself, but to be "unreligious, secretly anti-religious."

This possibility did not disturb Carlyle, who kept an eye on the project. In the spring of 1827 it had matured to the extent of advertisement for professors; whereupon he wrote on May 15 to Crabb Robinson, one of the founders, explaining his intention to apply for a chair of moral philosophy, rhetoric, mathematics, physics, or even metaphysics, in which he could offer "the oddest mixture of Scotch and German, Dugald Stewart and Immanuel Kant." [22] He also applied to Jeffrey, who was influential through long association with Brougham. Jeffrey gladly granted support, though informing Carlyle that the rhetoric chair was probably pre-empted by Campbell, and that his Kantianism might disqualify him for moral philosophy. Indeed the Benthamites considered Transcendentalism, of which they knew very little, as a kind of mysticism seducing back to religion. Taking the hint, Carlyle stressed, in his account of German thought for the *Edinburgh Review,* the point that Kant and his followers were not obscurantist mystics, but strictly logical and scientific thinkers, though he did not conceal his preference of their conclusions to those of Locke. On completing the article he sent a copy in advance of publication directly to Brougham as evidence of his qualifications for a university post. Jeffrey exerted pressure on Brougham, for he knew and disapproved of the Craigenputtock scheme, thinking it Carlyle's "misfortune not to have mixed sufficiently with intelligent men of various opinions, and open and intrepid minds."

Such society was at last open to him in Edinburgh. Jeffrey

introduced him to leading Whigs and he was equally welcome among the Tories. Although Lockhart had gone to London to edit the *Quarterly,* and Goethe's plan to acquaint Carlyle with Scott miscarried because of Scott's financial worries, he saw much of John Wilson ("Christopher North"), the unofficial editor of *Blackwood's Magazine,* and his remarkable contributor, De Quincey. The sight of the pitiful victim of opium, diminutive, soft-voiced, and apologetic in manner, made Carlyle forget his anger at De Quincey's "brutal review" of his *Wilhelm Meister,* that had attributed alleged crudities and coarseness of diction to the translator's "insufficient acquaintance with good society." This forgiveness established Carlyle in Wilson's good opinion. He was invited to one of the celebrated *Noctes Ambrosianae,* where he sipped diluted port while plying Wilson, whose tongue was loosened by prodigious potations of whiskey punch, with questions concerning the chief contemporary men of letters. When he reached home well after three in the morning, he was surprised to find Jane awake, waiting for him over a book: a silent reminder that he beware of the heavy drinking almost universal among Edinburgh gentlemen. To their Wednesday evening high teas at Comley Bank came many interested in German: the philosopher Sir William Hamilton to talk of Kant, De Quincey, who had introduced Richter to Carlyle through translating passages from his work for the *London Magazine,* Bess Stodart's husband the Reverend Mr. Aitken, recently returned from Germany, and a native German, Madame Viaris. Jane, born to adorn a salon, found it hard to think of abandoning such intelligent company for the solitude of Craigenputtock, and hoped for a reprieve.

But an unexpected family burden threw its weight unfavorably in the scale. Possibly from influence of Celtic traditions came the family communism of the Carlyles, to which Thomas subscribed by saying that the earnings of all should be considered as belonging to a chest to be drawn upon by the least fortunate members in emergencies. Since 1822, when the Buller tutorship made him the most affluent, he had contributed about three hundred pounds to his father's farming and to his brother John's medical education. Now John, having become a full-fledged doctor while living with the married pair at Comley Bank, disconcertingly announced his unwillingness to practice and his intention to follow Thomas's profession of authorship. Knowing its dangers, the elder brother was naturally opposed. But he could reconcile John to medicine only by agreeing to finance a year of specialized study at Munich.

In this emergency Jeffrey, having found Brougham unreceptive to Carlyle's London University candidacy, suggested as a last resort the professorship of moral philosophy at the Scottish University of St. Andrews, just vacated by Dr. Chalmers, who had accepted the chair of theology at Edinburgh. The St. Andrews post had hitherto been reserved for Church of Scotland clergymen, but on this occasion the University was making the liberal gesture of announcing that it would be given to the best qualified applicant, regardless of religious affiliation. Edinburgh intelligentsia, eager to find insincerity in this announcement, flocked to the support of Carlyle's candidacy. Although Goethe's letter came too late, Carlyle was recommended by Whig and Tory, devout Christian and sceptic; by John Wilson, who occupied the corresponding chair of moral philosophy at Edinburgh, by Jeffrey, Edward Irving, Professor Leslie, Dr. Brewster, Procter, and others. This array of names had the expected effect of unmasking disingenuousness. The post went to a mediocrity of approved orthodoxy, the Reverend Dr. Cook.

Meanwhile Charles Buller, now in his last year at Cambridge, had sounded out James Mill on the London University situation, and found this right-hand man of Jeremy Bentham hostile to Carlyle's "German metaphysics." Could Mill have been perfectly frank, he would have added that Carlyle was suspiciously intimate with the fanatical clergyman, Edward Irving. Caught between the opposed camps of Christian orthodoxy and scientific scepticism, Carlyle found every kind of university in the British Isles closed to him. Craigenputtock was inevitable, especially if he and Jane were ever to carry out the plan of widening their culture by six months at Weimar "for the study of music and painting, *artes perditae* in this political and economical and man of business land."

On the eve of their departure in May, 1828, Edward Irving arrived to be the preaching sensation of Edinburgh. The Carlyles did not have the heart to attend the public dinner in his honor, and hear praise of his views on the Apocalypse. Thomas told John: "I do not think he will go altogether mad, yet what else he will do I cannot so well conjecture. Cant and enthusiasm are strangely mingled; he preaches in steamboats and all open places, wears clothes of an antique pattern (his waistcoat has flaps or tails midway down the thigh)." Irving was in Edinburgh almost a week before he made a brief call at Comley Bank, friendly but strangely distraught and self-conscious. Thomas and Jane were pained by his formality and stilted Biblical phraseology, but neither could put him at his ease or bring back the old footing of intimacy. At parting he insisted on standing to pray for them. His last words were strange: "Farewell, I must go then and suffer persecution as my fathers have done." Despite this hint of his inner disquietude, Jane could not help reflecting upon the standards of a society that rewarded Irving with public dinners and five hundred pounds a year, and condemned her husband, with his enlightenment, brilliance, and solid industry, to poverty and exile.

While the carts conveying their household goods got the necessary start, the Carlyles spent two days at Jeffrey's elaborate new house in Moray Place, the most pretentious section of the New Town, before setting out for the lonely farm in the high moorlands.

CHAPTER IV

ROMANTICISM IN A MACHINE AGE

➤➤➤ ◄◄◄

§ 1

THE journey from Dumfries to Craigenputtock holds a breath-taking surprise. For ten miles the road follows the narrow fertile valley of Cairn Water to the straggling village of Dunscore. At Dunscore there opens for an instant a panorama of Galloway mountains as the road crosses the stream to turn westward over slightly rising ground. Suddenly, as if a cloud had moved across the sun, the view is blotted out by hills that have closed in on both sides and ahead; the treeless ground is darkened by heather, furze, and bracken. There are no more cultivated fields, but beyond the gray stone fences sheep lift their heads curiously from bracken fronds, grouse cluck and whir, and curlews wheel about with calls that intensify the wild stillness. Surely, one thinks, Craigenputtock must be that pleasant white house just before hills block the road. But one does not stop there, or later at a private gate where the road ends. Here, three miles from Dunscore, one passes through to follow an unfenced track across the heath, mounting steeply toward some high pass. The way winds among hill spurs that threaten continually to fasten it in their trap. Three more miles of desolation, with no prospect of an end. Then a second gate before a grove of firs. From among the firs emerges a group of stone buildings, nestling on the slopes of two great hills. That is Craigenputtock farm.

Such is the passage to-day by automobile to one of the least accessible of literary shrines. One approaches from the rear and enters a snug paved courtyard enclosed on three sides. Thomas and Jane Carlyle made a much slower journey on horseback, struggling to the front door of their new home over a boggy track long since abandoned. But the commodious stone house with gracefully severe lines promised to be a civilized dwelling, although carpenters were pounding away in the upper storey. Alick and his wife greeted them heartily, and led them into a spacious drawing-room where burned a peat fire that was welcome even in summer at an altitude of 700 feet in Scotland. Behind was a smaller room, also with a fireplace, looking to the rear through the open side of the courtyard upon broad heathy slopes. That would be Thomas's study. A hall divided these rooms from the rest of the house; a dining room that matched the drawing-room and a kitchen giving ample space for several women to work together. Upstairs were two large bedrooms, with a dressing room between. Such was the central building; the two wings contained a dwelling for Alick's household and the servants, and various outbuildings. Solidly built and protected by hills, Craigenputtock could defy winds that would uproot nearby fir trees in winter.

No other human dwelling was visible, but a climb across boggy heaths led to the 882-foot Glaister's Hill, where Carlyle was to take Emerson for the magnificent view: the stern granite mountains of Galloway arrayed to the northwest, southward a broad strip of seacoast with the Isle of Man lying faintly beyond, eastward the Dumfries road, Dunscore Church steeple, and the hills concealing the dale of the river Nith which passed Mrs. Welsh's dwelling at Thornhill, about twenty miles distant. This wild region on the Galloway border had been the refuge of nonconformists for centuries. Here the last of the Lollards had kept Wyclif's protest alive until John Knox came. Here the Covenanters had resisted the Stuarts; in sight of Glaister's Hill was the manor house of one of the most hated of their persecutors, Grierson of Lag, whose memory had been recently revived by Scott's novel *Redgauntlet*. The background was congenial to Carlyle's stubborn defiance of the current values of the literary market-place: "I came for this one reason," he explained to Goethe, "that I might not have to write for bread, might not be tempted to tell lies for money."

Alick took responsibility for the large sheep farm of 1,000 acres, with a small amount of arable ground that yielded potatoes and turnips. Thomas was free to read and write all day long in the quiet of the desolate hills, with frequent intervals of meditation over his favorite clay pipes. For exercise he cut firewood, wandered indifferent to cold and rain among the boggy hills in the wooden clogs of his childhood, and in fair weather rode on horseback with Jane. Jane was kept busy directing her maid-of-all-work, and planning for the needs of a household dependent upon a weekly carrier from Dumfries for food supplies as well as mail. Now and then she had to turn her hand to cooking some special dish for her husband, whom a delicate stomach made fastidious about cleanliness and quality. Unable to eat bread made by the maid or the Dumfries baker, Carlyle, accustomed to seeing his mother and sisters turn their hands to anything, casually asked his wife to bake some for him. Jane, whom a frail constitution had excused from all but the lightest household tasks, was naturally dismayed, even injured by such a request. But her husband relentlessly argued that a woman of brains could do anything and handed her Cobbett's *Cottage Economy*. Jane always remembered her resentment when, in her ignorance, she had to stay up alone until three in the morning waiting for the bread to rise and be ready for the oven. Happily, during the lonely night hours came the comforting reflection that she, in a situation similar to that of Cellini's when he cast his celebrated Perseus, was another kind of creative artist, and her self-pity was lost in the triumph of excellent bread at the first trial.

"My Apprenticeship is ending, and yours still going on," Carlyle had written her just before their marriage. Bread-making was but one episode in his efforts to free her from stultifying conventions. They were so far successful that four years later she advised a young woman of Irving's London congregation: "Render your daughters for ever impracticable to *ennui*. Shame that such a malady should exist in a Christian land: should not only exist, but be almost general throughout the whole female population that is placed above the necessity of working for daily bread. If I have an antipathy for any class of people it is for *fine* ladies. I almost match my husband's detestation of partridge-shooting gentlemen. Woe to the fine lady who should find herself set down at Craigenputtock for the first time in her life left alone with her own thoughts—no 'fancy bazar' in the same kingdom with her; no place of amusement within a day's journey; the very church, her last imaginable resource, seven miles off. I can fancy with what horror she would look on the ridge of mountains that seemed to enclose her from all earthly bliss; with what despair in her accents she would inquire if there was not even a 'charity sale' within reach. Alas, no! no outlet whatever for 'lady's work'; not even a book for a fine lady's understanding. It is plain she would have nothing for it but to die as speedily as possible, and so relieve the world of the expense of her maintenance." Thomas described to his brother John Jane's daily life in this period: "She manages all things—poultry, flowers, bread-loaves; keeps a house still like a bandbox, then reads, or works (as at present) on some translation from Goethe. I tell her many times there is much for her to do if she were trained to it; her whole sex to deliver from the bondage of frivolity, dollhood, and imbecility, into the freedom of valor and womanhood." The change from Haddington drawing-rooms decidedly improved her health. Unfortunately the boggy environs discouraged walking, but there was a riding horse at her disposal, and she often cantered down the heathy tracks, going with her husband sometimes as far as Dumfries, or to visit her mother at Thornhill.

Winter shut Craigenputtock off from the world; there were months when no visitor came to the door. But evenings passed pleasantly with reading aloud or study of Spanish, Italian, and especially German, the Continental trip being constantly in view. Isolation was not oppressive in a household numbering nine;

the four Carlyles, Alick's three farm hands, two male and one female, and a maidservant for each family. Alick was excellent company, with the humor and proud spirit of his family. Thomas listened intently to his discourses on the bad state of farming, that was feeling the effect of the 1825 crash, and shared his radical views of the economic structure of the country. He now and then ventured practical advice, and invented a horseshoe that would not slip on ice. There was plenty of peat to be dug from the bogs, and fires kept the house snug on the bitterest days. Carlyle felt his strength renewed by this quiet life, and his meditations quickened and deepened in the silence of the barren hills.

§ 2

LIVING expenses were under a hundred pounds a year, less than half what they had been at Edinburgh. Two fifty-page articles yearly would supply this; but he must earn at least twice the amount, for John must be maintained in Germany, and money be saved for occasional trips to Edinburgh to keep in touch with the literary market and escape the worst of the winter, and also for the project of six months in Weimar. His chief employer during the early years at Craigenputtock was the *Foreign Review,* published by the London importing booksellers Black, Young, and Young to arouse an interest in their wares of Continental literature. It appeared at the beginning of 1828 as a rival of the *Foreign Quarterly Review* established the previous year by the German firm Treutel, Würtz, Treutel Jr., and Richter. Since the founder and principal contributor of the competing review was Pearse Gillies, whose *German Stories* had been one of the four collections that anticipated Carlyle's *German Romance,* it was natural that the *Foreign Review* should turn to Carlyle for contributions. During his last months in Edinburgh he had written for it three articles, *The Life and Writings of Werner, Goethe's Helena,* and *Goethe,* which brought him a total of one hundred and thirty-five pounds. At Craigenputtock he contributed *The*

Life of Heyne (1828), *German Playwrights, Voltaire, Novalis* (1829), and *Jean Paul Richter* (1830). Although its payment, sixteen guineas for a "sheet" of sixteen pages (about three cents a word), was lower than the *Edinburgh Review's* twenty (about four cents a word), and its financial condition so poor that it went out of existence early in 1830, still it offered freedom from the political and religious restrictions which Whig party purposes imposed. Through Jeffrey's friendly interest came occasional commissions from the *Edinburgh, Burns* (1828), *Signs of the Times* (1829), which might have been more numerous if Carlyle had been willing to compromise with the Whigs, whose blue and buff colors the *Review* bore on its cover.

The *Edinburgh* and the *Foreign* Reviews were dignified periodicals for serious upper- and upper-middle class readers, who, unlike those of present-day journals, did not require ideas to be diluted or pre-digested and presented under catchy headings. The anonymity of all contributions gave young men the opportunity to build reputations on their merits without the initial handicap of competition with famous names, and the custom of making the books reviewed mere texts for long disquisitions on general topics offered ample scope for the display of original talent. With their solid, unadorned pages dealing with serious themes, politics, religion, science, literature, and travel, the *Quarterly* and *Edinburgh* Reviews of the eighteen-twenties and thirties stand as testimony of a rather wide, unspecialized, and genuinely aristocratic culture that has perished from English-speaking countries. Under these attractive conditions, Carlyle entered journalism.

Sending a biography of the missionary Henry Martyn to his mother as an 1827 New Year's gift, he had asked her to "believe that *your* son is a kind of missionary in his way—not to the heathen of India, but to the British heathen." Exposition of the lives and writings of various foreign figures gave him occasion to discourse by way of illustration and contrast upon the intellectual and social shortcomings of contemporary Britain. Gradually the topics yielded to the commentary as he gathered

confidence in his thought and experience. His chief efforts during
these formative years were directed toward raising the standards
of the literary profession and incidentally of literary criticism,
and attacking the mechanistic theories of science with their far-
reaching philosophical and social implications.

He found in Voltaire a symbol of the power of literature
"to clear away old superstitions." Closer at hand, he noticed that:
"The true Church of England, at this moment, lies in the editors
of its newspapers. These preach to the people daily, weekly;
admonish kings themselves; advising peace or war, with an
authority which only the first Reformers, and a long past class
of Popes, were possessed of; inflicting moral encouragement, consolation, edification, in all ways diligently 'administering the
Discipline of the Church.'" He added the satiric parallel: "It
may be said, too, that in private disposition the new Preachers
somewhat resemble the Mendicant Friars of old times; outwardly full of holy zeal; inwardly not without stratagem and
hunger for terrestrial things." The steam press, employed by the
London *Times* since 1814, was increasing the cheapness and
rapidity of printing, and radical newspapers like Cobbett's *Political Register,* evading the stamp tax, had attained unprecedentedly
large circulations by reaching the poor. Carlyle reminded upper-
class subscribers to the reviews of the great potentialities of
literature for good and evil, and of their responsibility for making
it a civilizing influence.

Here Germany offered an inspiring example. From what
Carlyle had learned through books and inquiries, it seemed to
give the man of letters a better social standing than England,
and to liberate him more frequently from ignominious dependence on publishers. The Germans made literature a subject of
serious study, while the British, following Locke, regarded it for
the most part as a source of amusement and relaxation, or shared
the opinion of Macaulay (whom Carlyle hints at without naming) that with the advance of civilization poetry almost necessarily declines. In Germany Novalis's *Schriften* ran into four
editions, while in England the far less difficult *Biographia*

Literaria of Coleridge was "triumphantly condemned by the whole reviewing world as clearly unintelligible." The Germans stimulated serious literary workers by clear-sighted and profound criticism. With them, criticism endeavored to become "a science," employing a precise analytic vocabulary. August and Friedrich von Schlegel were not content, like Dr. Johnson and the Scottish Lord Kames (here Carlyle hints at his contemporaries Jeffrey, Gifford, and Lockhart), with superficial considerations "concerning the coherence of metaphors, the fitness of sentiments, and the general logical truth of a work of art."

In his essay on *Goethe* (1828) Carlyle made an admirable statement of the new methods of criticism: "First, we must have made plain to ourselves what the poet's aim really and truly was, how the task he had to do stood before his own eye, and how far, with the means before him, he has fulfilled it. Secondly, we must have decided whether and how far this aim, this task of his, accorded,—not with *us,* and our individual crotchets, and the crotchets of our little senate where we give or take the law, —but with human nature, and the nature of things at large; with the universal principles of poetic beauty, not as they stand written in our text-books, but in the hearts and imaginations of all men." The first of these procedures had already been introduced into England, largely by way of Germany, by Coleridge, Hazlitt, Lamb, and others as a means of defending the new Romantic literature against the hangover of eighteenth-century judicial criticism represented by Jeffrey, by Gifford and Lockhart of the *Quarterly Review,* and other established and influential writers. But in the second, involving historical perspective and acquaintance with what the Germans called world-literature, Carlyle was largely a pioneer. His flair for historical interpretation is almost as evident in his admirable treatment of both parts of *Faust* in *Goethe's Helena,* as it is in a subject so intimate to his experience as the *Burns* of the same year. He exposed the insularity of most British periodical criticism, with its "genteel" snobbery (a reviewer of Goethe's autobiography in the *Edinburgh* in 1816 had said: "He appears to us to be always deficient in literary good-breeding, in literary decorum; in short he does not display a real aristocratic feeling in mind and habits"), and its prudery (operating against many works Carlyle admired, such as Burns's *Jolly Beggars,* Byron's *Don Juan,* and Goethe's *Wilhelm Meister*). He condemned prudery and snobbery as the results of catering to a public taste that demanded "elegance" to the discouragement of healthy realism and intellectual vitality. Already in the summer of 1827 the aged Goethe had perceived the precise nature and the significance of Carlyle's efforts in literary criticism: "It is admirable in Carlyle that, in his judgment of our German authors, he has especially in view the mental and moral core as that which is really influential. Carlyle is a moral force of great importance. There is in him much for the future."

The introduction of German philosophy to the British public permitted Carlyle an oblique attack upon mechanistic science and empirical philosophy; but his exposition of the technicalities of Transcendentalism was neither lucid nor accurate. It was quite otherwise when he called German literature to his aid with the first chapter of Richter's *Siebenkäs,* which presents the horror of atheism with an intensity unsurpassed in world literature, and with the second chapter of Novalis's *Lehrlinge zu Sais,* which describes the irreconcilable conflict of human desires with the current scientific views of nature. He entered so completely into the spirit of these passages that his translations have the eloquence and beauty of original work. He was thus gathering his forces to confute what Irving called "the Pharisee of intellect or reason (of whom Edinburgh is the chief city)" and of whom "scepticism of all things that cannot be expressed with logical precision is the characteristic, and an utter abhorrence of all mystery."

The social influence of physical science he attacked with a sureness contrasting agreeably with his fumbling with metaphysics. In *Signs of the Times* he emphasized the incongruity of the dynamic energies which were bursting the bonds of feudalism, with the mechanical means of building a new society proposed by Benthamite Radicals and many Whigs. He characterized the contemporary spirit in words that largely hold true of our own slightly disillusioned age: "Our true Deity is Mechanism. It has subdued external Nature for us, and we think it will all other things." The methods of physical sciences had become the methods of the sciences of man. The Lockian philosophy, thus led astray, "is not a philosophy of the mind; it is a mere discussion concerning the origin of our consciousness, or ideas, or whatever else they are called, a genetic history of what we see *in* the mind." Since Locke, theories of the mind had gone further in the same course, from "Hartley's vibrations and vibratiuncles" to Dr. Cabanis's posthumous *Rapports du Physique et du Morale* (1825) with its crude thesis that "as the liver secretes bile, so does the brain secrete thought." Likewise, from De Lolme to Bentham, government was considered "emphatically a machine: to the discontented 'a taxing machine': to the contented 'a machine for securing property.' Its duties and its faults are not those of a father, but of an active parish constable." Carlyle urged that this conception was dangerously inadequate, now that industrialism had brought a pressing problem: "Wealth has more and more increased, and at the same time gathered itself more and more into masses, strangely altering the old relations, and increasing the distance between the rich and the poor," thus constituting "a question for Political Economists ... much more complex and important ... than any they have yet dealt with." But this masterly analysis of the intellectual trends of the time and the social effects of the Industrial Revolution, was followed by a peroration pleading for the tempering of the mechanical spirit with the dynamic spirit of patriotism and individual virtue that has the vagueness of Carlyle's weakest pulpit manner. John Stuart Mill, then passing through a spiritual crisis similar to Carlyle's, was misled by such perorations into thinking Carlyle's essays "insane rhapsody" in favor of old forms of religious and political belief.

The most effective of these early essays were those which, like the *Life of Schiller,* offered sympathetic biographical topics from which Carlyle could preach the lessons of his own life. The

Life of Heyne narrates without comment the terrible struggles of a weaver's son who rose against every handicap of eighteenth-century society to be the professor in the University of Göttingen whose edition of Virgil had opened the eyes of the ill-taught Thomas Carlyle to the possibilities of humane study of the classics. But Carlyle did stress the contrast, sharpened by his own recent experience with St. Andrews, of the assiduity with which German universities sought out the best men for their faculties with the lethargy and bigotry of English educational institutions. A second essay on *Richter* (1830) presented a more congenial figure than the plodding scholar. The son of a poor Lutheran pastor, studying theology at Leipzig University, finds himself assailed by doubts. Lacking means to study for another profession, he turns to his pen for livelihood. Without books, and living in one room with his widowed mother, he persists in writing against manifold discouragements, saving money by cutting off his queue and discarding his neckcloth, to the scandal and protest of respectable neighbors. Yet want does not sour him; his writings overflow with uproarious and fantastic humor that finally wins the attention of the local aristocracy and the Weimar literary group. Carlyle compared Richter's unabashed confession of poverty with the pretentiousness of his fellow-craftsmen in Great Britain, where there were "no Men of Letters now, but only Literary Gentlemen" who boasted that they derived their materials from having "frequented the society of the upper classes." Excerpts from Richter point other of Carlyle's favorite morals, including satire on mercenary marriages.

Best of these biographical studies is that of *Burns* (1828), the earliest of Carlyle's writings which has become a classic. Here was a great Scotchman, of whom he was reminded every time he went to market at Dumfries, reared close to the soil like himself, with a heart full of the wrongs of mankind. Burns was for him a symbol of what befell a gifted soul of humble origin in the snobbish and mercenary Scottish society of "an age the most prosaic Britain had yet seen." His battles were Carlyle's own. Carlyle saw that the measure of Burns's greatness was not his poetry only; it was his accomplishment without access to the intellectual heritage accumulated by society. He summed up the poet's achievement in a magnificent sentence: "A dwarf behind his steam-engine may remove mountains; but no dwarf will hew them down with the pick-axe; and he must be a Titan that hurls them abroad with his arms." Only when Burns had performed this miracle did the French culture of Edinburgh notice him, and then in such a way as to be his ruin. His fate was eloquent of the intolerable injustice, the topsy-turvydom of a decaying feudal society out of which the democratic movement was born. Whoso to-day is disillusioned of democracy may regain sympathy for its origin and ideal aims by reading Carlyle's essay on Burns.

§ 3

THE *Burns,* written for the *Edinburgh Review,* proved strong meat for its editor. Jeffrey, whose contributors steadily complained of his liberties with their manuscripts, returned the proofs with considerable deletions. Of the nature of the cuts we can only judge from their occurrence chiefly in the first third of the article, containing preliminary generalizations as to the social significance of Burns's life and a comparison with Byron's, which had all the initial advantages. Carlyle resolutely restored most of the omitted passages and removed Jeffrey's softening qualifications, such as "It is but fair to say," risking the severance of the best paying and most influential of his literary connections. Genuinely fond of Carlyle, the powerful Jeffrey acquiesced, not without warning that the article was "on a subject by no means new— not interesting in itself to readers, and now treated in a manner of which many, though I think unjustly, will disapprove." He reminded his unruly contributor that the duty of an editor was to "promote the popularity, circulation, and effect of the review." Yet he generously gave *Burns* the leading position in the December number, 1828. A year later he offered full liberty to speak out on the contemporary social situation in *Signs of the Times,* but that was at the less responsible moment when he was resigning his editorship to accept non-partisan appointment as Dean of the Faculty of Advocates (head of the Scotch Bar Association).

Jeffrey was persistent in his good offices. In the autumn of 1828 he brought his family in a great carriage over the long and dreary way to Craigenputtock; in 1829 he endured a Dumfries inn "opulent in bugs" for the sake of meeting the Carlyles. At the close of the latter year he entertained them for a fortnight in his restored Gothic castle at Craigcrook in the outskirts of Edinburgh, which after Abbotsford attracted the most distinguished literary society in Scotland. He would not abandon the effort to convert Carlyle to his political opinions, being surprised that one who hated the Tory aristocracy did not share his enthusiasm for the approaching victory of the Whigs. Liberal opinion had been making great gains in England since the revulsion of feeling against Peterloo and the effort of the dissolute George IV to divorce his Queen, and Scotland was moving in England's wake toward a reform of Parliament which would destroy the political monopoly of the landed classes.

The return of freedom of assembly and of the press seemed immense progress to Jeffrey, who had witnessed the state trials of 1793-94. He had been one of the little group of Whig lawyers that alone dared open opposition to Tory despotism. He had attended dinners in commemoration of the birthday of the notorious defender of the French Revolution, Charles James Fox, when a sheriff at the door, with sinister ostentation, took down the names of all who entered; and he had suffered for his bravery by lack of legal employment. The reversal of fortune which now made him head of the Bar, and presaged a Whig government which would probably appoint him to rule Scotland as Lord Advocate, seemed sufficient reward for the discouragements of his early life.

But Carlyle saw little advantage in exchanging rule by the landed aristocracy for rule by the commercial and manufacturing middle-classes with whom his profession and comfortable income associated Jeffrey. The circumstances of his life, which were sufficiently remote from Jeffrey's to seem "romantic," put a gulf between them. The logic of humble birth and poverty had early made Carlyle go beyond Whiggism to radicalism. He could not forget the misery he had seen in Glasgow, which was largely under the control of the class Jeffrey would place in power. He had been told that Tom Paine and William Cobbett were mischievous demagogues; he now read them delightedly, having discovered that they were friends of the poor. Jeffrey chaffed him for being a zealot, but Jeffrey had a zeal of his own for political economy, which Adam Smith had made a cherished Scotch tradition. He had solicited Malthus to contribute to the *Edinburgh Review* and had given Dr. Chalmers ample space to proclaim the virtues of his effort to do away with assessments for the support of the poor and rely upon voluntary contributions to the churches, an effort that had roused Carlyle's ire in 1817-20. He was himself author of a pamphlet denouncing labor unions and demonstrating the impossibility of a successful strike, since it would run counter to the wage-fund law of the infallible economic science based on free competition. The middle-class economic prejudice which Jeffrey represented seemed as inimical to social welfare as Tory political prejudice.

The worldly lawyer at Craigenputtock, observing the poverty and isolation of the resolute husband and wife, and blind, perhaps, to the light of hope which keeps up the courage and rashness of the young, urged caution. He insisted that Carlyle could at least coöperate with the Whigs for immediate political ends, and keep silence about his other views until those ends were attained. His own life, passed in times of political tyranny, had been a continual compromise, beginning by an adaptation of his youthful dreams of a literary career to the drudgery of law, and by abstinence from voting, out of regard for a Tory patron, Lord Glenlee, when Henry Erskine was being ejected from the Deanship of the Faculty of Advocates because of his Whig opinions. His editorial policy with the *Edinburgh Review* sought a middle ground between High Toryism and democracy, its alternate attacks on these extremes being cleverly described by James Mill in the *Westminster Review* as "see-saw." Jeffrey urged the advantage of this "tolerating and moderate system of politics," which had brought him reputation and fortune, over the inflexibility that had already exiled Carlyle to the moors. They prolonged their debates into the late hours that both loved; the diminutive, dapper man of the world in his late fifties, with courtly eighteenth-century manners and artificial high-pitched speech acquired at Oxford, neither English nor Scotch, though with exaggerated English pronunciation ("heppy," "my Lud"), bantering his tall gaunt opponent, in his early thirties, with rustic accent and abrupt ways, for being "so dreadfully in earnest." Carlyle would not yield an inch to his superior in experience and reputation, even though he perceived that the celebrated critic, lawyer, and politician was a "thin-skinned sensitive man, with all his pretended pococurantism and real knowledge of what is called the world." Occasionally this ruffled the surface of Jeffrey's urbanity, once obliging him to write an apology "for the little burst of irritability which came upon me by surprise during our late vigil. . . . It seemed to be a necessary part of my warning against your public apostleship." Carlyle readily understood the kindness of Jeffrey's intention; he had told Procter: "There is a glance in the eye of the man which almost prompts you to take him in your arms." He accurately gauged his position as "midway between God and Mammon." It is on this account that Jeffrey remains an indistinct figure despite the bulk of his publications and letters, a sympathetic biography by his life-long friend Lord Cockburn, and the observation of such a masterly portraitist as Carlyle. Carlyle's repeated attempts to characterize him are unsuccessful. He eluded him, and eludes us, by his very typicality. He was the legal mind, pseudo-classical literary taste, the upper-middle class; he was Whig commonplace made flesh. In the allegory of Carlyle's life he stands as Mr. Worldly Wiseman.

There remains to individualize Jeffrey his well-known liberality to struggling authors. In March, 1830, he offered to make up the difference in living expenses of a hundred pounds a year if Carlyle would return to Edinburgh. He tactfully reminded him that he "would have been richer at this moment if you too had not been a giver, and where there was less call." The reference was to John Carlyle, who had drifted from Munich to London, still looking toward literature rather than the practice of medicine. Continued subsidizing of the brother had not only made Weimar impossible, but had kept the Carlyles away from Edinburgh except for their short stay with Jeffrey. The winter had been unusually severe at Craigenputtock, and Jane had spent New Year's day in bed with a prolonged sore throat. In February she had written to her old friend Bess Stodart (now Mrs. Aitken): "Oh for a sight of the green fields again, or even the black peat moss, anything rather than this wide waste of blinding snow! The only time when I can endure to look out (going out is not to be dreamt of) is by moonlight, when the enclosure before the house is literally filled with hares, and then the scene is really picturesque, the little dark forms skipping and bounding over the white ground so witch-like!" Jeffrey did not mention her in his note, but he had in the back of his head her comfortable nurture and sociable nature, and could not bear to think of her being sacrificed to the Quixotic notions of her husband. Those notions, he also thought, might be toned down if Carlyle returned to normal social life.

§ 4

CARLYLE was adamant in refusing aid, for he prized independence above all things, though he had little ready money. Toward the end of 1829, when his periodical connections were becoming precarious through the accession of a new editor of the *Edinburgh* and the prospect of the speedy failure of the *Foreign Review,* he had gladly closed with a proposal for a three-volume history of German literature made by one of the *Foreign Review* staff on behalf of London publishers. Eager to return to the congenial occupation of writing solid books, he sought little journalistic employment and lived on his savings in order to devote his energies to the history.

At the time of Jeffrey's offer, he was well into the first volume, which was completed in June. He was moving into later history in which he could increase his speed by utilizing his previous work, when bad news came. Just as the book trade seemed picking up from the aftermath of the 1825 panic, it felt the effect of another general depression. Crops were poor, and rot was destroying sheep. Rents remained at their post-war level; Carlyle thought them thirty percent too high. Alick, who had been losing about eighty pounds a year from sheep-farming, planned to leave Craigenputtock in May, 1831. In the southern counties of England conditions were worse; the official standard of subsistence for agricultural laborers had dropped one-third below that calculated at Speenhamland in the war year of 1795 as just sufficient to support life. Industrial wages had been declining steadily, although the cost of living had remained stable since a slight fall in 1826.[28] Attempts to lower wages were causing widespread strikes in the cotton industry about Manchester.

The consequent tightening of the money market made publishers nervous. Early in July, Carlyle was informed that the order for the literary history was withdrawn. He tried another London firm, Colburn and Bentley, then turned to Edinburgh. Tait, whose fingers had been burnt by *German Romance,* gave a firm refusal: "Every one of the books on German literature has been a failure; most of them ruinously losing concerns. The feeling in the public mind is that anything German is most especially to be avoided.... As to a collection of your pieces in the Reviews, etc., I am quite clear that such a thing should not be attempted. Sir Walter Scott's *Selected Prose Writings* have scarcely sold at all." Over six months' labor, representing more than two hundred pounds in value, had been turned back upon Carlyle's hands. His funds were low, and John was still dependent upon him. He pointed to John the obvious moral concerning professional authorship: "Often, as in the case of this 'Literary

History of Germany,' you anchor on some slumbering whale and it ducks under and leaves you spinning in the eddies."

Simultaneously with Tait's discouraging letter came news from France that still further unsettled the literary market. In the last days of July the French dethroned their Bourbon King Charles X, and put in his place the "Citizen King" Louis Philippe, who was under the control of a middle-class plutocracy. This second French Revolution had the opposite effect to that of its predecessor on English opinion, for it showed that anarchy was not the inevitable result of political change. The death of George IV on June 26 now seemed a symbol of the passing of the old regime, and a general election occasioned by the accession of his popular sailor brother William IV was held in August in an atmosphere unfavorable to the Tories, who were weakened by factional feuds. Capitalizing economic discontent and hopes for Constitutional change, the Whigs made decided gains of Parliamentary seats wherever the obsolete system of representation permitted the popular voice to be heard.

Just as the election was over, the country was further disturbed by a revolt of agricultural laborers. In late August news of the revolution in which peasants across the Channel had burned the ricks of their landlords penetrated to the miserably paid farm hands of Kent, who were being thrown out of work by Irish immigration and the introduction of threshing-machines. They rose as they had risen under John Ball four centuries before, smashing machinery, frightening off the Irish, and forcing farmers to raise wages. The revolt spread swiftly through fifteen counties of southern England.[24] Meanwhile at Birmingham, the centre of the iron industry, a "Political Union" of workers and employers joined the Benthamite Philosophical Radicals of London in agitation for universal male suffrage. From other industrial regions came rumors that workingmen were drilling secretly on the moors in preparation for armed revolt if the Tories did not yield.

Fear of a revolution, and speculation as to what the new Parliament would do when it met in November, turned attention away from literature. The book trade was paralyzed. In great need of money, Carlyle found he must descend into "the valley of the shadow of Magazine Editors," whose payment and standards were distinctly below those of the Reviews. His most ready recourse was *Fraser's Magazine,* recently founded as a London Tory periodical to match *Blackwood's* in Edinburgh. Its editor, William Maginn, had been on the *Blackwood's* staff, and its financial backer, Hugh Fraser, from whom it took its name, had contributed to the *Foreign Review.* Its printer was another Fraser, James Fraser, with whom Carlyle was to have a long association. *Fraser's Magazine* was ugly and undignified as compared to the reviews to which Carlyle had contributed. Its small type, close set in double columns on a poor quality of paper, corresponded to its contents, a largely ephemeral farrago of political articles, verse, prose fiction, facetious personal literary gossip, and slashing reviews of current literature. But it had dash and flavor, and was fearlessly independent, if a trifle vulgar and more than a trifle cruel. The proprietor, Hugh Fraser, knowing Carlyle through their mutual connection with the *Foreign Review,* had secured from him for his first number, February, 1830, a translation of Richter's review of Madame de Staël's *De l'Allemagne,* and had prefaced it with a complimentary editorial reference to Carlyle's article on Richter in the *Foreign Review* of the previous month. Now reluctantly obliged to lower the standard of his output, Carlyle used his brother John as an intermediary to copy and send anonymously to Fraser inferior work of his 'prentice years: the short story "Cruthers and Johnson" and various poems, serious and facetious. He asked John also to withdraw an article on Schiller from the *Foreign Review* office and give it to Fraser along with *Thoughts on History* that were a by-product of meditation on the unlucky literary history, at the same time pressing him for payment, long overdue, of the Richter transla-tion. Cutting up the completed portion of the literary history into articles, he began to peddle them among periodicals, the first, on the *Nibelungen Lied,* being accepted by the *Westminster Review* in February, 1831. Pocketing his pride, he also applied to MacVey

Napier, the new editor of the *Edinburgh Review,* who had hitherto shown no disposition to employ him. He assured Napier that, although "no Whig in the strict sense," he had "no disposition to run *amuck* against any set of men and opinions." Napier, who had read the outspoken *Signs of the Times,* made assurance doubly sure by commissioning an article on the non-political topic of Taylor's *Historic Survey of German Literature.* In this hour of need, John nobly returned his brother's aid. Continuing to live on the pittance from his own periodical publications on medical and German topics, he sent to Craigenputtock in November and December thirty pounds, which Thomas noted suspiciously to be twice the value of what Fraser, who was "on the hunt for attractive subjects, adapted to the passing moment," [25] had hitherto printed.

National events and the logic of his financial situation had deepened Carlyle's interest in politics and economics since *Signs of the Times.* Soon after completing that article he had written in his Journal: "Is it true that of all quacks that ever quacked (boasting themselves to be somebody) in any age of the world, the political economists of this age are, for their intrinsic size, the loudest? ... Could they tell us how wealth is and should be *distributed,* it were something: but they do not attempt it." Alick's failure and the fiasco of his literary history now added personal bitterness to these musings.

In late July, 1830, the shadowy existence of Craigenputtock, where, Jane wrote, all but food, air, and bed were "a dream of the absent and distant, of things past and to come," was invaded by a package forwarded from Edinburgh directed to the anonymous author of *Signs of the Times.* It contained several publications in French and a letter from a certain Gustave d'Eichthal of Paris. The letter congratulated the author on his insight into the evils of the age, and bade him find in the accompanying writings the gospel of the Count de Saint-Simon, the new Jesus, which was their remedy. The writings were *Le Nouveau Christianisme,* by Saint-Simon, and various works by his followers, including the

Exposition of his doctrines by Bazard and Enfantin which was appearing in their periodical *l'Organisateur.*[26]

Carlyle looked curiously at these foreign books. In their pages he found stated clearly and systematically his own throbbing resentment against the economic order. Saint-Simon had broken the bondage of the Church, the Bible, and mechanistic science. He announced that every age had its special revelation; that the mark of inspiration was the enunciation of the truth most needed by humanity at a given time. For the nineteenth century the essential revelation was the rediscovery of the brotherhood of man, of the social gospel of Jesus stripped of theological accretions. This gospel was not incompatible with science, but would employ science to bring about "the quickest and most complete improvement of the moral and physical existence of the most numerous class in society." Indirectly this would benefit all classes, and thus achieve the purpose of God, whose existence could neither be proved nor disproved, yet was a necessary guarantee of the moral and aesthetic demands of humanity. Though he could not accept Saint-Simon's claim to be a new messiah, Carlyle hailed with delight this humanitarian, aesthetic, and nonmetaphysical religion, which crystallized much that he had already found afloat in literature in German.

Le Nouveau Christianisme enunciated general principles of social reform; the development of Saint-Simon's doctrines by his pupils presented detailed means of putting them in operation. Carlyle had been hampered by lack of statistics concerning the economic condition of the masses; Bazard and Enfantin made use of the facts concerning the functioning of the industrial system collected by the Swiss Sismondi from observation of the British overproduction crisis of 1819-20 which had made Carlyle sympathize with the insurrectionary Glasgow workers. These facts revealed industrialism as cruel and wasteful: cruel in its ethics of warfare and its neglect of workers superseded or enslaved by machinery; wasteful in its toleration of compulsory and privileged idleness, overcrowding of certain industries and professions, and periodical overproduction. As engineers and financiers, the Saint-Simonians were irritated by the waste; as preachers of a new Christianity, they were distressed by the cruelty. Obviously the "invisible hand" upon which Adam Smith, with his deistic prepossessions, had relied for the evolution of social welfare out of individual egoism, was failing to operate.

Recourse must be made to scientific direction of the processes of industry for the improvement of every member of society. Justice and efficiency demanded the confiscation of private property by the State, and the redistribution of its income according to the formula: *"Á chacun selon sa capacité, á chacque capacité selon ses œuvres"* (To each according to his ability, to each ability according to its accomplishment). To prove that no injustice would be done by abolishing what the economists called the "sacred right of property," unconditioned by responsibility to society for its use, the Saint-Simonians brought forth two arguments, one from history, the other from orthodox political economy itself. The feudal system had made tenure of land by the aristocracy contingent on at least theoretical obligation to protect the serf and the burgher. Now that national governments had assumed this obligation toward the general population, it was logical that they, and not the descendants or plunderers of a functionless aristocracy, should succeed to possession of the land. Furthermore the term "rent," which the bourgeois economists since Ricardo had been blithely turning against the landlords, was equally dangerous to the industrial and commercial capitalists, for it could be expanded consistently from its original meaning of monopoly advantage from the best lands when the worse were forced into cultivation, to include every sort of income from monopoly, from inheritance and every other kind of chance or luck, from interest on loans, and from investments in industries not directed personally by the recipients. Thus there could be no moral or legal obstacle to the revival of the functional conception of property and abolition of inheritance.

In the new order, industry would have central direction and planning, enlightened by comprehensive statistics. *"Chefs de l'industrie"* (captains of industry) would have a privileged position in the hierarchy of labor, but their tenure would be contingent upon continued capacity and diligence. They would not own factories any more than colonels their regiments, nor would they be able to hand down their power or superior income to their children. Man would no longer wage competitive war upon man; but a world of brothers would coöperate in exploiting the resources of the planet.

Hardly had Carlyle begun to read the Saint-Simonians, when the news of the second French Revolution came pat. To his thankful acknowledgment to D'Eichthal on August 9, he added a postscript expressing joy that Charles X had been driven into exile, and congratulating the Saint-Simonians that they had plans of social reconstruction compared to which such merely political revolutions were superficial.

Jeffrey visited Craigenputtock in September, exultant over the approaching victory for the Whigs, who had been out of office, save for the one year 1806-7, since 1783. Urging Carlyle to join the swelling movement for Parliamentary Reform, he was met by hot attacks on private property and inheritance which shocked his middle-class convictions profoundly. Driven in his turn to being dreadfully in earnest, he followed up their debate by a letter of November 13, arrayed in full panoply of Malthusianism and the wage-fund theory: "I wish to explain to you the grounds of my horror of radicalism. It is nothing but the old feud against property, more formidable by the greater intelligence and conceit of those who have none.... It is only by protecting and assuring the right of property that we have emerged from that condition [universal poverty], and are still kept out of it, and though its ultimate establishment produces many evils, and a most revolting spectacle of inequality, I do not see how you can touch it, without bringing in still greater evils.... A rich man after all spends almost all his income on the poor, and except a very little *waste* of food among his servants and horses, is a mere distributor of his rents among industrial and frugal workmen." The alarm he dared not show Carlyle was confided in a letter of January 31, 1831, to his Whig friend Empson: "The great battle that is soon to be fought ... is not between Whigs and Tories, Liberals and Illiberals, but between property and no property—Swing and the law. In that battle our Tory opponents must be on the same side with us."

This would have confirmed Carlyle's contention that the contest between the two leading parties was largely a sham. At the time of this letter to Empson, the Whigs were close to their political goal. With the help of dissatisfied Tory groups, they had overturned the Duke of Wellington's majority in mid-November. Jeffrey was Lord Advocate of Scotland in the new Whig Ministry of Earl Grey, whose Home Secretary, Lord Melbourne, was protecting the party against the charge of being revolutionary by crushing the revolt of agricultural laborers with great severity, while the Tories looked on with a certain irony. Yet Carlyle knew well how personal generosity tempered Jeffrey's economic principles. During the visit to Craigenputtock a note had been forwarded to Jeffrey: "Dear Sir, I am dying. Can you send me £100, and consummate your many kindnesses to me?—W. Hazlitt." He requested John Carlyle to offer medical attention in London, and hurried off to his bankers at Edinburgh, whence he sent a first installment of fifty pounds. Before this aid arrived, Hazlitt was dead.

Jeffrey had carried away Carlyle's history of German literature with the hope of interesting a publisher, but he had no success. The only encouraging news came from Germany, where Goethe was writing a preface to a translation of *The Life of Schiller* and was having the essay on *Burns* reprinted. In early February, Carlyle confided to his Journal: "I have some five pounds to front the world with, and expect no more for months. Jack, too, is in the neap tide. Hand to the oar."

Undeterred by Goethe's repetition of Jeffrey's warning against the Saint-Simonians, Carlyle had continued to read eagerly all their publications he could lay hands on: the *"Simonienne"* [27] John promised to send from London in early December was probably the collection in book form of the lectures printed in the *Organisateur*. In December he had translated *Le Nouveau*

Christianisme but could find no publisher, not even the Radical *Westminster Review.* In late January he had asked John to rescue from Fraser an essay, *Thoughts on Clothes,* that had been begun immediately after Jeffrey's visit. He was resolved to expand it into a book that would lead "through Religion and the Nature of Society and Lord knows what." "I fear perfect anonymity is now out of the question," he added; "however, swear every one to secrecy, for I mean to speak fearlessly if at all." Although Napier failed to pay for the review he published in March, and John's straits required the loan of the returns from the *Westminster Review* article in July, pot-boilers for *Fraser's* maintained Carlyle while he wrote steadily on the ambitious book for seven months, not knowing "in the least whether I shall ever gain the price of my paper."

The Craigenputtock solitude became oppressive when Alick and his household departed in May, but John kept up his courage with discerning and prophetic praise. "It is not for the purpose of flattering you with fine words," he wrote on June 9, "that I state my deep and sincere conviction, that you require only to find your place among men in order to exercise more influence on the present age than any living writer. Even the little fragments you have published show an extent of knowledge, a keenness and depth of insight, a clear and fearless liberty that I find in no English writer of these times. You are not chained in any den, like Irving plunging and floundering. You have not dreaded to explore the thick darkness with perfect freedom, and having come through it all and known it all your light is only the more constant and serene on that very account. You may depend upon it you will meet response from many hearts even in these times of Mammon. The only fault, if it may be so named, of your writing is that it is too high and sustained for almost all English readers. There are few who can bear to have so much intense and continued thought put upon them as any of your papers require. The fault I think rises almost entirely from your isolation and consequent want of knowledge of the audience you have to address. You fire well and stoutly, but have to take aim in the twilight, and can never rightly discern whether you have hit or missed the mark." [28] On the completion of the book in August came the immense satisfaction of his clear-headed wife's verdict: "A work of genius, my dear." Such also has been the verdict of posterity on that strange work, *Sartor Resartus*.

Sartor Resartus sums up the best ideas in Carlyle's previous work, and looks forward to the fuller development of his thought in politics, economics, and history. It is a brilliant exhibition of the variety of his talents; a medley of humor, pathos, moral exaltation, poetic upliftment, irony, playfulness, and sardonic satire. It also marks the accomplishmen of a change in manner that had been coming on gradually. The style of the *Life of Schiller,* though with Romantic touches, had the firm, clear framework of eighteenth-century English and French prose. Later, following his favorite humorists Richter and Sterne, and indulging his temperamental urge to preach and teach with metaphorical warmth, the style of his essays becomes increasingly rhapsodic and unconventional. Articles close in perorations; their contents are arranged less in a logical, and more in an emotional order. These tendencies culminate in *Sartor Resartus,* where Carlyle, free from the restraint imposed by the editors and audience of periodicals, took "aim in the twilight" even more than he was wont. The Romanticists delighted in inventing literary forms to express their idiosyncrasies; Carlyle had the precedent of Richter and *Don Juan,* though *The Prelude, Apologia pro Vita Sua,* and *The Ring and the Book* were yet to come.

He gave himself the utmost liberty by providing for his ideas the mouthpiece of an eccentric German professor, Diogenes Teufelsdröckh, whose philosophy had been fished out by a British editor from twelve bags into which it had been carelessly thrown. The supposed editor and translator has arranged these materials in three books which, bearing the marks of the original chaos, tend to overlap. However, Book I is chiefly concerned with an attack on mechanistic science, garnering the best ideas from Carlyle's review articles; Book II is romanticized autobiography developing the manner of the abandoned *Wotton Reinfred;* and

Book III presents recently developed social doctrines. The style outdoes this arrangement in eccentricity. Sentences are jerky, disjointed, with unexpected quirks and a few Germanisms to give verisimilitude; in their midst arise purple passages in exalted poetic rhythm, such as the early description of a sleeping city from an attic window, and periods of exhortation, in which Carlyle adopts the tone and rhythms of the Hebrew prophets to drive his social gospel home. In 1829 he had written to John Wilson: "I have some thoughts of beginning to prophesy next year, if I prosper; that seems the best style, could one strike it rightly."

The unifying idea of the book was the clothes metaphor adopted from Swift's *Tale of a Tub* and reflected in the title (Sartor Resartus meaning Tailor Retailored). The metaphor is employed in two ways: to indicate that the material world is the mere clothing of the spiritual, or that institutions are clothing that must be periodically cast off and replaced by society, whose nature it is to change. In its development in the first sense, chiefly Book I, Carlyle achieved magnificently by literary art what he had failed to do in fumbling attempts at Transcendental philosophy, and had hitherto attained only through translations from Richter and Novalis. Many passages, such as the chapters *The World without Clothes* and *Natural Supernaturalism,* carry, at least for the moment, conviction of a spiritual world even to the sceptical, the words being the thing they paint. The sphere of science dwindles before the immensity of man's ignorance, and ample breathing space is opened for Wonder, Reverence, and Heroism. Yet Carlyle avoids the pitfall of obscurantism; the chapter on *Natural Supernaturalism* rejects the orthodox conception of miracles as well as the dogmatism of narrow scientists.

Book II shows the steps whereby Professor Teufelsdröckh escaped the bondage of mechanistic science and arrived at the spiritualistic philosophy thus described. Without regard to literal chronology and circumstance, it follows the main outlines of Carlyle's dramatic life. This puts the reader in emotional sympathy with his attitude toward science and with his struggles against social barriers that motivate the social theories to be expounded in Book III. The brilliant description of the spiritual crisis and conversion is an historical document of European significance, paralleling similar accounts in Goethe's *Dichtung und Wahrheit,* Wordsworth's *Prelude,* and Tennyson's *In Memoriam.* The latter eighteenth and early nineteenth centuries were full of such crises, resulting from the clash of traditional and scientific views of the world. There had probably been no comparable conflict since the period when Christianity arose in the Græco-Roman world.

Two lessons of Carlyle's spiritual experience bear marks of their testing at Craigenputtock. The preservation of the honesty of his pen through the rejection of conventional middle-class standards of living lay behind Professor Teufelsdröckh's discovery that *"the Fraction of Life can be increased in value not so much by increasing your Numerator as by lessening your Denominator.* Nay, unless my Algebra deceive me, *Unity* itself divided by *Zero* will give *Infinity.* Make thy claim of wages zero then; thou hast the world under thy feet. Well did the wisest of our time [Goethe] write: 'It is only with renunciation (*Entsagen*) that Life, properly speaking, can be said to begin.'" This was but the "Passive half" of the good life. The active had been found in the steady absorption in literary tasks which made solitude bearable and banished the hobgoblins of introspection and discontent. Hence the exhortation: "Be no longer a Chaos, but a World, or even Worldkin. Produce! Produce!...Whatsoever thy hand findeth to do, do it with thy whole might. Work while it is called To-day; for the Night cometh, wherein no man can work." The duty of man was compressed in these gospels of Renunciation and Work, which Carlyle was never to tire of preaching.

Book III contains the latest development of Carlyle's thought: criticism of contemporary institutions, the old clothes of humanity. It bears strong imprint of the doctrines of the Saint-Simonians, the debates with Jeffrey, and the exciting events of 1830-31. A sweeping Reform Bill that would throw political control into the hands of the upper middle class having encountered stubborn opposition, the Whig ministry had appealed to the country. A general election in May, 1831, had left no doubt of the popular verdict where it had chance of expression; the Whigs returned with a majority for the Bill in the Commons, though the House of Lords was still to be reckoned with. But a Reform Act was to Carlyle only a beginning of the removal of the remnants of feudalism, which must be completed by the Benthamite Radicals before a new social framework could be built. Carlyle's summary of his position seems an echo of conversation with Jeffrey: "The English Whig has, in the second generation, become an English Radical; who, in the third again, it is to be hoped, will become an English Rebuilder."

The detailed development of this conception requires for clearness a regrouping of Carlyle's materials that disregards the rather haphazard order of his chapters. Church clothes and political clothes are outworn. The bishops do not care for their flocks, and the effete aristocracy wastes its time in shooting, hunting, and social frivolity, acquiescing in Malthus's principle that population tends to outrun means of subsistence instead of leading forth the people to the unoccupied lands of the globe. The chapter *Helotage* shows the masses deprived of education and less cared for than horses; and *The Dandiacal Body* makes an effective contrast, with Carlyle's characteristic mingling of pathos and humor, of the extremes of society, the Dandies and the Irish Poor Slaves. Government has so far decayed under the influence of *laissez-faire* theories that "there is no Social Idea extant... each, isolated, regardless of his neighbor, clutches what he can get, and cries 'mine,' and calls it Peace, because, in the cut-throat scramble, no steel knives, but only a far cunninger sort, can be employed."

But Carlyle did not despair. After *laissez faire* had done its worst, a new society would arise, based on the Saint-Simonian and Christian doctrine of the brotherhood of man. The railroad and the steamboat were already bringing men closer together. Recognition of the dignity of labor would remove the chief motive for their exploitation of their fellows. Elemental political forces, pointed out in a chapter on *Symbols,* would burst the stop-gap mechanism of representative government, and drive onward, not to illusory independence, but to obedience to a real aristocracy of ability, the Heroes. For the guidance of these leaders inspired men of letters would continuously provide new bibles for new times. At this climax of optimism Carlyle hesitated. He remembered the sad fate of metaphorical tailors who had attempted to make better social garments for mankind. Man had so often rejected and martyred his benefactors. In the final chapter, Teufelsdröckh disappears in search of the Saint-Simonians, who may have solutions for such riddles.

§ 5

CARLYLE had the satisfaction of having written a book that would cause "ears to tingle." But his financial situation was desperate. For the journey to London to market *Sartor Resartus,* he was obliged to borrow sixty pounds from Jeffrey, and to leave Jane behind at Craigenputtock with one of his sisters for company, now that a stranger was grazier in Alick's place. He set out the first week of August, 1831, going by steamboat to Liverpool, but by stagecoach thence to London, not being able to afford a ride in the new "steam coaches" he saw for the first time. John welcomed him to London on August 9, and they dined "at an eating house among Frenchmen, one of whom ceases eating to hear me talk of the St. Simonians."

The next day Carlyle called on Jeffrey, who gave him a complimentary letter of introduction to the famous publisher, John Murray. Murray received him pleasantly, but procrastinated irritatingly with his decision on the manuscript. Other publishers, Fraser, Longman, were discouraging when sounded out as to the literary history and *Sartor Resartus;* so it seemed best to wait until Jeffrey brought pressure upon Murray, who appeared "very anxious to keep well with Ministers."

Carlyle began to realize more fully than in his rural solitude how hard the publishing business had been hit by the political and economic crisis. Irving confessed to loss of money on his recent publications. Allan Cummingham, a fellow Annandalesman in the Fraserian group, told him it was "almost 'madness' to press forward a literary work at this so inauspicious season and not to wait for a while." We now know the correctness of this view from manifold sources, of which a statement by the established publisher William Blackwood (October, 1831) is typical: "There has never been so slack a year in our trade since I have been in business." But Carlyle could not wait, for he needed money badly. Besides, he was burning to get his opinions before the world.

He watched indignantly the means which publishers and authors were employing to force sales against adverse conditions. In face of the slump of 1825-6, Constable had imitated with considerable effect the advertising methods recently developed for large-scale production in industry. Now London publishers were trying the same expedient with unprecedented lavishness. Dignified houses like Murray and Longman spent freely, but they were outdone by the firm of Colburn and Bentley, whose reputed yearly expenditure of £9,000 on publicity was the scandal and admiration of the literary world. Naïve surprise as well as disapproval may be detected in a rhetorical question concerning Colburn in *Fraser's* for April, 1830: "Does he not keep clerks and writers whose exclusive employ is, as he says, 'solely to look after the papers and advertisements'?" This firm ensured favorable reviews of its publications by owning three organs of critical opinion: the *New Monthly,* the *Court Journal,* and the *Sunday Times,* besides one-third interest in the weekly *Literary Gazette.* The rival *Fraser's Magazine* for February, 1831, pointed out that of the forty new novels on the current Colburn list, eighteen were puffed extravagantly by the *Court Journal,* and eleven more by the *Literary Gazette.* This subtly concealed self-criticism had been outdone by the *Athenaeum* during the brief period of Colburn's half-ownership in 1828, when it devoted a leader to laudatory review of the entire Colburn list for the season. The *Literary Gazette,* supreme among weeklies, had its publicity copied extensively as news by provincial newspapers. The *New Monthly* pushed Colburn's specialty of novels of fashionable life, including those of Bulwer, for which a great vogue had been created by the desire of the post-war newly rich to ape the manners of the aristocracy.[29]

Colburn had taken temporarily a half share in the *Athenaeum,* founded as a rival weekly to the *Literary Gazette,* in order to discipline his partners in the latter, the publishing house of Longman and Company and the veteran editor, William Jerdan. "I cannot any longer consent," he wrote Jerdan on December 1, 1827, "to see my best authors unfairly reviewed and my own property injured." Jerdan, looking over the past year's files, could find only one Colburn novel unfavorably noticed: "It might be thought," he reflected in his *Autobiography,* "that such a series of panegyric should have satisfied the most exigent expectations." He was not squeamish in his editorial policy, for earlier in the same year he had made a significant overture to the Tory Prime Minister Canning: "Should you ... find me eligible for any mark of favor which would enable me to associate an efficient coadjutor in the *Literary Gazette,* and take a somewhat higher station in society, I would without doubt or fear of success undertake to produce very beneficial consequences throughout the whole periodical press. It requires but cultivation." Yet publishers were insatiable. When G. B. Whitaker threatened to withdraw his advertising on account of unfavorable comments on his publications, Jerdan had replied somewhat pathetically, "It is utterly impossible to produce a review which shall always be puffing." The crusading *Westminster Review* outlined the state of journalistic criticism without mincing words: "A publisher in a large way can put in or direct from the pockets of any newspaper proprietor many hundred pounds a year. Here is the secret of laudatory critiques, of favorable quotations, of sly allusions, of grossly eulogistic paragraphs, paid or unpaid for, inserted as the impartial suggestions of the editor." *Fraser's* repeated the accusation with picturesque detail: "The uninitiated may ask— How does it happen that the teachers best of moral wisdom, the newspapers, reviews, magazines, etc. inform us day after day, week after week, month after month, that one novel is the most splendid effort ever produced—another, so touchingly pathetic as never was heard of—a third, comic 'to a degree'—a fourth 'one in which the sensibilities of genius so blend with the ideality of illusion, that the perfection of fact shines in all the essence of soul'—in a fifth—see the last *Literary Gazette.* We say this may perplex the uninitiated, but the initiated know better. You may tell it to the marines."

Fraser's Magazine itself employed a more subtle and legitimate method of bringing its contributors and other literary figures to public notice by inaugurating from June, 1830, a *Portrait Gallery,* in which monthly drawings of authors by Maclise were accompanied by a page of comment on their personalities and writings. Some portraits, like that of Carlyle appearing as No. 37 in 1833, are dignified, but others set examples of theatrical posing that have not been outdone by present-day publicity. Sometimes an author was encouraged to carry his pose into daily life, as in a case humorously described by Carlyle during this visit to London: "Hogg the Ettrick Shepherd is walking about here; dining everywhere, everywhere laughed at.... He appears in public with a grey Scotch plaid, the like of which was never seen here before; it is supposed to be a trick of his Bookseller (a hungry *shark,* on the verge of bankruptcy) who wishes to attract notice from the Cockney population, and thereby raise the wind a little."

Authors used every means to push their own wares. John Wilson ("Christopher North") wrote to his friend De Quincey, who was about to review his works in 1829: "If you think the *Isle of Palms* and *The City of the Plague* original poems (in design) I hope you will say so.... If you think me a good private character, do say so.... Base brutes have libelled my personal character...I have wished to speak of humble life and the elementary feelings under the light of a veil of poetry. Have I done so? Pathos, a sense of beauty, and humor, I think I possess. Do I? In *The City of the Plague* there ought to be something of the sublime. Is there?" [and more in the same strain]. The popular novelist Edward Bulwer wrote to Napier (September 8, 1830) to complain that his books had not been noticed by the *Edinburgh;* three days later, fearing he might have only provoked hostile comment, he wrote again in tactful and verbose supplication. In 1833, protesting against an unfavorable review in the *Athenaeum,* he went so far as to hint to its proprietor, Charles Dilke, a reward for better treatment by stating casually that he had presented Jerdan of the rival *Literary Gazette* with a silver inkstand. The poet Robert Montgomery sent a gift of his complete works to Dilke's private residence; they were returned with the explanation: "It has ever been a rule with me since my first connection with the *Athenaeum* to decline presents of books from authors and publishers."

The inconsistency of Montgomery in permitting his publishers to employ for his own works the kinds of publicity he had denounced in his satire *The Puffiad* (1827) offered a shining mark to other satirists, especially to those honestly concerned in improving literary ethics. Macaulay's castigation of Montgomery in the *Edinburgh Review* for April, 1830, illuminates with not too much exaggeration the market to which Carlyle had brought *Sartor Resartus:* "All the pens that ever were employed in magnifying Bish's lucky office, Romani's fleecy hosiery, Packwood's razor strops, and Rowland's Kayldor, all the placard bearers of Dr. Eady, all the wall-chalkers of Day and Martin, seem to have taken service with the poets of this generation. Devices which in the lowest trades are considered disreputable are adopted without scruple, and improved upon with despicable ingenuity by people engaged in a pursuit which never was and never will be considered as a mere trade by any man of honour and virtue.... It is for his honor as a gentleman that his works should come before the public recommended by their own merits alone, and should be discussed with perfect freedom." The *Westminister Review,* commenting on *Puffing, and the Puffiad* in April, 1828, had expressed itself in terms that might have been Carlyle's own: "Title-pages, prefaces, advertisements, and even critiques, may be clubbed together as one great LIE. The practice of puffing your property brings on the practice of puffing yourself, and hence all kinds of egotism and vanity, especially in the tribe of authors, editors, and critics. The fact is, that puffers have an advantage over the world; the public gives them partial credit for honesty, and believes two thirds of what it reads in honor of typography." With even the respectable London *Times* invaded by inspired eulogies of Montgomery, the discerning few among the bookbuyers tended to keep "aloof from all modern books."

The *Westminster* suggested a remedy in the launching of literary periodicals by honest and independent men. A start was made on this plan by Charles Dilke, scholar and friend of Keats, when in 1830 he purchased a three-quarters share in the *Athenaeum*. He enforced Spartan discipline on his reviewers, forbidding them to comment on books with whose authors or publishers they were personally acquainted, to accept advance sheets or other favors from publishers, or to frequent literary salons; and he took the same precautions himself. On May 28, 1831, he stated editorially that some publishers had refused to advertise in the *Athenaeum* or sell copies of it in their bookstores because it would not admit *trade* criticism or *paid* criticism. But by the revolutionary step of lowering its price from eightpence to fourpence it took the lead of the *Literary Gazette* in subscribers from 1832 onward. It became a considerable force in raising the standards and reliability of criticism during the early Victorian period; how far this still fell short of the ideal in 1860 may be read in Matthew Arnold's *Function of Criticism in the Present Time.*[30]

Carlyle had tea with Dilke about a fortnight after his arrival in London, and discussed with him the evils of the literary world. He found the worthy journalist "not without a sense for the good, but with little power to follow it and defy the evil." "That is the temper in which I find many here," he informed Jane; "they deplore the prevalence of dishonesty, quackery, and stupidity; many do it (like Dilke) with apparent heartiness and sorrow; but to believe it can be resisted, that it will and shall be resisted, herein poor Teufelsdröckh is wellnigh singular." Carlyle's impatient idealism was unfair to Dilke, whom long experience with literary conditions and a year's valiant effort with the *Athenaeum* had taught how strongly intrenched evils were, and how slow must be the progress against them. In reaction against impudent self-advertisement Carlyle clung to the old practice of anonymous writing that was passing out. He was super-sensitive when Dilke gave harmless publicity to his name in connection with a translation of a few lines from "Faust": "Last Friday I saw my name in large letters at the *Athenaeum* office in Catherine Street, Strand; hurried on with downcast eyes as if I had seen myself in the pillory. Dilke ... asked me for a scrap of writing with my *name*. Inclined now to believe that I did wrong; at least imprudently. Why yield even half a hair's breadth to puffing? Abhor it, utterly denounce it, and kick it to the Devil."

Carlyle applied to Jeffrey for some minor government position that would put him above the vicissitudes of literature, but found that his not being a Whig excluded him from a share in the party spoils. Jeffrey, however, intervened effectively in other ways. In late August he secured for John Carlyle the post of travelling physician to the Countess Clare at a salary of three hundred pounds that made him independent of his brother. Early in September he won Murray to a reluctant offer to print 750 copies of *Sartor Resartus* if Carlyle would share half of whatever profits or losses this edition would bring. Murray urged Carlyle to try elsewhere for better terms before accepting this arrangement; accordingly he applied even to the malodorous Colburn and Bentley: "After waiting a weary hour in the Bentleian apartments saw a muddy character, to whom I explained myself.... The muddy man uttered the common cant of compliments, hinted at the sole object of publishers being money, the difference between talent and popularity, etc., etc." The next day he closed with Murray, who began to print with the intention of publishing early in 1832.

Relieved of John's drain on his purse, Carlyle joyously called his brave wife to spend the winter with him in London: "My love for you does not depend on looks, and defies old age and decay, and, I can prophesy, will grow stronger the longer we live and toil together. Yes, Jeanie, though I have brought you into rough, rugged conditions, I feel that I have saved you, as Gigmaness you could not have lived; as woman and wife you need but to see your duties in order to do them." Before she could complete preparations for travel, came the bad news that the wavering Murray had turned *Sartor Resartus* back on her husband's hands. She was told to come, nevertheless, for there was plenty of employment on periodicals to sustain a winter in London.

Early in October, Jane arrived to share two comfortable rooms in the house of one of Irving's parishioners. She found Irving with "grizzled" hair, conferring at his home with fanatics who claimed to have received the apostolic Gift of Tongues and of casting out devils. As Irving greeted his old friends, a shriek came from somewhere in the upper storey. Exclaiming, "There is one prophesying; come and hear her," he forced them upstairs, where they saw a woman raving with a "shrieky hysterical lah-lah-lal" that continued almost ten minutes. The strong-minded Jane almost fainted, and was in a bad state of nerves all night.

The Carlyles were greatly concerned for Irving when they heard the report that he had permitted such "Prophetesses," recent English converts, to break forth in open meeting the preceding Sunday. Carlyle had begun writing a letter of warning, when he discovered that the newspapers had called upon Irving's original Scottish congregation "for the honor of Scotland to leave him or muzzle him." He then gave up the letter as useless, for he knew that newspaper interference would make Irving determined not to draw back, "lest it seem fear of men rather than of God." That the congregation would remove him seemed equally certain. Carlyle could not help confessing privately that there was poetic justice in that "he who believed without inquiry should now believe against all light, and portentously call upon the world to admire as inspiration what is but a dancing on the verge of bottomless abysses of madness."

Yet affection and gratitude prompted him to accede to Irving's brother's earnest request that he take the first occasion to make a solemn oral protest against risking so much for a theory "founded solely on a little text of *writing* in an ancient book," which yet "soared above all known experience and flatly contradicted" it. Irving listened patiently and kindly, but it was impossible to save him. The Carlyles could only look with sorrow on the scenes of the final four years of Irving's life: the eviction from his pastorate, the trial for heresy in his native Annan, the founding of the sect which still bears his name, and his premature death in 1835, at the age of forty-three, from constant religious excitement. Carlyle wrote a moving obituary for *Fraser's,* of which one sentence epitomized the significance of Irving's life: "The Spirit of the Time, which could not enlist him as its soldier, must needs, in all ways, fight against him as its enemy."

Jane met new London friends of her husband who indicated how definitely he had, for his own part, cast in his lot with the spirit of the time. Early in November Charles Buller, now "a great tower of a fellow, six feet three in height, a yard in breadth," called at their lodgings. He was in Parliament, voting for the extinction of his uncle's pocket borough, for which he was sitting, and going against strong Whig family connections in professing himself a Benthamite Radical. He rejoiced that a more tolerant attitude toward Benthamism was indicated in Carlyle's recent friendship with John Stuart Mill, son of the James Mill who had opposed his candidacy for a London University chair. While Buller was talking, Mill dropped in. He was "a slender, rather tall and elegant youth" of twenty-five, "with small clear Roman-nosed face; modest, remarkably gifted with precision of utterance, enthusiastic, yet lucid, calm." Discussion of current events developed into what Jane described as "a pleasant forenoon call of seven hours and a half."

On coming to London Carlyle had sought the anonymous author of a series of articles that had appeared in the *Examiner* earlier in the year, bearing striking resemblances to what he was then writing in *Sartor Resartus.* He discovered, to his surprise, that the writer was one of the chief Benthamites, John

Stuart Mill. Already out of sympathy with orthodox Utilitarianism, Mill was studying German, and had actually met D'Eichthal, the Saint-Simonian. Interest in the Saint-Simonians at once formed a strong bond between Carlyle and Mill, who were approaching agreement, from very different backgrounds. Mill had been subjected to a forcing system of home education by his father that had made him a precocious convert to the doctrines of Philosophic Radicalism, including mechanistic science and Ricardian political economy. Without religious instruction, he had not Carlyle's need to break away from orthodox Christianity. But he had revolted against an overdose of eighteenth-century rationalism. His "conversion," begun in 1826 and still in progress, was thus similar to Carlyle's: the discovery of a satisfying emotional outlet in English and German Romantic literature, and in the synthesis of Romanticism and science attempted by the Saint-Simonians. In this synthesis science bulked more largely for Mill, Romanticism for Carlyle; the source of a divergence that would increase as they grew older. In 1831 their minds were at the point of closest approximation in politics and economics; though here again Mill was more political and Carlyle more economic in emphasis.

D'Eichthal had introduced Mill in 1828-9 to the Saint-Simonian outlook by means of Auguste Comte's briefer *Traité de Politique Positive* (1822). Comte revealed the error of Benthamite Radicalism, inherited from the French *philosophes* and Jacobins, in a brilliant sentence: "It consists in attributing an organic character to the negative principles which served to destroy [in France] the Feudal and Theological System; in other words, it takes mere modification of the Old System as the foundation of the system to be established." Mill's awakening to the weakness of the allied political economy had come later through meeting Bazard and Enfantin in Paris after the revolution of July, 1830. Mill continued to be a Benthamite to the extent of thinking wide extension of the suffrage necessary to give the masses a weapon for securing economic rights, though he wished to offset it by providing in some way for the aristocracy of talent dear to the Saint-Simonians. This undemocratic side of his opinions was prominent in his articles on *The Spirit of the Age,* which Carlyle had enjoyed for their insistence on the incapacity of the average man to contribute to the reconstruction that would be necessary after the political revolution of a Reform Act.

Mill had just returned from a summer pilgrimage to the homes of Wordsworth and Southey in the Lake region, and under the spell of their personalities had strayed farthest from his inherited political creed. He was writing to his friend John Sterling in the West Indies: "The Toryism of Wordsworth, of Coleridge (if he can be called a Tory), of Southey even, is *tout bonnement* a reverence for *gouvernement* in the abstract; it means that they are duly sensible that it is good for man to be ruled; to submit both his body and mind to the guidance of a higher intelligence and virtue. It is, therefore, the direct antithesis of Liberalism, which is for making every man his own guide and sovereign master, and letting him think for himself, and do exactly what he judges best for himself, giving other men leave to persuade him if they can by evidence, but forbidding him to give way to authority; and still less allowing them to constrain him more than the existence and tolerable necessity of every man's person and property renders indispensably necessary. It is difficult to conceive a more thorough ignorance of man's nature, or what is necessary for his happiness, or what degree of happiness and virtue he is capable of attaining, than this system implies. But I cannot help regretting that the men who are best capable of struggling against these narrow views and mischievous heresies should chain themselves, full of life and vigor as they are, to the inanimate corpses of dead political and religious systems, never more to be revived."

This position between the contending Tory, Whig and Radical parties, identical with Carlyle's, drew the earnest idealists strongly together.[31] Carlyle, ten years the elder, took the lead and somewhat mistakenly regarded Mill as one of the disciples he was eager to enlist. Mill and Buller were the first of the younger generation of thinkers and writers whom Carlyle, having missed his own generation by his retarded development in Scotland, began to gather about him at the threshold of the Victorian era. Mill introduced him to young men in Parliament and the diplomatic service, and Carlyle was encouraged by the admiration of these youths for *Sartor Resartus,* which he circulated in manuscript.

In December the Carlyles were delighted by the unexpected appearance of the Saint-Simonians Detrosier and D'Eichthal, the latter "a little, tight, clearly pure lovable *Geschöpchen;* a pure martyr and apostle, it seems to me; almost the only one (not belonging to the Past) whom I have met with in my pilgrimage. Mill goes so far as to think there might and should be martyrs; this is one." The cool middle-aged Crabb Robinson gives a revealing glimpse of Carlyle at this period: "His voice and manner and even the style of his conversation are those of a religious zealot; and he keeps up that character by his declamations against the anti-religious. But then—if not the God of his idolatry, he has a priest and prophet of his church in Goethe, of whose profound wisdom he speaks like an enthusiast. . . . But in strange union with such idolatry is his admiration for Bonaparte. Another object of his eulogy is—Cobbett, whom he praises for his humanity and love of the poor!!!" Carlyle retrospectively called his portrait by Maclise in 1832 "the Dominie," stressing correctly his pedagogic manner that merged with the prophetic when the schoolmaster was in training for the pulpit. Literature combined for him the opportunities to preach and to teach.

In the hectic atmosphere of late 1831, prophecy seemed a natural mode of utterance, and even Irving's sort not entirely abnormal. In October the House of Lords enraged the nation by rejecting the Reform Bill after its passage in the Commons. Political unions sprang up in greater numbers. There was terrible rioting in Bristol. Unemployment and starvation made manufacturing and agricultural workers break out in sporadic acts of violence throughout the United Kingdom. Numerous special constables were sworn in to protect the dwellings of London notables; the Duke of Northumberland fortified his house. To make apprehension greater, an epidemic of Asiatic cholera arrived by way of the Continent. On November 13, Carlyle wrote to his brother John in Italy: "Truly the political aspects of England give even me alarm. A second edition of the French Revolution is distinctly within the range of chances; for there is nowhere any tie remaining among men. Everywhere, in court and cathedral, brazen falsehood now at length stands convicted of a lie, and famishing Ignorance cries, Away with her, away with her! God deliver us. Nay, God will deliver us; for this is His world, not the Devil's." The social shoddiness was reflected in the newer building in London: "You are ill-lodged, in brick houses, thin as shells, with all the floors twisted, and every article indicating its showiness and its weakness. The Tradesman, in every department, has become an eye-servant; and could not help it, without being a martyr, as indeed all men should be." Carlyle found it "almost positively painful to walk these streets, and see so many cold and hungry and naked and ignorant beings, and have so little power to help them." Everywhere was "the most crying want of government, a true all-ruining anarchy."

§ 6

CARLYLE's reflections on the chaotic state of England and its influence upon literature found public expression in his review of Croker's edition of Boswell's *Life of Johnson* (*Fraser's Magazine*) and in his essay *Characteristics* (*Edinburgh Review*), both written in his London lodgings during this winter of 1831-32. The topic of Samuel Johnson, the first important English author to support himself entirely from the sale of his writings, offered an opportunity to discuss the financial conditions of authorship. Looking backward over the experience of a century, Carlyle wondered whether the transition from dependence on wealthy patrons to dependence upon publishers and the general public deserved to be called a "happy change." For if patronage had led to flattery and cringing, the new system had led to the probably greater dishonesty of advertising and kindred practices. Now puffery, ceasing to deceive the best class of readers, was making them hesitate to buy any new book. Literature seemed "working pretty rapidly toward some third method, the exact conditions of which are nowhere visible"; perhaps toward a coöperative guild of authors. Carlyle regretted that there was so little exact knowledge of the past to guide this step into the future. "In these days, ten ordinary histories of Kings and Courtiers were well exchanged against the tenth part of one History of Booksellers," that would tell, for example, who *"first* paid copyright in England." Meanwhile Carlyle saw encouragement for honest literary workers in Dr. Johnson's conquest of "a two-fold problem: How to keep alive by writing, and to keep alive while writing the truth." Johnson's patience under attack: "Sirs, if they should cease to talk of me, I would starve," was but one example of the gigantic calmness with which he faced the realities of his profession. "By popular delusion," he said on another occasion, "illiterate writers will rise into renown."

Napier, continuing his policy of keeping Carlyle off political and economic topics, permitted him to review a metaphysical work, Thomas Hope's *Origin and Prospects of Man.* But Carlyle adroitly converted the article into a profounder *Signs of the Times* by contrasting Hope's book, "the apotheosis of materialism," with Friedrich von Schlegel's *Philosophical Lectures.* The plight of those who, like Schlegel rebelled against materialism and struggled "to be persons, not machines," Carlyle developed in an eloquent passage that is a classic document in the spiritual history of the period.

"They have to realize a Worship for themselves, or live unworshipping. The God-like has vanished from the world; and they, by the strong cry of their soul's agony, like true wonder-workers, must again evoke its presence. This miracle is their appointed task; which they must accomplish, or die wretchedly: this miracle has been accomplished by such; but not in our land; our land yet knows not of it. Behold a Byron, in melodious tones, 'cursing his day'; he mistakes earth-born passionate Desire for heaven-inspired Free Will; without heavenly lodestar, rushes madly into the dance of meteoric lights that hover on the mad Mahlstrom; and goes down among its eddies. Hear a Shelley filling the earth with inarticulate wail; like the infinite, inarticulate grief and weeping of forsaken infants. A noble Friedrich Schlegel, stupefied in that fearful loneliness, flies back to Catholicism; as a child might to its slain Mother's bosom, and cling there. In lower regions, how many a poor Hazlitt must wander on God's verdant earth, like the unblest on burning deserts; passionately dig wells and draw up only the dry quicksand; believe that he is seeking Truth, yet only wrestle among endless Sophisms, doing desperate battle as with spectre-hosts; and die and make no sign!

"To the better order of such minds any mad joy of Denial has long since ceased; the problem is not now to deny, but to ascertain and perform. Once in destroying the False, there was a certain inspiration; but now the genius of Destruction has done its work, there is now nothing more to destroy. The doom of the Old has long been pronounced, and irrevocable; the Old has passed away; but, alas, the new appears not in its stead; the Time is still in pangs of travail with the New. Man has walked by the light of conflagrations, and amid the sound of falling cities; and now there is darkness and long watching till it be morning."

This spiritual suffering was matched by the "Physical diseases of Society" aggravated by *laissez faire:*

"Wealth has accumulated itself into masses; and Poverty, also in accumulation enough, lies impassably separated from it; opposed, uncommunicating, like forces in positive and negative poles. . . . How much among us might be likened to a whited sepulchre; outwardly all pomp and strength; but inwardly full of horror and despair and dead men's bones! Iron highways, with their wains fire-winged, are uniting all ends of the firm Land; quays and moles, with their innumerable stately fleets, tame the ocean into our pliant bearer of burdens; Labor's thousand arms, of sinew and of metal, all-conquering everywhere, from the tops of the mountain down to the depths of the mine and the caverns of the sea, ply unweariedly for the service of man; yet man remains unserved. He has subdued this Planet, his habitation and inheritance; yet reaps no profit from the victory. Sad to look upon; in the highest stage of civilization, nine tenths of mankind have to struggle in the lowest battle of savage or even animal man, the battle against Famine."

Thus a major problem had arisen "from the increase of social resources, which the old social methods will no longer administer." Where Toryism had failed, the Reform Bill would not succeed, for it was based on the fallacious mechanistic theory of politics.

Carlyle proposed instead a method for the social sciences based on the conception of society as an organism: "The vital articulation of many individuals into a new collective individual. ... To figure Society as endowed with life is scarcely a metaphor, but rather the statement of a fact by such imperfect means as language affords." Since his escape from the domination of deductive science, he had been groping in the domains of scarcely born biology. This new science was fruitful of a psychology at variance with the analytic, static Lockian variety taught at Edinburgh University and recently presented in an extreme form by James Mill's *Analysis of the Phenomena of the Human Mind* (1828), that attempted to make mental functioning "as plain as the road from Charing Cross to St. Paul's." The intellect was no longer seen as lord and lawgiver, but only as an instrument whereby the human organism adjusts itself to its environment. Mental activity was evidence of imperfect adjustment; Carlyle instanced the aphorism, "Life is ... a working excited by suffering." Furthermore, he pointed out, "of our thinking, we might say, it is but the mere upper surface that we shape into articulate Thoughts;—underneath the region of argument and conscious discourse, lies the region of meditation.... These curious relations of the Voluntary and Conscious to the Involuntary and Unconscious, and the small proportion which, in all departments of our life, the former bears to the latter,—might lead us into deep questions of Psychology and Physiology." In fact, they led to the chief line of development in psychology since Carlyle's time. This type of psychology, though contrary to the prevalent atomic theory of society, harmonized completely with Carlyle's organic theory: "It is in Society that man first feels what he is; first becomes what he can be. In Society an altogether new set of spiritual activities are evolved in him, and the old immeasurably quickened and strengthened."

This remarkable essay, *Characteristics,* subversive of the politics and economics of individualism, stated the basic principles of Carlyle's social theory. Its belittlement of the logical intellect began a disagreement with John Mill that finally led to the parting of their ways in the eighteen-forties. Its immediate effect was irritation of the Whigs.

Napier had employed Carlyle in order to please Jeffrey. He did not suspect the drift of Carlyle's comment on Hope's book as "the highest culminating point of the mechanical spirit of this age; as it were, the *reductio ad absurdum* of that whole most melancholy doctrine"; or of his frank statement, in submitting the article, that Napier might wish to reject it. Apparently he was disarmed by Carlyle's saying: "A mighty work lies before the writers of this time. I have a great faith and a great hope that the *Edinburgh Review* will not be wanting on its own part, but stand forth in the van, where it has some right to be." Bewildered by the aphoristic style which, Carlyle informed him while writing, needed "an incessant watchfulness to keep from being abstruse," the solid Edinburgh lawyer pronounced *Characteristics* on hasty perusal "inscrutable," yet decided to print it, since it had an indefinable power. In so doing he brought down upon himself the laughter and anger of his chief contributors.

Macaulay wrote Napier gaily on February 1, 1832: "As for Carlyle, he might as well write in Irving's unknown tongue at once. The *Sun* newspaper, with delicious absurdity, attributes his article to Lord Brougham." Lord Chancellor Brougham, who had disliked the drift of Carlyle's writing ever since he had received the manuscript of *The State of German Literature* as evidence of his qualifications for a London University chair, was consequently enraged with Napier. Even Jeffrey lost much of his patience, and advised him on February 7: "I fear Carlyle will not do, that is, if you do not take the liberties and pains with him that I did, by striking out and writing in occasionally. The misfortune is that he is very obstinate, and, I am afraid, conceited, and unluckily in a place like this [London], he finds people enough to abet and applaud him, to intercept the otherwise infallible remedy of general avoidance and neglect. It is a great pity, for he is a man of genius and industry, and with the capacity of being an elegant and impressive writer." Napier had at hand a request from Carlyle, dated the day previous to Jeffrey's letter, for the opportunity to review the anonymous "Corn-Law Rhymes" recently brought to his attention by Mill, which had "more of sincerity and genuine natural fire than anything that has come my way of late years." Possibly wishing to give him rope enough to hang himself, he disregarded protests in granting the request.[32] In any case, the article on the *Rhymes* (July, 1832), in which Carlyle consciously glanced "in a poisonous manner, at Whiggism itself," put an end to his connection with the *Edinburgh Review*.

Breaking with the Whigs threw Carlyle into closer association with London radicals. Leigh Hunt, with the eye for genius that had discovered Keats, Shelley, and very recently the young Alfred Tennyson, sought the acquaintance of the author of *Characteristics*. Dr. Bowring of the *Westminster Review,* who had printed the *Nibelungen Lied* article, introduced him to the editor of the *Examiner,* Anthony Fonblanque, who seemed "the best of the Fourth Estate now extant in Britain." John Mill, who was becoming Carlyle's intimate friend, projected a meeting with the aged Jeremy Bentham which the latter's bad health rendered impossible. These congenial connections made Carlyle eager to remain in London, but he could find no firm financial foothold. He learned that lecturing was done only by quacks, and the book trade showed no sign of reviving. Periodicals alone continued to flourish.

In October, 1831, Blackwood had added to his pessimistic account of the year's business: "Maga (*Blackwood's Magazine*) has, however, carried on triumphantly, and the sale and popularity are as great as ever." In January, 1833, he was to write again: "There has never been such a year of stagnation.... Our business has felt it more than any other; and had it not been for the magazine, which keeps on flourishingly, I do not know what I should have done." Carlyle's situation may be also illuminated by a letter of Mrs. Shelley to the publisher Murray concerning her father, William Godwin, in May, 1832: "You are but too well aware of the evil days upon which literature has fallen, and how difficult it is for a man, however gifted, whose existence depends upon his pen, to make one engagement succeed another with sufficient speed to answer the calls of his situation. Nearly all our literati have found but one recourse in this—which is the ample scope offered by periodicals. A kind of literary pride has prevented my father from mingling in these." Carlyle shared some of this literary pride, but periodicals were his only recourse. The *Edinburgh Review* connection was tenuous, the *Foreign Review* was dead; but *Fraser's* was induced by the decided success of his review of Croker's *Johnson,* more penetrating and sympathetic than Macaulay's, to pay him twenty guineas a sheet. Bulwer, who was giving Colburn's *New Monthly* a radical tone since becoming its editor in November, 1831, sought his services. Periodicals would keep him alive, but on the condition that he return to Craigenputtock.

§ 7

THE retreat to Craigenputtock in late March, 1832, had a deeper coloring of sadness from the news, as the Carlyles were passing through Dumfries, of Goethe's death. "I feel as if I had a second time lost a Father," Thomas wrote John; the death of their own father having come as a great blow in January, when both were far from him. The literary interregnum was emphasized by the passing of giants; of Bentham and Scott before the year was out, and of Coleridge soon thereafter. Of Romanticism Carlyle saw only "dying embers, kicked to and fro under the feet of innumerable women and children in the Magazines." [38]

Craigenputtock was lonely without Alick: "Our new Neighbors have nothing to do with us, except little kind offices of business; articulate speech I hear little; no wiser man than William Corson [a neighboring farmer] visits me," Thomas wrote. But the brown fields, lately visited by sleet and whirlwinds of snow, now gleamed with freshly plowed furrows, and the men were busy with road-cleaning and hedge-cropping. In spite of the unsold *Sartor Resartus,* no hint of discouragement crept into the letters of either husband or wife. Jane's breathed elation mixed with sermons from Goethe. Thomas's the familiar: "My sole comfort and remedy is Work! Work!" Work was urgent, for Jeffrey had not been repaid.

The *Corn-Law Rhymes* review, stating boldly that the country suffered from far worse ills than the landlords' "bread tax," was completed in May, just before Carlyle heard that threats of armed insurrection by the Political Unions, and of a run on the Bank of England engineered by Benthamite Radicals, had frightened the House of Lords into accepting the Reform Bill. When its enactment gave Carlyle a vote, he paid the half-crown necessary for registration, even though he thought the political gain slight as compared with the economic problem ahead.

Poverty continually hampered his writing by lack of books. He queried in his Journal: "Why is there not a Majesty's library in every county town? There is a Majesty's jail and gallows in every one." This suggested an essay on Authors, toward which he jotted down: "Authors are martyrs—witnesses for the truth— or else nothing. Money cannot make or unmake them. . . . Yet for the world whom they address . . . money, as the epitome and magic talisman of all mechanical endeavor whatsoever, is of incalculable importance. Money cannot hire the writing of a book, but it can the printing of it. The existence of a public library, or the non-existence thereof, in the circle where a thinker is born, will forward his thinking or obstruct and prevent it. When the thinker has discovered truth, it depends on money whether the world shall participate in such discovery or not participate." Napier, having had enough of Caryle's economic views, was not interested in such an article, and it was never completed. Mill came to Carlyle's aid, sending bundles of books and interesting economic documents including the reports of two Parliamentary committees for the investigation of child labor in factories that caused a sensation in 1832 and 1833.

Such contact with the great world was precious to the solitary thinker, who wrote in his Journal in September: "It never wholly seems to me that I shall die in this wilderness; a feeling is always dimly with me that I am to be called out of it, and have work for me before I depart.... Let not solitude, let no silence and unparticipating isolation make a savage of thee." He was now thirty-seven, and the problem of his future was serious.

The long article on Diderot begun in September for the *Foreign Quarterly* illustrates the handicaps of his conscientious thoroughness and brooding meditation in the journalistic market. Before sitting down to write, he read the twenty-six octavo volumes of Diderot's works and correspondence at the rate of one a day. Then he spent a month in composing one of the most profound and balanced of his essays. For this he was paid about thirty pounds for each month of actual work, and had to wait four months for payment. Fortunately John repaid him enough to wipe out his debt to Jeffrey, so that the income from various articles could be expended on a much needed return to civilization in Edinburgh, January to May, 1833.

After "the boiling roar of London," Edinburgh seemed "village-like." Its literary market was stagnant, except for the penny magazine Robert Chambers had recently launched to reach the barely literate. No publisher wanted *Sartor Resartus*, whose message Carlyle burned to give the world. But he found the Advocates' Library very useful for an article on the quack Cagliostro and similar investigations into the origins of the French Revolution, in which the reading of Diderot had re-kindled his interest. He was eager to write another book, but whether his subject should be the French Revolution, which meant a removal to London or even Paris, or John Knox and Scotch Presbyterianism, which would keep him in Edinburgh, was hard to determine. But unsatisfactory society in Edin-burgh turned him toward the French subject. He saw little of Sir William Hamilton; De Quincey was ill; John Wilson avoided him, probably, he suspected, because of the current rumor that he "was living in closest sworn-league, last winter," with Fonblanque and other dangerous radicals. Napier's reluc-tance to pay for the *Rhymes* article, and his refusal of other con-tributions, showed that the Whigs were as skittish as the Tories. He was thrown upon the society of mediocre men, intent upon "getting on" in conventional grooves. He felt them saying behind his back: "Carlyle is wasting his considerable talent on impossi-bilities, and can never do any good."

He was amazed at the indifference of Edinburgh to main problems of the day, such as the regulation of factory labor. For intelligent interest in these matters he had to write to Mill, or to his brother Alick, whom difficulty in making a living by agri-culture made an especially sympathetic audience. He had sent Alick the *Corn-Law Rhymes* essay, and now he was laying before him evils that the Reform Act had not touched, especially the tragic plight of Scotland, caught between the upper millstone of ruthless manufacturers and the nether millstone of greedy landlords: "Millions of mortals are toiling this day, in our British Isles, without prospect of rest, save in speedy death, to whom, for their utmost toiling, food and shelter are too high a blessing. When one reads of the Lancashire Factories and little children laboring for sixteen hours a day, inhaling at every breath a quan-tity of cotton *fuzz,* falling asleep over their wheels, and roused again by the lash of thongs over their backs or the slap of 'billy-rollers' over their little crowns; and then again of Irish White-feet, driven out of their potato-patches and mud-hovels, and obliged to take to the hillside as broken men—one pauses in a kind of amazed horror, to ask if this be Earth, the place of Hope, or Tophet, 'where hope never comes!'.... One grand remedy against the worst still lies open: America and its forests, where you have only the wild beasts to struggle against. I understand there never was such emigration from these parts, at least from Edinburgh, as this year. People of all sorts are going: laborers, shop-keepers, even Writers to the Signet [lawyers] and country Lairds. They are right. But in the mean time go on tilling: surely the Government will apply itself in earnest to Emigration, as the sole remedy for all that immediately presses on us." He told Mill of his disgust at the general interest in the emancipation of the Negro in the British Colonies, to the neglect of more important domestic evils of the same sort: "We have two blustering turkey-cocks lecturing here on the Negroes: one an Anti-slaver; the other a Slaver that follows him Ibis-like to destroy his Crocodile eggs. They fill the emptier head with vague horror and jarring. While we, under soft names, have not only slavery but the fiercest *Maroon War* going on under our noses, it seems to me philan-thropy and eleutheromany might find work nearer home. But names *do* change things." This paradox, though stated now and then by writers in *Fraser's* and other periodicals of the time, was to shock the public, and even Mill, when pushed to an ex-treme by Carlyle in *The Negro Question* in 1849.

Carlyle's opinions now isolated him as effectually in Edin-burgh as his social origin had isolated him formerly. As he walked its streets in discouragement, he remembered the words of Jesus: "Be of good cheer, I have overcome the world," and tears almost sprang into his eyes. Although he had abandoned orthodox Christianity, the heroic story of the Gospels remained his chief inspiration.

In hopeful moods he thought of London, where he had found comprehension and sympathy. His correspondence with Mill was a great satisfaction: [84] "Besides the comfortable available intelligence your Letters bring, there is a most wholesome feeling of communion comes over me in your neighborhood; the agreeable memento: 'Thou art not alone then!' " Mill responded with a suggestion: "Your picture of Edinburgh is *triste* enough, and might serve for all other provincial towns; there is an *odor* of literature and intellect about Edinburgh; at Glasgow, Liverpool, and the like, there is little else than the *stench* of trade. London is better, tho' bad. There are here some true believers, among whom your thoughts would not fall like hand-grenades and put them to flight. If you determine to leave Craigenputtock, there is surely no place so eligible as this."

Even with allowance for London complacency, Mill's advice was sound. The intellectual glories of Edinburgh were passing as able Scots were drawn more and more to London by greater prizes in politics and literature. "From about 1800," noted the shrewd observer Lord Cockburn, "everything purely Scotch has been fading." Scott had immortalized his "own romantic town" of Edinburgh in "Marmion" at the ironic moment of her decline. Campbell had settled in London in 1801. Of the original *Edinburgh* reviewers, Brougham and Sydney Smith were established in England before 1808, leaving Jeffrey, who had tried in vain for a literary opening in London in 1798, to follow in the period of his Lord Advocateship (1831-34). Their contemporary at Edinburgh University, James Mill, had begun in 1802 the journalistic career that made him a leader of the Radical Party launched by the *Westminster Review* in 1824. Of the Tory chiefs, Scott was dead, and his son-in-law Lockhart had gone to London in 1825 to edit the *Quarterly*. The immediate future promised a further provincialization of Edinburgh. The Reform Act was bringing a large part of the Scottish population into active participation in English politics, and the newly invented railroads would make Scotland amazingly closer to London.

Carlyle returned to Craigenputtock in May, pondering on Mill's advice, which would be discussed at length on his friend's vacation visit in August. His thoughts turned more definitely toward the French Revolution as Mill, who had collected a mass of books and pamphlets on the subject, decided not to treat it because he would incidentally be obliged to disclose his lack of faith in Christianity. Mill sent him some of these books, and he pondered without writing all summer. He was subsisting on the proceeds of *Sartor Resartus,* which had at last been sold for serial publication in *Fraser's* at a reduced rate which yielded a trifle over eighty-three pounds. This incoherent and profound book, sprung from the satire of Swift and the humors of Sterne and Richter, to which had been added wayward fancies encouraged by Craigenputtock solitude, was totally unsuited to a magazine audience, as the event proved. But in his eagerness to get his views published, Carlyle seized the only available vehicle.

In August came the disappointment that Mill could not get leave from his employers at India House in time for a visit. Instead, there arrived unexpectedly a pilgrim from America, bearing letters of introduction from Mill and D'Eichthal.

In October, 1832, the Reverend Ralph Waldo Emerson, on the eve of resigning the pastorate of the Second Unitarian Church of Boston because of doubts, was pleased to find a kindred spirit in the anonymous author of a review of *Corn-Law Rhymes.* "My Germanic new-light writer," he wrote in his Journal,... "gives us confidence in our principles. He assures the truth-lover everywhere of sympathy. Blessed art that makes books, and so joins me to that stranger by this perfect railroad." Now, after much difficulty, he had discovered him in this remote spot, having made, as Jane Carlyle remarked humorously, "the first journey since Noah's deluge... to Craigenputtock for such a purpose." The thirty-year-old American was charmed by the Carlyles: "Truth and peace and faith dwell with them and beautify them. I never saw more amiableness than is in his countenance." Emerson's lean face lighted with shrewdness and nobility was indeed welcome. He was persuaded to spend the night at Craigenputtock.

While Jane prepared dinner, Thomas led their guest to the top of Glaister's Hill to display the sternly grand panorama of his domain. The high-minded enthusiasts covered a wide range of topics, of which Emerson preserved an account in his *English*

Traits. Having recently lost his wife, he introduced the topic of immortality, from which Carlyle sheered off. But he was curious about America. Although he feared the American political principle was "mere rebellion," it was good to know one country in which the poor man could have "meat for his labor." He preferred London to any other place to live in, and instanced Mill, "the best mind" he knew, as one whom "London had well served." Upon their return to the house, Jane revealed some of the cares of the household, especially the disappointment when the repudiation of the order for the literary history had postponed indefinitely the journey to Weimar. When Emerson mentioned the essay on Burns, she exclaimed with wifely pride that it always happened that her husband heard of the effect of such writings two or three years after they came out.

Carlyle always remembered Emerson's departure: "I saw him go up the hill. I didn't go with him to see him descend. I preferred to watch him mount and vanish like an angel." It was immensely consoling that work rejected in Edinburgh was reaching pure spirits across the Atlantic. Emerson, in Liverpool, waiting to sail to Boston, summarized in his Journal the results of his European tour. He had seen the four Englishmen he most admired; Landor, Coleridge, Carlyle, and Wordsworth: "The comfort of meeting men of genius such as these is that they talk sincerely, they feel themselves to be so rich that they are above the meanness of pretending to knowledge they have not, and they frankly tell you what puzzles them. But Carlyle—Carlyle is so amiable that I love him." Thus began the long friendship whose record can be read in the celebrated correspondence.

The French Revolution seemed "the subject of subjects" for a history that would be "the grand Poem of our Time," but Carlyle could not afford a trip to Paris, or even to Edinburgh, this winter. Fortunately, a gentleman living eight miles away at Barjag generously opened to him his excellent private library at the end of September: "For the first time in my life I have free access to some kind of Book-collection. I a Book-man." The ends of a Paris trip were partially served by Mill's going there in

October and obligingly doing errands about books and maps. Before the close of the year Carlyle had written a long account of the Diamond Necklace scandal, that revealed hidden springs of Court life under Louis XVI and Marie Antoinette.

There remained the problem of supporting himself while writing a book of such proportions. His periodical connections seemed in danger of breaking. The *Foreign Quarterly,* on the verge of bankruptcy, had declined *The Diamond Necklace* without seeing it. James Fraser reported that the first installments of *Sartor* were meeting with "the most unqualified disapproval," a hint that his best outlet might be closed. So he strove once more for some salaried position independent of literature, such as Mill had at the East India House. Hearing that the new astronomical observatory at Edinburgh University needed an Observer, he wrote in the middle of January, 1834, to Jeffrey, who controlled the appointment. Jeffrey, who probably knew nothing of Carlyle's early scientific training, replied at once that it would be useless to apply. Secretly irritated that Carlyle should apparently intend to impose on their friendship to obtain a post for which he was insufficiently qualified, he added a frank and vigorous statement of the attitude of the Whigs toward his recent writings. Soon thereafter he warned him that he need not apply for the chair of Rhetoric and English Literature that would also be open at the University. Carlyle suppressed his indignation, but because of this misunderstanding was never again on intimate terms with his benefactor.

The severing of this last link with Edinburgh was decisive for London. During the correspondence with Jeffrey, Mill had written of plans for a Radical Review controlled by a younger group dissatisfied with the narrow Benthamism of the *Westminster*. He invited Carlyle to contribute if it came into existence. Welcoming the opportunity, Carlyle mentioned his uncompleted essays on *Authors* and *John Knox*. He added a shrewd suggestion that the younger Radicals make use of the purely literary appeal which the old Benthamites, in their long feud with literature as a "seducer," had scorned: "I approve greatly of your purpose to discard Cant and Falsehood of all kinds; yet there is a kind of Fiction which is not Falsehood, and has more effect in addressing men than many a Radical is aware of. This has struck me much of late years in considering *Black-wood* and *Fraser;* both these are furnished as it were with a kind of theatrical costume, with orchestra and stage-lights, and thereby alone have a wonderful advantage; perhaps almost their only advantage. ... The Radicals, as you may observe, appear universally *naked* (except so far as decency goes); and really have a most prosaic aspect." Carlyle hoped that Mill might choose him to carry out this policy as editor, and he added that to his chances of a foothold in London. Meanwhile, although Alick owed him two hundred pounds without much prospect of repaying, he had somewhat over that amount in savings on which to live while beginning the History. If the History failed, he would emigrate to America, a step from which he no longer dissuaded Alick.

The history of the French Revolution was to be no academic exercise, but a warning to the British nation of a revolution that would scourge it also if it did not rebuild its social structure. A rhetorical question in the *Corn-Law Rhymes:* "How were it if we surmised, that for a man gifted with natural vigor ... especially if in the way of Literature, as a Thinker and Writer, it is actually, in these strange days, no special misfortune to be trained up among the Uneducated classes, and not among the Educated; but rather of two misfortunes the smaller?" reveals Carlyle half-consciously taking stock of his own qualifications as a social prophet. He had seen a wide range of Scottish society, agricultural, industrial, professional, from the simplest to the most complex and cultivated minds, from the proletariat to the fringes of the aristocracy; and what Emerson was to call his "devouring eye" had seized every significant detail. At Edinburgh University he had found the most original philosophy and best organized scientific research in Great Britain; in Chalmers, Irving and Coleridge, he had met the most characteristic religious phenomena of the time; he had known the best literary society in London and Edinburgh; and in Jeffrey he had seen incarnated the middle-class philosophy made dominant by the Reform Act. He had measured himself against these notable men, and believed himself their superior. From his wide reading he was conscious that his rise from obscurity, his discovery of the humbug of the professions and of institutions generally, his spiritual crisis, and his conversion had a general European significance, were typical of the age of transition through which Western civilization was passing. To preach the lessons of his life he had used strikingly parallel incidents in the lives of Schiller, Richter, Heyne, Burns, Goethe, Diderot, and Johnson, as well as romanticized autobiography under the guise of Diogenes Teufelsdröckh. He had developed a political and economic philosophy, and found for it in Mill and other London Radicals promising disciples, or at worst allies. He was ready to take a last chance to make it prevail. He was almost thirty-nine, and possibly at the catastrophe of the literary career that had opened so promisingly with the *Schiller* and *Meister* ten years before.

He announced his decision to Mill in late February: "Except in the little circle of my own kindred I know of no soul out of London whose society cheers and fortifies me; in *this* circle free working is impossible; why *not* London then?" "To go thither seems inevitable; palpably necessary," he told John, "yet contrasted with these six years of rockbound seclusion, seems almost like rising from the grave. Like an issuing from the Bastille at least: and then the question is, whether we shall not, like that old man, request with tears to be *taken back!* On the whole, I hope; and my little Dame (whom I often call 'Spairkin, Despairkin) declares naïvely that 'she is not a coward, for all that she is desperate.'" Mill wrote a hearty welcome, and Leigh Hunt offered to find the Carlyles a good house neighboring his own in the suburb of Chelsea.

Breaking family ties was painful. Carlyle's mother took the news stoically, but Mrs. Welsh burst into tears at the thought of her daughter so far away. Jane, however, was to remain with her until Thomas found a house in London. Alick and Jamie accompanied him to his steamer as he went by way of Liverpool in the middle of May. On the road to London, the Liverpool coach passed a Trades Union procession. Somehow it seemed symbolic, and Carlyle saluted it. As he caught sight of the "huge smoky Babylon" in which he must win a place or else emigrate to the New World, he found himself humming defiantly one of his mother's Border ballads:

> "For there's seven foresters in yon forest,
> And them I want to see, see,
> And them I want to see."

CHAPTER V

THE PROPHET

◆》》《《◆

§ 1

FINDING a comfortable home in the welter of overgrown London was a vexatious preliminary to the last effort of the Scotch prophet to conquer recognition in the English capital. In his ignorance of ways on the other side of the Border, he had hurried ahead of his wife under the impression that the renting season was late May, as in Edinburgh. His leisure was spent in a wide survey of possibilities in many old villages that were being swallowed up by the great city. The most eligible house seemed to be No. 5 Great Cheyne Row in Chelsea, then unfashionable and reputed unhealthy, with no hint of its present-day Bohemianism. The disadvantages of fog from the Thames and close proximity to Leigh Hunt, who might interrupt work by injudicious calls, made Carlyle await Jane's judgment on her arrival early in June. The rent of thirty-five pounds a year, ten below that of a similar house in Dumfries or Annan, decided her to risk these unpleasantnesses. They took possession on June tenth, little thinking they would end their days there.

Chelsea was to the west of London, two miles from Piccadilly and five from the factories of east London, whose smoke rarely drifted that way. A "Shilbeer" horse omnibus passing near his door every quarter of an hour took Carlyle to the centre of town for sixpence, though he generally preferred walking for exercise. He enjoyed the contrast of the "Craigenputtock silence" of the house, which lay "safe down a little bend of the river, away from all the great roads," with "the world-hubbub of London and its people into which a few minutes will bring you." The rear windows looked over his snug walled garden, where he could smoke and lounge in a dressing-gown, across grccn meadows once a bishop's pleasure grounds, to the distant smoke-cloud in which only Westminster Abbey and the gilded dome of St. Paul's were visible, unless a wind revealed "faint ghosts of spires." At night this became a great "gas-lit shimmer," variegated with rockets from Vauxhall Gardens. Across the street to the front were garden walls surrounding an ivied house. By putting their heads out the front windows the Carlyles could see the Thames with its darting pleasure craft. The quaint wooden Battersea toll-bridge gave a halfpenny crossing to the green knolls of Surrey with their villages, among which Carlyle delighted to walk.

Number 5 was one of twelve houses originally built on Cheyne Row in 1708, with the eighteenth-century substantiality of brick and wood Carlyle respected. It had three full storeys, with seven rooms, besides an attic half-storey and a kitchen floor partly sunk beneath street level. The rooms were large and high-ceiled, white wood panelling rising the height of the walls increasing the effect of light and spaciousness. Carlyle admired the "broadish stair, with massive balustrade (in the old style) corniced and thick as one's thigh; floors firm as a rock, wood of them here and there worm-eaten yet capable of cleanliness, and still thrice the strength of a modern floor." The heavy old-fashioned Scotch furniture from Craigenputtock was at home here; but the paintings that would have completed the eighteenth-century harmony were missing. In the second floor drawing-room that became Carlyle's study were a French print of Belisarius with sentimental associations for Jane, two old Italian engravings, and a cheap colored lithograph, sent by John from Italy, of a ragged *segretario ambulante* writing letters for illiterate passers-by; a symbol to Carlyle of "Literature in its simplest quite steadfast condition, below which it cannot sink." The years brought more engravings, chiefly portraits, which finally cluttered the walls. Color was conspicuously absent or else generally off-shade and in bad design, like the Turkey-red table cover of Tait's 1855 picture, that was probably akin to the red carpet brought from Craigenputtock for the study floor. Jane kept house with the assistance of a maid-of-all-work, and was willing to turn her hand to anything. One day this summer she told Mrs. Leigh Hunt that she had been busy painting. "What," she was asked, "is it a portrait?" "No," was the reply, "something of more importance—a large wardrobe." Mrs. Hunt, maintaining the fine-lady attitude in the midst of disorderly poverty, was unable to comprehend Jane's "patience for such things."

Living expenses would be about two hundred pounds a year, nearly the total of Carlyle's savings. To escape undue haste with his history, he looked about for other literary employment. As in Edinburgh, nothing seemed to thrive except "Penny Journals." Cochrane, the editor of the *Foreign Quarterly,* received him very kindly, but gave no commission—from want of funds, Carlyle suspected. James Fraser said that *Fraser's Magazine* was losing money. He was honestly perplexed about *Sartor Resartus,* whose final installment was to appear in August. The English public was clearly hostile; one of his oldest subscribers had threatened to withdraw if there was "any more of that damned stuff," but an American had ordered the magazine "so long as there was anything of Carlyle's in it." He was willing to publish the *French Revolution* on the profit-sharing arrangement Murray had proposed for *Sartor Resartus,* but refused the *Diamond Necklace* for the magazine, though considering its later publication as a sort of advance notice of the history.

There remained Mill's Radical quarterly, with the possibility of its editorship. Mill seemed "almost fonder than ever" in welcoming him to London. Charles Buller gave a dinner at which Carlyle met Sir William Molesworth, the financial backer of the project, who apparently liked him. Nevertheless in August he heard the rumor that the editor was to be the Reverend W. J.

Fox, whom Mill had named as the probable choice when first mentioning the periodical. Carlyle suspected one of Fox's parishioners, Mrs. John Taylor, of having influenced Mill, who had introduced her as his "dearest friend." Buller said Mill was in love with her, though she had a husband and children. But reflection suggested that Fox, who had experience as editor of the *Monthly Repository*, in which some of Mill's essays had been appearing, and could be depended upon not to break too sharply with Philosophic Radical tradition in ideas or manner, had seemed "the safer man." Disappointment was somewhat assuaged when Carlyle read in "Mill's embarrassed face when Fox happened to be talked of," that he had divined his friend's unspoken desire for the editorship and had considered it.* Mill made it clear that he would welcome Carlyle's contributions when the *London Review* was launched early in 1835. His tactful request to print the *Diamond Necklace* at his own expense was refused, but Carlyle accepted the loan of one hundred and fifty books on the French Revolution, some of which he suspected to have been bought expressly to help him.

Since July 6 he had settled down to intensive reading on the subject. With three hundred volumes on his shelves since Mill's gift, he needed to stir to the British Museum only once or twice a week to consult reference works. He walked thither through the extremes of wealth and misery—the fashionable Belgrave Square and the unspeakable Irish slums of St. Giles. One day banking business took him farther eastward, and he chanced upon "a strange anarchy of a place—the Stock Exchange. About a hundred men were jumping and jigging about in a dingy, contracted apartment, and yelping out all manner of sounds, which seemed to be auctioneers' offers, not without much laughter and other miscellaneous tumult. I thought of the words 'trade's contentious hell.'" He stored such incidental observations of London life in his memory against the day when he would speak out again upon the social situation.

* The final arrangement did not give the editorship to Fox after all, but to Mill as the supervisor of various sub-editors.

His reading matured so rapidly that he wrote his first two pages on September second. Although he had planned only a bird's-eye survey of the great subject, by the end of January, 1835, he found that he had completed the first volume of what had grown under his hands to a three-volume history. With his savings melting away and no journalistic employment available, he felt the pressure of haste. But his conscientiousness as to fact and form stood in the way: "I cannot write it fast; I could write it fast enough if I wrote it ill; but that I have determined not to do—wilfully." Emerson wrote encouraging news of good opportunities for lecturing in America, which might be a last financial resort. Carlyle felt his health much improved as he passed forty, and his mind "quite young yet, and *growing,* as when I was eighteen."

Fears of interruption by Leigh Hunt proved groundless. He never came unless invited, and then charmed with his melodious voice, and the boyish beauty and eagerness which remained with him when turned of fifty. He was a gentleman in the midst of the poverty to which improvidence and the collapse of the literary market had drawn him down. In his study, on the floor above a living room littered, dirty, and full of "wild children," there were "only two chairs, a bookcase, and a writing table." Yet "the noble Hunt receives you ... in the spirit of a king, places you in the best seat, takes a window-sill himself if there is no other, and there folding closer his loose-flowing 'muslin cloud' of a printed nightgown in which he always writes, commences the liveliest dialogue on philosophy and the prospects of man (who is to be beyond measure 'happy' yet); which again he will courteously terminate the moment you are bound to go."

In Hunt Carlyle encountered unshaken by events the faith of the eighteenth-century philanthropists for whom the French Revolution had opened boundless vistas of human perfectibility. His "fantastic framework of agreeabilities" offered a perfect foil to Carlyle's grim facing of facts. Their friendly debates, continuing until Hunt left the neighborhood in 1840, were the delight of hearers. A Scotch friend of Hunt's was fascinated by the collision of Carlyle's "sonorous eloquence...illuminated...by the coruscations of a splendid fancy, sometimes lurid enough...and heated to boiling fervor by the inextinguishable fire of deep emotion that is forever gnawing his heart and brain" with Hunt "all light and air, glancing gracefully over all topics, and casting the hues of his own temperament on every subject that arose." [35] Unfortunately Hunt exaggerated Shelley's Quixotism and Keats's sensuousness until the former became silly and the latter repulsive; which explains Carlyle's preposterous conception of both poets. At times Hunt was hurt by the vigorous demolition of his cloud castles, but he appreciated the generosity of Carlyle's aid in his unfortunate journalistic enterprises, and initiation in 1836 of the movement that finally in 1847 brought him a pension from a Whig government in recognition of his sufferings in the cause of liberalism. A bust of Shelley, the work of Mrs. Hunt, remained in the Carlyle house as a memorial of this friendship.

Almost every Sunday John Mill came for a long walk, full of lively discussion ranging from the *French Revolution* to current topics, such as the behavior of the small group of Radicals in Parliament whose policy Mill was hoping to direct with his *London Review*. Mill's was a different strain of radicalism from Hunt's, deriving from the newly formulated social sciences. Melioristic rather than utopian, it relied upon the gradual improvement of the masses by universal education and the exercise of political rights and responsibilities. With this doctrine Carlyle was more in sympathy, though disapproving of the Lockian psychology that made man a creature of environment and of argument and denied innate, ineradicable differences between individuals, and of the deductive method that had based the social sciences prematurely upon a narrow conception of human nature. Mill illustrated its limitations in the rather mechanical manner of his speech, sometimes so slow as to indicate a mind working by syllogisms, as well as by his ignorance of the world, the result of the restriction of his experience to a circle of middle-class intellectuals.

His pathetic innocence of the illogical and guileful ways of women came out in his infatuation for Mrs. Taylor. Fox had brought them together, seeking in Mill a competent answerer of the metaphysical questions raised by her inquisitive mind. Mill was attracted by what he considered her remarkable mental powers, unaware of the part played by her dark eyes and melancholy beauty. Her husband, an intelligent wholesale druggist, seemed dull beside the earnest young philosopher. So she encouraged Mill, who enjoyed the novelty of a flattering female audience, until gossip obliged Mr. Taylor to remonstrate. They protested innocence and agreed not to see each other; but they had found it impossible to keep their promise. Since there were children to be considered, the magnanimous husband compromised by absenting himself from dinner on the evenings Mill called. Mill and Mrs. Taylor considered the sex relation a private matter in which society had no right to interfere, but were unwilling to act upon this belief until divorce should be granted for incompatibility. This attitude was shared by Fox, whose unconventionality in keeping his secretary, Miss Eliza Flower, in his house while he was separated from his wife had caused a secession of part of his Unitarian congregation in 1834. Leigh Hunt also preached free love in the manner of his friend Shelley, although infidelity to his tippling and slatternly wife did not go beyond public kissing of quite proper ladies, among them Jane Carlyle, heroine of his familiar lyric "Jenny Kissed Me" (1838).

Observation of the lives of these reformers strengthened Carlyle's conviction that duty should be put above personal happiness: "Though the *world* is already blooming (or is one day to do it) in everlasting 'happiness of the greatest number,' these people's own *houses* (I always find) are little Hells of improvidence, discord, unreason. Mill is far above all that, and I think will not sink in it; however, I do wish him fairly far from it, and though I cannot speak of it directly would fain help him out; he is one of the best people I ever saw." After a first gush of enthusiasm, Jane Carlyle was becoming irritated by Mrs. Taylor's patronizing airs and affectation of profundity, but Thomas had to admit the intellectual and social attraction of the men in her group. A dinner party at the Taylors' was "the cleverest (best gifted) I have been at for years: Mill, Charles Buller (one of the gayest, lightly-sparkling, lovable souls in the world), *Repository* Fox (who hotches [fidgets] and laughs at least), Fonblanque, the *Examiner* editor, were the main men. It does one good." [86]

This party took place in late February, 1835, when the March number of *Fraser's* was prepared to advertise the *History of the French Revolution* as "getting ready," and Mill had borrowed the manuscript of the completed first volume to annotate it with criticisms. As the Carlyles were sitting at tea on March 6, they heard Mill's characteristic short rap at the door. Jane opened to find him "unresponsive, pale, the very picture of despair; ... half-articulately gasping, that she must go down and speak to 'Mrs. Taylor.'" One thought rushed through the minds of both Carlyles—"They are eloping." Jane hurried outside to the cab containing Mrs. Taylor, while Thomas led Mill to a chair and waited with sympathetic inquiring looks until the explanation came out after "considerable additional gasping."

Mill had carelessly left the borrowed manuscript lying about; a maid had mistaken it for waste paper, and had burned it, except for "some four tattered leaves." Carlyle felt a curious relief that it was not the disaster of Mill's self-exile from society. He threw all his effort into consoling his friend, who kept saying that nothing of the sort had ever happened before. It was useless to remind him of Newton's dog Diamond, for he replied without his usual tact: "Newton went mad over it." Too stunned to move, he remained for three hours after the departure of Mrs. Taylor, who did not enter the house. With Spartan self-control, the Carlyles succeeded in turning the conversation into pleasant channels.

It was almost midnight before they were alone to lament their terrible loss. Jane threw her arms around her husband: "*She was very good to me, and the thing did not beat us. I felt in* general that I was a little Schoolboy, who had laboriously written out his Copy as he could, and was showing it not without satisfaction to the Master; but lo! the Master had suddenly torn it, saying: 'No, boy, thou must go and write it better.'" The task seemed impossible, for he had destroyed his notes and lost the mood in which he had written.

For Carlyle the night was "full of emotion, occasionally of sharp pain (something cutting or hard grasping me about the heart)." He could not pray, but kept a sort of composure by repeating "Walk humbly with thy God." When at last he fell asleep there came a nightmare of his father and his favorite sister Margaret, "alive, yet all defaced with the sleepy stagnancy, swollen habitude of the grave, and again dying as in some strange rude country." Awaking to the full horror of the blank day, he forced himself to write in his Journal: "This morning I have determined so far that I *can* write *a* book on the French Revolution, and will do it. Nay, our money will still suffice. It was my last throw in the monstrosity of this life—for too monstrous, incomprehensible it has been to me."

He at once communicated this decision to Mill, whom he knew it would soothe, adding, "Is there anything that I could do or suffer or say to alleviate you? For I feel that your sorrow must be far sharper than mine; yours bound to be a passive one." He considerately provided him with an occupation in searching for Madame de Campan's *Memoires*. This note was crossed by one from Mill passionately entreating to be allowed to repair the irreparable, as far as money could. After some hesitation Carlyle consented, but reduced the two hundred pounds Mill sent to one hundred, his living expenses during the time of writing. Mill added the gift of a biographical dictionary, and continued the loan of books. He was eager to aid with the history, not only for his friend's sake, but also because of the radical point of view which it would embody. He continued his walks with Carlyle, and their friendship was unimpaired by the terrible mischance, which was kept a close secret in the Carlyle family.

§ 2

FRASER had to be told in confidence of the unexpected delay in the preparation of the book, but Mill was not mentioned. Carlyle finished his chapter in the second volume within a week, then returned to the lost first. The recapture of its mood was even more difficult than he had thought. He cleared his mind by reading light literature for two weeks, and was back at his task by the end of the month. Working against time, he made good his loss before October. The completion of the second volume in April, 1836, left him exhausted: "The mind is weary, the body is very sick; a little black speck dances to and fro in the left eye like a signal of distress."

Fortunately at this juncture his brother John, whose letters had been full of good advice as to measures of health and of efforts to dissipate worries about money by reminders of their compact as to a "common fund," [37] arrived from abroad. They spent a six weeks' vacation walking about the environs of London. Having been conservatized by the circle of the Countess Clare, John could not help remonstrating against the tone of the history as he read it in manuscript. Thomas replied vigorously: "Jack, there are some ten million of men on this Island, who generation after generation spend their lives in *supporting* Conventionalities of one sort or the other,—why should there not once be one man who spent his life (were it his *life* even) in declaring openly to whatever quackhood he met, Behold thou art a quackhood!"

He was cheered by the news that Emerson had got out *Sartor Resartus* in book form in the United States, selling one hundred and fifty subscription copies before the date of publication. On John's departure he bolstered up his finances by two pot-boilers, by-products of the history, for Mill's periodical, which by absorbing the *Westminster* had become the *London and Westminster Review*. In so doing he expended the benefit of his vacation, and was tired when he began his third volume in July. Since Jane was in Scotland, the watchful Mill suggested the diversion of a week-end visit to his country house at Dorking, which he shared with a sister. Carlyle hesitated, saying: "My state is very unsure. I work all day, and awake occasionally at five or even at three in the morning; I am so dreary of mood (like a ghost rather than like a man), and alive nowhere except over the paper, that it often seems quite foolish in me to think of going anywhither."

He nevertheless made the visit, which proved anything but restful because of even greater psychological disturbance on Mill's part. The death of James Mill three weeks before had removed the last restraining influence on his son's infatuation with Mrs. Taylor. The strain of sexual temptation was bringing John Mill toward a nervous breakdown, already manifesting itself in physical danger-signals. Unable to mention what was preying on his mind, he bewildered his friend by an unexpected barrier of reserve. Carlyle described the visit to his wife: "They were as hospitable as they could be. I was led about, made attentive to innumerable picturesqueness, etc., etc., all that evening and the next day.... There was little sorrow visible in their house, or rather none, nor any human feeling at all; but the strangest *unheimlich* kind of composure and acquiescence, as if all human spontaneity had taken refuge in invisible corners. Mill himself talked much, and not stupidly—far from that—but without emotion of any discernible kind. He seemed to be withering or withered into the miserablest scrae,* body and mind, that I almost ever met with in the world. His eyes go winking and jerking with wild lights and twitches; his head is bald, his face brown and dry—poor fellow after all. It seemed to me the strangest thing what this man could want with me, or I with such a man so *unheimlich* to me. What will become of it? Nothing evil; for there is and there was nothing dishonest in it. But I think I shall see less and less of him. Alas, poor fellow! It seems possible, too, that he may not be very long seeable; that is one way of its ending, to say nothing of my own chances."

* Dialect for "old shoe."

Soon everything was explained by Mill's collapse, and gossip as to its cause. He was given three months' leave of absence from the India House, and his brothers accompanied him to Switzerland, where they left him in the care of Mrs. Taylor for a tour of convalescence in Mediterranean sunshine. In October Carlyle acquainted their mutual friend John Sterling with a report of Mill's condition that had come from Nice: "His health is a little, and but a little, improved. Mrs. Taylor, it is whispered, is with him or near him. Is it not very strange, this pining away into dessication and nonentity, of our poor Mill, if it be so, as his friends say, that this charmer is the cause of it? I have not seen any riddle of human life which I could so ill form a theory of. They are innocent, says Charity; they are guilty, says Scandal: then why in the name of wonder are they dying broken-hearted? One thing only, is painfully clear to me, that poor Mill is in a bad way. Alas, tho' he speaks not, perhaps his tragedy is more tragical than that of any of us: this very item that he does not speak, that he never could speak, but was to sit as in thick ribbed ice, voiceless, uncommunicating, is it not the most tragical circumstance of all?"

Sterling, whom Carlyle had met on dropping in to see Mill at the India House in February, 1835, was also in France for his health, which had likewise psychological complications. The son of the chief editorial writer for the London *Times,* he had begun a literary career by editing, with Frederick Denison Maurice, the *Athenaeum* in the interval between Colburn and Dilke. Both these young editors had come under the influence of Coleridge, which was evident in Sterling's novel *Arthur Coningsby* (1829-30). Soon after his marriage in 1830 Sterling had fallen dangerously ill of tuberculosis, from which he was recovering in the West Indies, when the terrible news arrived that his cousin, Lieutenant Boyd, and thirty-five others had been executed by a firing squad for complicity in the expedition of the exiled General Torrijos against the despotic King Ferdinand of Spain. Like many English liberals, including Tennyson, Sterling had been a backer of this enterprise. He would have shared the fate of his cousin had not Susannah Barton's tears at his farewell detained him for marriage. Feeling the executioners' bullets tearing his own brain, he vowed atonement for these deaths by a life of service. Coleridge's symbolical interpretation of the Thirty-nine Articles of the Church of England, that made its priesthood compatible with liberal thought, directed this desire for service into religious channels. Sterling returned to England, was ordained deacon, and in June, 1834, entered upon the duties of curate for his friend Julius Hare at Hurstmonceaux in Surrey.

But doubts rearose as he recovered from the shock of the Spanish tragedy. When Carlyle met him, he was resigning his post, ostensibly because of ill-health, which took him to France the following year. Before this journey Sterling became intimate with Carlyle, whose dark moods were dissipated by his ebullient hopefulness. Sterling's father offered Carlyle a position on the *Times,* which had to be refused because it involved subordination of personal convictions to the newspaper's Tory policy. Through Sterling Carlyle had come to know the leaders of the Broad Church movement, Maurice and Hare. In April, 1836, he described these new friends to Emerson: "There are two or three of the best souls here I have known for long; I feel less alone with them.... These friends expect mainly that the Church of England is not dead but asleep; that the leather coaches, with their gilt panels, can be peopled again with a living aristocracy instead of the simulacra of such. I must altogether hold my peace as to this, as I do to much. Coleridge is the Father of all these. *Ay de mi!"* Notwithstanding this dissent from their aims, Carlyle was to exert considerable influence on the Established Church through these clergymen.

The purpose of using the French Revolution as a means of oblique comment upon contemporary British affairs was kept strong by Carlyle's daily observation while he wrote. In October, 1834, he had watched fire destroy the Parliament Buildings: "The crowd was quiet, rather pleased than otherwise; whew'd and whistled when the breeze came as if to encourage it: 'there's a flare-up for the House o' Lords!'—'A judgment for the Poor-

Law Bill!'—'There go their hacts (acts)!' Such exclamations seemed to be the prevailing ones. A man *sorry* I did not anywhere see."

The New Poor Law enacted this year was an especial grievance of the working classes. Drafted chiefly by Nassau Senior, Professor of Political Economy at Oxford, and Edwin Chadwick, formerly Bentham's secretary, it applied the principles of orthodox economic science to the problem of pauperism, which had been increasing steadily in proportions since 1795, when the central government had guaranteed subsistence by supplementing wages out of taxes. The evils of this method had been long apparent. The laboring population was being demoralized by a dole which gave the independent worker no advantage over the pauper; paupers increased in number; taxes rose. The new legislation struck at the root of these evils by abolishing the dole, and aiding only those who would submit to the custody of workhouses, where food and lodging were designed to be worse than those of the most miserable workers outside. The ration of food was somewhat difficult to establish without killing the inmate, since the independent farmhand, according to Chadwick's calculation, "could expect, in the average, to obtain for his own consumption only 17 ozs. of bread per day and ½ lb. of bacon per week." But there was hit upon the ingenious plan of supplying food sufficient for nourishment but in forms so unpalatable that the workhouse would be chosen only in the extremity of need.

The crowd that watched the burning of the Houses of Parliament was murmuring at the harshness of incarceration in what, thinking like Carlyle of the French analogy, they dubbed "Bastilles." Only later did the working classes see the full injustice of such legislation, that took no account of physical incapacity and of involuntary idleness through overproduction crises in industry. Carlyle explained to Alick that the failure of agriculture was partially due to the lack of a good home market in "a population sinking deeper and deeper into destitution and inability to purchase anything but Potatoes."

Worst of all was the blind complacency of the propertied

classes: "Everybody, Radical and other, *every* body here tells me that the condition of the Poor people is—improving! My astonishment was great at first, but now I look for nothing else than this: 'improving daily.' 'Well, gentlemen,' I answered once, 'the Poor, I think, will get up some day, and *tell* you how improved their condition is.' " One night at a social gathering, as he heard the celebrated Whig wit Sydney Smith "guffawing, other persons prating, jargoning," it seemed to Carlyle that through the "thin cobwebs" of the drawing-room walls "Death and Eternity sate glaring." Then in sudden contrast he found himself walking "homewards along Regent Street, through street-walkers, through —*Ach Gott!* unspeakable pity swallowed up unspeakable abhorrence." On a similar occasion he observed what the reaction against the French Revolution had done to another Whig soul. He met the poet Samuel Rogers, who in 1792, at the age of twenty-nine, had applied for membership in the Constitutional Society that included Tom Paine, but on cautious second thought had withdrawn his name before it could be voted upon. Prudence and success in the banking business that supported his avocation of literature had left their mark indelibly upon him at the age of seventy-three. Carlyle found him "a half-frozen sardonic Whig-Gentleman: no hair at all, but one of the whitest bare scalps, blue eyes, shrewd, sad, and cruel: toothless horse-shoe mouth drawn up to the very nose: slow-croaking, sarcastic insight, perfect breeding."

Such was the generation that ruled the country with Lord Melbourne. The Whigs had the power they had fought for, and opposed the efforts of the Benthamite Radicals for further curtailment of aristocratic privilege. Although he disagreed with their economic policy, Carlyle could coöperate with the Radicals in their attempt to supply the want of popular education in England, so shocking to a Scotchman. In 1833 Mill's friends Grote and Roebuck had secured the first government appropriation for the purpose of secular education, less than one-tenth of one percent of the yearly budget, and not half the amount voted for the construction of the Queen's stables in 1839. After

the burning of his manuscript in 1835, Carlyle had applied
through Charles Buller for employment by the committee administering this fund. "If I stir in any public matter," he told
John, "it must be this of public education.... Woe the while if
the people are not taught; if not their wisdom, then their brutish
folly will incarnate itself in the frightfullest reality." This was
the lesson of the French Revolution as he saw it.

Fortified by a hundred pounds from the articles sold to the
London and Westminster, and by the prospect of returns from
the American edition of *Sartor Resartus,* which with the aid of
Emerson's generous introduction had exhausted its entire five
hundred copies by September, 1836, Carlyle kept doggedly at his
final volume. As the Benthamite Radicals had offered a convenient parallel to the Girondists, so now he found insight into
the psychology of the Jacobins who were to play the chief rôle
in the third volume through acquaintance with two exiles in
London,—Godefroi Cavaignac and Joseph Mazzini. Cavaignac
had carried out the republican principles of his father, a member
of the Convention, by leading the Parisian workingmen in the
street fighting of the Revolution of 1830, and thereafter by repeated plots against Louis Philippe that finally drove him to
refuge in England. Mazzini, whose mild manners and fervent
belief in God contrasted with the fire-eating atheistic Frenchman,
was quite as courageous in organizing the anti-clerical and republican secret society "Young Italy" against the Pope and the
foreign masters of his divided native land. Mazzini and Cavaignac gave Carlyle contact with the democratic and nationalistic
aspirations of Continental peoples that prepared him for the
great year of revolutions, 1848.

Volume III was planned on a different scale from its
predecessors: "splashed down in large masses of colors, that it
may look like a smoke-and-flame conflagration in the distance,
which it is;" an impression maintained by writing "with the
force of fire, with the speed of fire." Such intensity aggravated
the old complaints of insomnia and dyspepsia, which in turn
brought worry about money. The arrangement with Fraser gave

no prospect of returns from the history, whatever its fortune with the public, until over a year after publication. Meanwhile there remained saleable only the *Diamond Necklace,* which Fraser would print in his magazine for January and February, 1837. Emerson's suggestion of a lecture tour in America was a final resort.

In late October, 1836, he wrote despondently to John: "My chief pity, in these circumstances of mine, is for Jane. She hoped much of me; had great faith in me; and has endured much beside me, not murmuring at it." Grimly persisting in the fog and darkness of a London winter, he wrote the last sentence of the history at ten o'clock on the night of January 12, 1837. Then a flash of his old self-confidence returned. He said proudly to Jane that he was ready to tell the world: "You have not had for a hundred years any book that comes more direct and flamingly from the heart of man. Do what you like with it, you—"

The reaction came as he toiled over revision and proofs, hearing Jane's cough from the other side of the wall. She had the influenza three times this winter; her physician whispered a hint as to tuberculosis. Influenza was epidemic in Chelsea, and it seemed to Carlyle that "the funeral bell never ceased jowling." At the end of March he was so alarmed that he sent for Mrs. Welsh. Fortunately she found Jane out of danger. With her mother's nursing she was able to venture out of doors under the brighter skies of late April, when proofreading was coming to an end.

By this time Carlyle's financial worry was being removed by the popular authoress Harriet Martineau and other friends, who came to the rescue on hearing of the American lecture project. They canvassed subscriptions for lectures on German literature, and engaged for the lecturer the incongruous setting of Willis's Room, "where the Almack balls are held, a painted and gilded saloon, with long sofas for benches." A woman admirer told Jane that she feared her husband would begin with "Gentlemen and Ladies," and thus create a bad impression at the very outset. Jane roguishly replied that he would be more likely to say "Men and

Women," or "Fool creatures come hither for diversion." Society
folk subscribed, including the Marchioness of Lansdowne and
even Lord Chancellor Brougham. The six lectures began on the
first of May, when final corrections of the history had left only
two days for preparation. Carlyle was obliged to "tumble in and
start." Jane was strong enough to accompany him to the hall
and mix a tumbler of brandy and water, which nevertheless
failed to dispel his nervous hesitancy. But sincerity and solid
information atoned for lack of fluency and polish. Carlyle managed to suppress the desire to interpolate unpalatable truths about
the English social situation, and the series closed successfully.
Lecturing brought insomnia and dyspepsia, but cleared him one
hundred and thirty-five pounds, enough to keep the wolf from
the door for the rest of the year.

The French Revolution: A History, the first book to bear
Carlyle's name on its title page, came out immediately after the
lectures. He was in his forty-second year, and his future hung in
the balance. Introduced by mottoes in Greek and German, and
selling at the high price of one pound, eleven shillings and sixpence, it would find readers almost entirely among the ruling
classes, toward whom its lessons were directed. For Carlyle, the
fate of the French aristocracy foreshadowed that of the British
aristocracy, the fate of the Girondists that of the respectable
moneyed middle class relying on political economy and parliamentary institutions. The last days of the Dauphin were given a
pointed British reference: "The boy, once named Dauphin, was
taken from his Mother while she yet lived; and given to one
Simon, a Cordwainer, on service then about the Temple-Prison,
to bring him up in principles of Sansculottism. Simon taught
him to drink, to swear, to sing the *carmagnole.* Simon is now
gone to the Municipality: and the poor boy, hidden in a tower
of the Temple, from which in his fright and bewilderment and
early decrepitude he wishes not to stir out, lies perishing, 'his shirt
not changed for six months'; amid squalor and darkness, lamen-

tably,—so as none but poor Factory Children and the like are wont to perish, and *not* to be lamented!"

The early chapters presented deftly the feebleness, stupidity, and indecision of the French Royal Family and aristocracy, the cupidity and unspirituality of the higher clergy. Upon the stubbornness of the Court, incapable or unwilling to see that the day of absolute monarchy was over and plotting constantly against Lafayette, Mirabeau, and other friends of limited monarchy, Carlyle laid ultimate blame for the Reign of Terror. Unable to rule, to care for the masses, it would not permit any other group from the upper classes to rule effectively. The Girondist majority in the Assembly wasted precious time making an elaborate Constitution and listening to oratory. Meanwhile the Jacobins, in touch with the needs of the people, gained steadily in power because they were willing to fight for what they wanted. Carlyle regretted the failure of a compromise that would have given reform from above without bloodshed. Mirabeau might have effected this, had he not died in the midst of his efforts. Even then popular feeling was sane enough to check Robespierre's fanaticism and welcome the stamping out of anarchy by military despotism.

Carlyle had no patience with the outcry against the September massacres and the Terror. Bad as both were, they were results of a state of war and the consequent popular suspicion and hysteria. Besides, respectability approved of war, which had been accountable for infinitely more bloodshed than prison massacres or the guillotine. The official lists of those guillotined contained less than two thousand names; had there been twice as many, they would not have amounted to a two-hundredth part of those killed in the Seven Years' War in the earlier part of the same century. Carlyle's dismissal of the supposed moral distinction between international war and class war was in his best satirical manner: "Fell slaughter, one of the most authentic products of the Pit you would say, once give it Customs, becomes War, with Laws of War; and is Customary and Moral enough; and red individuals carry the tools of it girt round their haunches, not without an air of pride,—which do thou nowise blame. While, see! so long as it is but dressed in hodden or russet; and Revolution, less frequent than War, has not yet got its Laws of Revolution, but the hodden or russet individuals are Uncustomary— O shrieking beloved brother blockheads of Mankind, let us cease shrieking and begin considering!"

Nor did he share the usual horror of the Parisian mobs, although admitting that their ignorance made them prey to rages of suspicion and blood-lust. The inertia of the masses was great; they had been patient for centuries. The Reign of Terror must be viewed with a sense of proportion. Normal life had gone on, even with arrests and bread lines; twenty-three theatres were open, sixty dancing places flourished, and the output of novels was notably brisk. For the majority of Parisians life was happier and economically easier during that brief period than before or after. The really bad moment came after the fall of Robespierre, when profiteers ruled and the people starved. Thus in an important respect the end of the Revolution was worse than its beginning: "Aristocracy of Feudal Parchment has passed away with a mighty rushing; and now, by a natural course, we arrive at Aristocracy of the Money-bag. It is the course through which all European societies are, at this hour, travelling. Apparently a still baser sort of Aristocracy? An infinitely baser; the basest yet known."

Nevertheless, there were certain solid advantages, victories over monopoly and respectability. The army had been democratized. "Shams are burnt up.... In France there are now Four Million Landed Properties; that black portent of an Agrarian Law is, as it were, *realized*. What is still stranger, we understand that all Frenchmen have 'the right of duel'; the Hackney-coachman with the Peer, if insult be given: such is the law of Public Opinion. Equality at least in death! The Form of Government is by Citizen King, frequently shot at, not yet shot!"

This interpretation of the Revolution challenged Sir Archibald Alison's *History of Europe during the French Revolution* and Sir Walter Scott's *Life of Napoleon,* which had chiefly shaped

British opinion. These were Tory in outlook, stressing warfare, politics, and the misfortunes of the upper classes. Carlyle had begun the difficult enterprise of writing the history of the common man and of mass movements. But to achieve this he would have needed access to documents partly closed to him in the British Museum for want of a catalogue, and partly still to be sought and collected in Paris, as in recent times by M. Aulard. For such research he had neither the time nor the money, though he pointed the way to it. He was forced back to a large degree upon a biographical approach, for which he was superbly equipped and toward which his admiration of great men naturally led. This involved a new style of writing history learned from Sir Walter Scott—not Scott the historian, but Scott the novelist. "The 'Historical Novels,' " Carlyle explained, "have taught all men this truth, which looks like a truism, yet was as good as unknown to writers of history and others, till so taught: that the bygone ages of the world were actually filled with living men, not by protocols, state papers, controversies and abstractions of men. Not abstractions were they, not diagrams or theorems; but men in buff or other coats and breeches, with color in their cheeks, with passions in their stomach, and the idioms, features, and vitalities of very men!" [38]

The subject lent itself to dramatic treatment, containing swift reversals of fortune and ironic clashes of events against an immense background. Carlyle's contrasts of the fate of men and classes on anniversaries has been a stock device of later historians, such as M. Madelin. Quotations from contemporary accounts are remarkably well selected and placed; often the reader is permitted to form his own judgment from conflicting evidence. The narration is swift, with abundant picturesque detail and compressed biographies of a multitude of actors. Certain great scenes stand out: the death of Louis XV; popular uprisings like the attacks on the Bastile, the châteaux, and the Tuileries; the last days and executions of Danton and Desmoulins. To pitiful events in the prisons are juxtaposed humorous episodes,—aristocratic conspirators with daggers drawn literally kicked out of the

Tuileries by the National guards, and the flight to Varennes, that left no doubt of the Royal Family's lack of common sense. The protagonists are the populace and the Heroes, the Heroes in a feverish swirl of events while the daily life of the masses goes on little disturbed. The Heroes, being French, are not idealized out of semblance to humanity; they are compounds of strength and weakness. Carlyle makes drama of Mirabeau's insights, Danton's eloquence, Napoleon's decisive acts. But the motive power of the Revolution is the cry of the people for bread.

Carlyle's method had the defects of its qualities. The vivid narrative, aided by rhetorical punctuation, in itself a stroke of genius, was a welcome change from the flat chronicle of the antiquarian for whom Carlyle borrowed Scott's nickname of Dryasdust, or the abstract analysis issuing from Bolingbroke's ideal of history as "philosophy teaching by experience"; but it was so breathless as to leave little room for critical examination of institutions and events. There is not enough reflection, and picturesque episodes are often allowed disproportionate space. Dependence upon accounts of eye-witnesses lost in reliability what it gained in intensity. Carlyle's didactic intention made judgments explicit when events should have carried their own moral. Catch-phrases and comments are repeated to weariness in the effort to reach and move lethargic readers.

The faults of personal bias were more serious. Carlyle assumed, without sufficient statistical evidence, that increasing misery of the people was responsible for the Revolution. He displayed Teutonic superciliousness toward the effusive side of the Latin character, not understanding the national earnestness expressed in the symbolic pageantry of the Feast of Pikes, and seeing the Lamourette Kiss as ridiculous. The Scotch Calvinism in him condemned the gaiety with which the Girondists prepared for death, and was so hostile to Roman Catholicism as to doubt even the sincerity of the counter-revolution in *La Vendée*. But these prejudices against French character and religion were likely to commend the history to its British audience.

Sales of the *French Revolution* were slow, for Fraser did not have sufficient confidence in Carlye's reputation to seek advance subscribers, or in the merits of the book to do much advertising. Its format was unattractive, the print rather small. Hasty reviewers in newspapers were puzzled by its unconventional manner, and the literary weeklies hostile, the *Athenaeum* objecting violently to the "three long volumes of misplaced persiflage and flippant pseudo-philosophy," and the *Literary Gazette* stupidly thinking their author "staunch for Church and King." [39] Carlyle's first encouragement came from acknowledgements of presentation copies, including generous praise from Jeffrey: "It is a book written most emphatically in your own manner, and yet likely to be very generally read, and which cannot be read anywhere, without leaving the impression that the author (whatever else may be thought of him) is a man of genius and originality, and capable of greater things than he has done even here. It is no doubt a very strange piece of work, and is really, as Coleridge I think said of something else, like reading a story by flashes of lightning."

In June Carlye went off alone on a visit to his family at Scotsbrig, to recuperate from the long nervous strain. As he leaned upon a milestone just out of Ecclefechan, the familiar view across the Solway to the mountains of Cumberland took the coloring of his depression: "Tartarus itself, and the pale kingdoms of Dis, could not have been more preternatural to me— most stern, gloomy, sad, grand yet terrible, yet steeped in woe." Solitary horseback rides and lounging "on the sunny side of hedges" brought a more normal vision. With the humor that always came to relieve contemplation of his woes, he wrote to Mill: "I can very well understand how old clergymen and such like, as I have known them, after working for forty years at some Commentary on the Revelation, have finished it, and then in a few weeks gone mad, and died." By procuring advance sheets from Fraser, Mill managed to anticipate the other quarterlies by an enthusiastic review in the July number of the *London and Westminster*. "It is the history of the French Revolution and the poetry of it, both in one," was his thesis, "and on the whole no work of greater genius, either historical or poetical, has been produced in this country for many years." Early in August came a notice in the much more influential *Times.* Alick and Jamie excitedly asked their brother to read it aloud. Although rather disapproving of the style, the reviewer found in the history "most extraordinary powers—learning, observation, and humor. Above all, it has no CANT.... It possesses genius, if ever a book did." He recommended it to the Tory readers of the newspaper as a lesson to English Radicals, showing something more necessary than "mad liberty." This friendly critic was William Makepeace Thackeray, "a half-monstrous Cornish giant, kind of painter, Cambridge man, and Paris newspaper correspondent," whom Carlyle had met through Buller and Sterling. Carlyle's aged mother ("very fond of newspapers, especially Radical ones, and stands up for the rights of man") toiled admiringly through her favorite son's work, though the French names were "a sad clog."

When he returned rested to Cheyne Row in September, Jane burst from behind the street door to surprise him, exclaiming, "You are famous." By the mysterious word-of-mouth process that defies the shrewdest publisher's predictions, the outstanding merits of his book had become known to discriminating readers indifferent to advertisements and the opinions of the periodical press; and the buzzing of their praise had reached his wife's expectant ears. Thoughtful Tories like Southey and young radicals like Dickens, just famous at twenty-five with *Pickwick Papers,* found general agreement in Carlyle's point of view. Clergymen, including Dr. Arnold of Rugby and F. D. Maurice, welcomed the thesis that God still worked righteous judgments in history. In December Fraser gave most tangible evidence of the book's success by proposing to revive the unfortunate *Sartor Resartus* and to publish a collected edition of Carlyle's journalistic articles.

The popularity of the history was evidence that the reaction against the French Revolution was largely spent, and that Englishmen were becoming somewhat capable of detachment.

Against this attitude Wordsworth, for whom it revived disturbing memories of a youth he had long endeavored to forget, delivered the denunciatory blast of a sonnet, beginning:

> "Portentous change when History can appear
> As the cool Advocate of foul device."

The official organs of the dominant parties were also hostile. The Whigs, having failed to silence Carlyle by neglect, were forced to meet him with argument. In July, 1840, the *Edinburgh* printed a review by the historian Merivale, attacking the handling of evidence as unscientific and deploring the dissemination of "gloomy speculations and unmanly alarms" as to the state of the masses. The *Quarterly* in September of that year reprimanded him for his lack of faith in Christianity and landed aristocracy.

The style and diction, though less unusual than in *Sartor Resartus,* aroused more resentment than the point of view in a period when Macaulay, having ground down the eighteenth-century sentence to an unmelodious simplicity that anticipated the click of the typewriter, represented the norm. The *Athenaeum,* guardian of the taste of the solid middle class, began a long battle for purism and conventionality by ruling out "the affected present tense" and the general "quaintness, neologism, and whimsical coxcombry." Thackeray in the *Times* granted the appropriateness of the manner to gloomy and bizarre subject-matter, but was uneasy at the affront "to admirers of Addisonian English, to those who love history as it gracefully runs in Hume, or struts pompously in Gibbon." The alleged attempt to domesticate Germanisms offended English national pride: the *Athenaeum* attacked the "compound-substantive" as encouraging obscurity, the *Edinburgh* proclaimed its "dislike to his bastard English," and the *Quarterly* scented a more insidious danger: "Learn to talk in German, and as Germans talk, and you will soon learn to think in German, and thinking in German, you will cease to think as an Englishman."

Carlyle was familiar with such objections, which had been urged with more point against *Sartor Resartus* by his friends

Sterling and Mill, especially by Mill in his efforts to tone down the article on Mirabeau to the sobriety of the *London and West-minster Review.* "As to my quarrel with the Nominative-and-verb," Carlyle had responded, "I do assure you it is one that I reflect on with great sorrow; but it is not a quarrel of my seeking. I mean that the common English mode of writing has to do with what I call the *hearsays* of things; and the great business for me, in which alone I feel any comfort, is in recording the presence, bodily concrete colored presence of things." To Sterling's objection against coining words such as *talented, environment, visualized, complected,* he replied with equal consciousness of what he was doing: "Do you reckon this really a time for Purism of Style; or that Style (mere dictionary style) has much to do with the worth or unworth of a Book? I do not: with whole ragged battalions of Scott's Novel English, with Irish, German, French, and even Newspaper Cockney (when 'Literature' is little other than a newspaper) storming in on us, and the whole structure of Johnsonian English breaking up from its foundations —revolution there as visible as anywhere else!" In anticipating objections to the style of *The French Revolution* Mill accepted these defences, though he still found it hard to stomach "phraseology borrowed from the spiritualist school of German poets and metaphysicians." The *Quarterly Review* admitted that the style was "not unlikely to become popular," for readers were "sick of the weak vapid slops with which the press is now inundated, when every one who can spell and write, and couple verbs with nominatives, thinks it his duty to publish." One of the earliest to grasp its possibilities for popular appeal was the young Tory adventurer Disraeli, who imitated it in a series of political articles signed Cœur-de-Lion in the *Times* for January 3-15, 1838.

§ 3

THE arrival of fame brought warning memories of Irving's downfall: "The liveliest image of Hell-on-Earth I can form to myself is that of a poor bladder of a creature blown up by popular wind; and bound to keep himself blown, under pain of torment very severe, and with torment all the while and the cracking to pieces of all good that was in him!" Carlyle described his own mood as "in general not a little relieved and quieted; yet with all the old features of Burton's Melancholic Man, to-day full of peaceable joy (ah no, not peaceable entirely, there is a *black* looks through it still!), then to-morrow for no assignable cause sunk into sadness and despondency. But verily the Book has done me great good. It is like a coal of fire burning my heart, which by Heaven's favor I have got thrown out of me." His only tempting of Nemesis was a review of Lockhart's *Life of Scott* for the *London and Westminster,* pronouncing triumphal judgment on the materialism of the Edinburgh of his youth. "One knows not what idea worthy of the name of great, what purpose, instinct, or tendency, that could be called great, Scott ever was inspired with. His life was worldly; his ambitions were worldly. There is nothing spiritual in him; all is economical, material, of the earth earthy." His books were "altogether addressed to the everyday mind," which he did not aim to improve, but only to amuse for the sake of money. Scott had "nothing of the Martyr"; his writings were nicely calculated to hit the taste of "an age at once destitute of faith and terrified at scepticism," a happy phrase which Carlyle was to repeat. Although he had an income of £2,000 without writing a word, Scott defiled artistic conscience by turning out slipshod work with great rapidity: "Walter Scott, one of the most gifted of the world, whom his admirers call the most gifted, must kill himself that he may be a country gentleman, the founder of a race of Scottish lairds." Carlyle was haunted by his tragedy: "Alas, his fine Scottish face, with its shaggy honesty, sagacity, and goodness, when we saw it latterly in Edinburgh streets, was all worn with care, the joy all fled from it; ploughed deep with labor and sorrow." [40]

Fame brought no immediate end to Carlyle's financial worries. When the second anniversary of its publication was near, *The French Revolution* had not yielded him a penny. In March,

1839, as Fraser was proposing a second edition to be published for both England and America, Carlyle displayed to him remittances from America of one hundred and fifty pounds for the history, besides lesser amounts for a second edition of *Sartor Resartus* and for a collection of his journalistic essays under the title of *Miscellanies*. Whereat the cautious Scotch publisher "actually blushed," and soon delivered half-profits on the first edition of the history, amounting to one hundred and ten pounds. In irritation at Fraser's dilatoriness Carlyle had meanwhile let Saunders and Otley have the English edition of *Sartor Resartus,* which he ironically prefaced with the unfavorable opinions of Murray's reader and the *Sun* newspaper, the obtuse solemnity of the *North American Review,* and finally Emerson's discerning introduction to the American edition. But now he gave Fraser the English rights of the *Miscellanies,* and would soon give him another book. "All the world cries out, why *do you* publish with Fraser?" he told Emerson, whose generous aid had procured quick returns from American publishers. " 'Because my soul is sick of booksellers, and of trade, and deception, and "need and greed" altogether, and this poor Fraser, not worse than the rest of them, has in some sort grown less hideous by custom.' " On account of the slowness of his English receipts he had continued to deliver courses of lectures: The History of World Literature (1838) and Revolutions of the Modern World (1839).

There was now no escaping the usual penalty of popularity —dining out. Carlyle estimated that there were 3,000 London houses at which a literary lion would always be welcome. In 1836 Charles Buller had introduced him to his college friend, Richard Monkton Milnes, heir of a wealthy Yorkshire family recently titled. Milnes subscribed to the 1837 lectures, but showed no lively interest in Carlyle until fame came to him a few months later; which Carlyle noticed in saying, "He looked at you out of the boxes." But Milnes was irresistible: "A most bland-smiling, semi-quizzical, affectionate, high-bred, Italianized little man, who has long olive-blond hair, a dimple, next to no chin, and flings his arms round your neck when he addresses you in public society!"

A minor poet with an inexhaustible appetite for literary society, he coaxed Carlyle into the company of celebrities. At a Milnes breakfast he met Landor, Tom Moore, Rogers, and other older and more established men of letters: "A brilliant firework of wits, worth being fretted into fever with for once," the last phrase typical of his complaints of the wear and tear on his nerves of public appearance. At a Rogers' breakfast this strain was banished by Macaulay, just returned from a lucrative judgeship in India, who monologued with prodigious volubility. Rogers privately proposed writing a new *Inferno* in which Macaulay would be gagged and surrounded by disputants. Milnes gave a dinner at which Carlyle found a varied company; the rising politician Gladstone, the astronomer Whewell, and two fellow historians, Hallam, an authority on the English Constitution, and Sir Archibald Alison, his Tory competitor on the theme of the French Revolution. Alison remembered Carlyle's remark when the conversation turned to Queen Victoria, who had come to the throne the year previous (1837): "Poor Queen! She is at an age when she would hardly be trusted with the choosing of a bonnet, and she is called for a task from which an archangel might have shrunk." Carlyle's desire to influence practical politics was furthered by such contacts, which already included the Whig Lord Monteagle, later Lord Chancellor, his son Stephen Spring Rice, and the Tory Bingham Baring, member of a great banking family. For over ten years after his achievement of recognition, Carlyle's interests and writings were to be increasingly political.

Although by 1839 he found himself "for the first time these twelve years..... free, almost as free as other men perhaps are, from the bewildering terror of coming to actual want of money," Carlyle did not forget the misery of most of the population. The better times that followed the settlement of the question of Parliamentary Reform had come abruptly to an end in the autumn of 1836. Over-ambitious railway expansion brought extensive bank failures, followed in 1837 by a serious falling off of manufactured exports. A series of bad harvests beginning in 1838 delayed recovery, and in 1839 resistance to the efforts of the Bank of the United

States to raise cotton prices by subsidizing the growers caused further shut-down of factories. In passing from an agricultural to a manufacturing economy England was becoming increasingly affected by international complications. Unemployment in the cotton industry lowered wages: Bowley's index number for all cotton wages in 1839 stands at 91, as compared to 100 in 1833-4, and 118 at the close of the Napoleonic Wars. Bad harvests, aided by the sliding scale of the Corn Laws, helped raise the general cost of living to an index number of 123 for 1839, as compared with 99 in 1835 and 128 in the panic year of 1825.[41] Factory workers were hard pressed, to say nothing of handloom weavers and stocking knitters competing blindly with hand labor against machines. For the unemployed yawned the doors of workhouses, just being built in the industrial North in accordance with the severe regulations of the 1834 Poor Law.

The economic weapon of the strike was useless, and the workingmen had no faith that the Whig government would come to their aid. The suspicion that they had been tricked into supporting the Reform Bill seemed justified when in the fall of 1837 Lord John Russell announced that the Whigs had no intention of extending the suffrage further, though he had promised the contrary in 1831. Having passed such important legislation as the Reform Act, the Factory Act of 1833, the New Poor Law, and the Municipal Corporations Act, the Whigs had shot their bolt. The loyalist landslide that greeted the accession of Victoria had greatly reduced the Radical seats in Parliament and left the Whigs, with a bare majority, fearful that progressive measures might return the Tories to power. Inaction suited the temper of the Prime Minister, Lord Melbourne, who met any proposal of change with his celebrated, "Why can't you let it alone?"

Thrown upon their own resources, the workingmen sought to remedy their condition by means which the middle class had found effective in 1832. In 1838 great mass meetings supported the People's Charter drawn up by Radical agitators, with its "five points" of universal manhood suffrage, annual Parliamentary elections, formation of electoral districts equal in population, abolition of property qualification for, and payment of salaries to, Members of Parliament. The Chartists, as its advocates were called, had their strength, not among skilled and unionized machine workers, but among unorganized handicraftsmen and miners goaded to desperation by hunger. For them, constitutional means of agitation were too slow. So while the Charter circulated for signatures to be presented to Parliament in 1839, there was secret drilling on the moors, forging of pikes, and accumulation of firearms. The ruling classes were alarmed; most looked to military protection, but many sought to remove the causes of unrest. The Tories of the *Times* demanded the repeal of the obnoxious Poor Law; Whig manufacturers countered with agitation for repeal of the Corn Laws that made food dear.

To Carlyle, Chartism seemed a portent of the proletarian revolution against which he had warned. He believed it would be madness to grant the suffrage to men so ignorant and rash, yet equally unwise to leave their grievances unremedied. As Chartism gathered strength in the summer of 1838, he proposed to Mill an article in the *London and Westminster* urging the necessity of meeting the crisis intelligently. But Mill feared the result of plain speaking upon subscribers from the commercial and manufacturing classes, whom he wished to rally after the Radical defeat of 1837. Carlyle introduced the topic into his May, 1839, lectures on *Revolutions of Modern Europe*. Leigh Hunt heard him place the industrial revolution beside Voltairianism as a cause of the breakdown of eighteenth-century society, and comment on its result in "the melancholy spectacle of a human being willing to labor but forced to starve." A vigorous defence of Sansculottism brought unexpected applause from an audience mainly Tory. This evidence of Tory interest in the welfare of the masses suggested to Carlyle a new outlet for the article Mill would not take. He wrote to Lockhart: "It will probably seem surprising that I of all persons should propose writing for you in the *Quarterly Review*......I have, and have had for many years a word to speak on the *condition of the lower classes* in this country. My notions on this subject differ intensely from those of the speculating Radicals, intensely from those of the Whigs; it seems to me the better class of the Conservatives are, on the whole, the persons to whom it were hopefullest, and in many ways fittest, to address myself." Lockhart conferred with him, and it was agreed that the article should be submitted in the autumn.

The chief difficulty in preparing it was to secure reliable statistics as to the economic and sanitary conditions of the proletariat. Carlyle sent special inquiries to Chadwick and other experts. When he went for a vacation early in July, he found that even Ecclefechan had its Chartists, who were "rattling a very slack old drum, and shouting round the rumble of it, passing 'resolutions,' I suppose." On July 12 the House of Commons, by an overwhelming vote of 237 to 48, refused to consider the Chartist petition presented with 1,200,000 signatures. The young Disraeli was prominent among the minority. The Chartists replied with serious rioting in Birmingham, which was quelled by the arrest of its leaders. Six thousand regular troops, paradoxically under Sir Charles Napier, who had offered to lead an armed revolt in favor of the Reform Bill of 1832, nipped in the bud other disturbances in the North. Returning to London in September, Carlyle passed through the disturbed area, embarking at the manufacturing town of Preston on the first railway journey of his life, which took him by way of Birmingham.

In October he set to work on the promised article. As it grew beyond article length he found himself saying things that he feared no Tory would print. This apprehension was justified when Lockhart returned it with apologies after keeping it for a week. Then unexpectedly Mill, having found his efforts with the *London and Westminster* fruitless, asked to publish it as "the last dying gasp of a Radical Review." Out of friendship he was inclined to comply, had not Jane and John, harboring resentment at the episodes of the editorship and the burnt manuscript, in which they suspected Mill of shielding the real offender, Mrs. Taylor, persuaded him that his work was too good to be identified with a lost cause with which he had never been too sympathetic. Carlyle confided to his mother his secret triumph: "I offered them this very thing two years ago, the blockheads, and they dared not let me write it then. If they had taken more of my counsel, they need not perhaps have been in a sinking state at present. But they went their own way, and now their review is to cease; and their whole beggarly unbelieving Radicalism may cease, too, if it likes, and let us see whether there be not a believing Radicalism possible."

Since the success of *The French Revolution,* Carlyle and Mill, though on good terms, had been going separate ways. Mill was preparing a book on logic, which Carlyle thought a misdirection of energies that should be employed in preaching "the new Aristocracy we have to look for." Carlyle was appearing in general society, while sensitiveness about Mrs. Taylor was confining Mill to a little group of rebels against the marriage laws. This group Carlyle had found increasingly uncongenial: "No class of mortals ever profited me less. There is a vociferous platitude in them, a mangy hungry discontent; their very joy is like that of a thing scratching itself under disease of the itch. Mill was infinitely too good for them; but he would have it, and his fate would. I love him much as a friend frozen in ice for me." The strain on Mill continued as Mrs. Taylor spent more and more time apart from her husband. He took another Continental trip for his health in the winter of 1838-39. In September, 1839, Carlyle informed Sterling, whose general survey of Carlyle's works Mill had published that month with the generous design of keeping both in the public eye: "Mill, whom I had not seen till that day at the India House, was looking but indifferently; he professed not to be sensibly better at all by his last year's journeying. Mrs. Taylor, he farther volunteered to tell me, is living, not at the old abode in the Regent's Park, but in Wilton Place, a street where as I conjecture there are mainly wont to be *Lodgings.* Can it be possible? Or if so, what does it betoken? I am truly sorry for Mill; he has been a most luckless man since I came hither, seeming to himself all the way to be a lucky one rather. He seems to fear the Review will have to cease.... He has no skill in 'concrete realities,' or less than I ever saw in a man so skilful about abstractions. Nature and Fact, as you remarked, first tell a man the truth about his philosophy." Carlyle did not foresee that Mill would have his turn of fame.

Although Mill's touchiness about Mrs. Taylor had caused him to cut his old Radical friends the Grotes, the Austins, Roebuck, and Miss Martineau, he clung to Carlyle in spite of Mrs. Carlyle's obvious distaste for the woman he loved. But by 1846 the intimacy had died a slow death; to the loss of England, which would have been better served by the coöperation of the dissimilar abilities of two important thinkers whom events were to drive into opposition. Carlyle did not forget his debt of gratitude to Mill. He wrote to him in 1841: "I may well value your approbation;—what man's more? It was mine at a time when I had few other men's in the world. That will be always memorable to me." In the thirty years that followed their last meeting in 1846, people observed that Mill seemed to grow "suddenly aged" whenever Carlyle was mentioned.[42]

In the last days of 1839 Carlyle's *Chartism* appeared as a five-shilling booklet of one hundred and thirteen pages with Fraser's imprint. The title of the first chapter, The Condition of England Question, was to be often on British lips in the ensuing decade. The comfortable classes could no longer ignore its existence, or be lulled by newspaper assurance that arrests of Chartist leaders and military repression had put an end to it. But Carlyle believed that more exact knowledge of the state of the working population would be necessary to prevent Melbourne's inaction from being succeeded by "legislating in the dark." As Cobbett in *Rural Rides* had acquainted the nation with the psychology of the agricultural laborer motivating the 1830 uprising, so Carlyle now endeavored to interpret the new and unfamiliar class of industrial workers. *Chartism* supplied abundant specific details, where *Signs of the Times, Sartor Resartus, Characteristics, Corn-Law Rhymes,* and incidental allusions in *The French Revolution* had only sounded a general alarm.

The high wages of skilled machine workers, such as cotton

spinners, to which the propertied classes pointed as evidence that factory labor had nothing to complain of, Carlyle showed to be illusory: "Economy does not exist among them; their trade now in plethoric prosperity, anon extenuated into inanition and 'short time,' is of the nature of gambling; they live by it like gamblers, now in luxurious superfluity, now in starvation." It was also unfair to cast suspicion on the motivation of strikes by pointing out that for the most part only the better paid workers joined in them. The unskilled were too near the starvation level, too destitute, to dare quit work. Consequently while the wages of skilled machine labor tended to rise, those of unskilled and hand labor steadily fell. Not only did the competition of steam machinery grind down handicraftsmen; the influx of Irish pauper labor made more miserable the pittances of the unskilled, whether factory hands or the "navvies" that built railroads. Legislators must know these things, and be guided by statistics concerning fluctuations of wages and employment, opportunities for saving or for rising into positions of authority.

Carlyle believed legislation must come from above, for universal suffrage under existing conditions would bring chaos. If it worked fairly well in America, that was a special and transitional case in which the masses had access to abundant cheap or free land. He interpreted eloquently the political meaning of the current unrest: "What are all popular commotions and maddest bellowings, from Peterloo to the Place-de-Grève itself? Bellowings, *in*articulate cries as of a dumb creature in rage and pain; to the ear of wisdom they are inarticulate prayers: 'Guide me, govern me! I am mad and miserable and cannot govern myself!' Surely of all 'rights of man' this right of the ignorant man to be guided by the wiser, to be, gently or forcibly, held in the true course by him, is the indisputablest." Yet such government must be wise, as the contemporary government was not when it strove for "the protection of property" without regard for the property of the poor man, which was his labor.

The Poor Law which the Benthamites had induced the Whigs to enact was a step in the right direction in protecting "the thrifty laborer against the thoughtless and dissolute"; yet its insistence that there was "no place for the idle man" would work hardship until it were applied likewise to the rich idler. In other respects the Benthamites were as indolent as the Whigs, constituting a "Paralytic Radicalism" that trusted in "time and general laws" of political economy to produce improvement without human interference. The landed aristocracy, abandoning its mediaeval tradition of paternal care of the people, had missed the golden opportunity to regulate the newborn machine industry by eighteenth-century Parliaments. It had been punished by the loss of political control through "the triumph of Cash" in 1832. The middle class, considering "cash payment . . . the universal sole nexus of man to man," had not yet learned the responsibility for ruling which would make it into a new aristocracy. To the old aristocracy of land and to the nascent aristocracy of money Carlyle made a solemn appeal for the active guidance of industrialism into channels of human welfare.

Industrialism held immense possibilities of good and of evil: of evil, if it were allowed to drift; of good, if it were regulated so as to increase the comfort of the entire population. An immediate palliative of the intolerable evils producing Chartism would be Government-directed emigration of surplus labor superseded by machinery, to fill the British Colonies and other empty lands of the world. Whereas Bentham had urged, "Emancipate your Colonies," Carlyle became a father of British imperialism. For the benefit of machine workers left in England he advocated adjustment of the Poor Law to fluctuations of the labor market, the repeal of the Corn Laws to make food cheaper, and universal free education on the model offered by Prussia. Education would prepare them to exercise the suffrage prematurely demanded by the Chartists "in about two centuries." If Parliament would thus provide for the future, Carlyle saw England the glorious head of a loyal empire.

Chartism was directed to a wider public than that of his previous writings. With three seasons of lecture audiences behind him, he no longer took "aim in the twilight," as in the days of

Sartor Resartus and *The French Revolution*. His name now commanded attention. The proverb, "It never smokes but there is fire," printed on the title page, set the tone of the book: and its five shilling price, a day's wage of the most skilled factory workers, made it accessible to the lower middle class and an occasional workingman. Carlyle achieved the knack of striking phrases that found their way into general circulation. Emerson told him: "As the words are barbed and feathered, the memory of men cannot but carry them whithersoever men go." The *Athenaeum* was roused to protest against "tampering with our beautiful language" by colloquialisms; it objurgated "makes nothing to no purpose" as the "finest Cockney." Carlyle was gratified by the almost immediate sale of two thousand copies, much the best circulation of his work hitherto, and by spirited critical attention.

He had published through Fraser in order to reach the Tories: "Tories," he told Emerson, "I often think have more stuff in them, in spite of their blindness, than any other class we have.... Walter Scott's *sympathy* with his fellow creatures, what is it compared with Sydney Smith's, with a Poor Law Commissioner's!" The Tory *Quarterly,* welcoming Carlyle as part of the reaction against eighteenth-century materialism and liberalism, agreed with his statement of the evils of the time, but not with his remedy: "When the forms remain after the spirit has departed, he who would invent new forms with a new spirit in them, instead of retaining the old and bringing the old spirit back into them, must be establishing a lie." The *Athenaeum,* on the other hand, attacked Carlyle as a Tory wishing to revive the feudal aristocracy, and the *Edinburgh* denied the power of a paternal government "to raise the poorer class altogether out of its present position by legislation.... The everyday utility of free institutions is, not that they guarantee the toiler against hunger—would it were otherwise;—but that they create a vast and powerful class interested in the maintenance of order.... They cannot ensure the laborer against want; but they give scope to his energy, if he has any; they cannot heal the evils of competition, but they secure to the competitors fair play." Fox and other Radicals were even more irritated than the Whigs. Carlyle exclaimed amusedly on February 11, 1840: "The people are beginning to discover that I am not a Tory. Ah no! but one of the deepest, though perhaps the quietest, of all the Radicals now extant in the world—a thing productive of small comfort to several persons."

Chartism, the *Miscellanies* (pioneer in what became a profitable fashion of collecting fugitive essays soon followed by Macaulay, Jeffrey, and Sydney Smith), *Sartor Resartus,* the second edition of *The French Revolution,* and a series of lectures on *Heroes and Hero-Worship,* brought him over £1,000 on which to live while preparing a book on the ambitious subject of England under the Commonwealth, abandoned in 1822 and now resumed since January, 1839. His style of living having advanced only from two hundred to some three hundred pounds a year (possibly $4,000 in New York to-day), he was freed from the lecture platform, to which he never returned after discoursing on *Heroes and Hero-Worship* in May, 1840.

The great man, the Hero, was a favorite theme of the Romanticists, in reaction against the psychology explaining genius by making differences between men merely quantitative, and against democratic theories exalting the wisdom of the majority over the wisdom of the exceptional individual.[40] An age that produced such grandiose figures as Beethoven and Napoleon provided convenient rebuttal to these theories by evidence of man's continued capacity to admire and obey. Carlyle's lectures, covering a vast historic sweep from the mythical Odin and the little-understood Mohammed to Napoleon and Burns, were not his best statement of his thesis, having been hastily thrown together by frugal use of Knox, Luther, and other unfinished portraits of his Craigenputtock days, various by-products of biographical essays and the view of Cromwell that was emerging from his study of the Commonwealth. But they were popular, and remain so, because they carry no difficult weight of argument, contain some of the brilliant portraiture of which *The French Revolution* had given a foretaste, and glow with a contagious moral fervor that makes the reader feel vaguely heroic.

Critical minds find them among the least satisfactory of Carlyle's work because of their looseness of structure and the self-contradictory illogicality to which his vehement temperament was prone in conversation and oral discourse. There was a mild sensation when Mill rose amid the audience to protest against a tactless and rather pointless derogation of his father's friend Bentham in comparison with Mohammed; but Mill and Carlyle were seen walking away in amicable discussion with Sterling at the close of the address. The previous groups of lectures had not been published, and Carlyle had his doubts about these. His opinion of the cold print was discerning: "This thing on *Heroes* proves to be a stranger kind of Book than I thought it would. Since men read without reflection, this too was worth writing. For men that read otherwise, it lay mostly legible in what I had long since written."

Having gained at the age of forty-five the security to write a solid book with leisure and reflection, he used his influence to improve the status of the profession of letters in which he had struggled so long. In 1839 he joined Wordsworth, Southey, Forster, and other prominent authors in support of Sergeant Talfourd's Bill extending copyright from twenty-six years from date of publication to sixty years after the author's death.* His petition published in the *Examiner* is still very readable for its Swiftian irony, its plain speaking of infringement as theft, and its honest confession, in an atmosphere of literary snobbery, that he wanted money as well as praise. In 1842 he supported Charles Dickens in petitioning the Congress of the United States in behalf of an international copyright that would outlaw the outrageous pirating of British works, which not only cheated their authors but subjected American writers to worse disadvantages by adding unfair competition of cheap editions of British authors to liability to piracy in England. American publishers had circumvented some of Emerson's best schemes to protect Carlyle's works,

---

* Largely through Macaulay's opposition, the Bill, in becoming a law, was pared down to protection for forty-two years from the date of copyright. See G. O. Trevelyan, *Life of Macaulay*, II, 119-123.

and Carlyle's return for his friend's many courtesies by writing a preface to an English edition of his *Essays* in 1841 had been handicapped by a cheaper English pirated rival against which there was no redress. The failure of the United States to respond remained a source of irritation during Carlyle's lifetime.

Carlyle's experience of the difficulty of poor authors in obtaining access to books led to the establishment of the London Library in 1840. His plea for a cheap public subscription library before a distinguished company at the Freemason's Tavern is a landmark in the movement toward free public libraries that culminated in the bounty of a fellow Scot, Andrew Carnegie. He outlined the demoralizing policy of the proprietor of the usual commercial circulating library: "The question for such a person to ask is not, 'Are you wanting to read a wise book?' but 'Have you got sixpence in your pocket for the reading of any book?' Consequently he must have an eye to the prurient appetite of the great million, and furnish them with any kind of garbage they will have. The result is melancholy—making bad worse—for every bad book begets an appetite for reading a worse one. Thus we come to the age of Pinchbeck in Literature, and falsehoods of all kinds."

But acquaintance with literary men of all sorts had convinced him that the association of authors for the improvement of the literary product, which he had dreamed of in his essay on *Johnson,* was little other than "a devout imagination." So he did not join the "British Author's Society" that got under way in 1843: "My decided idea is that 'Authors' will associate and become a most stupendous Body Corporate one day; but it will be, I think, 'when they cease to be a *canaille*'; nor while they continue one does it seem very possible! Hunting merely for pudding or praise, we have, like all animals of prey, to do it in a solitary manner. . . . 'Authors,' it seems to me, are somewhat difficult to lay hold of and define in these days, not all who talk with Printers' Types are authors now!" He invariably endeavored to dissuade young men who wrote to him for advice about entrance into the literary profession; to one he described it as "the frightfullest, fatallest, too generally despicablest of all trades now followed under the sun."

Yet his inflexibility during his journalistic years was bearing fruit; Thackeray commented upon the appearance of the *Miscellanies* in 1839: "Criticism has been a party matter with us till now, and literature is a poor political lacquey. Please God we shall begin ere long to love art for art's sake. It is Carlyle who has worked more than any other to give it its independence."

§ 4

THE choice of the period of the Civil Wars and the Commonwealth for his next important book had been actuated chiefly by a desire to become better acquainted with England, now Carlyle's permanent residence. There were difficulties in interpreting to his contemporaries seventeenth-century ways of thought and speech, and it was only at the beginning of 1842 that the figure of Oliver Cromwell, "a great man ... almost a kind of god," furnished the means of unifying and humanizing the huge subject. Yet this discovery did not speed Carlyle's progress, for his mind was constantly distracted from the past by a heart that could not shut itself to the distresses of his own time.

The conditions that had moved him to write *Chartism* had grown worse, and the Tory ministry of Sir Robert Peel, in power since 1841, showed no more disposition than the Whigs to adopt the constructive policy he had urged. Industrial depression had been continuous since 1837. Real wages in the cotton industry had remained at the unprecedentedly low level of 1839. Wheat, which had sold at just under two pounds a quarter in 1835, reached a peak of three and a half in 1839, and had not since fallen below three. The increased price of bread alone increased the average working family budget by fourteen percent. Severe winters aggravated the sufferings of the poor. In February, 1842, Carlyle observed: "Here at Chelsea, for the first time, I notice the garden palings torn up this winter and stolen for fuel—a bitter symptom, for the poor in general are very honest." The official count of paupers in England and Wales for March 25, 1842, totalled

1,429,089, or one out of every eleven in the population; 221,687 had to be cared for outside the overflowing work-houses. In May appeared a terrible report on working conditions in the mines which, summarized in a speech by the Tory philanthropist Lord Ashley, moved Members of Parliament to tears.

In the same month Carlyle was greatly distressed by what he saw and heard on returning from Scotland, where he had been settling the estate of the recently deceased Mrs. Welsh, through the industrial districts: "The most tragic circumstance I noted there was *want of smoke;* Manchester was never in my time third-part as clear. What a strange country we are at this hour! Two thousand men and women assembled the other night before the Provost's door in Paisley and stood, without tumult, indeed almost in silence; when questioned as to their purpose, they said they had no money, no food nor fuel, they were Fathers and Mothers, working men and women, and had come out there to see whether they could be saved alive. The police withdrew to a distance, there were soldiers hard by to have checked any riot. By dint of great efforts the Provost collected a sum which yielded one penny farthing to each, and at sunrise they gradually dispersed again." His pity and alarm increased when skilled workers of the Manchester district, union men who had not been Chartists, declared a general strike for the anniversary of the Peterloo massacre in August. He told Jane: "We seem to me near anarchies, things nameless, and a secret voice whispers now and then to me, 'Thou—behold thou too art of it—thou must be of it!'" He was much relieved when this "Manchester Insurrection," which had succeeded in stopping almost all the factories remaining active, ran its course with very little violence and bloodshed, while achieving its purpose of peacefully impressing the nation with the magnitude of the economic crisis.

To write on Cromwell became increasingly difficult. He wrote to Emerson at the close of August: "One of my grand difficulties I suspect to be that I cannot write two Books at once; cannot be in the seventeenth century and in the nineteenth at one and the same moment.... For my heart is sick and sore in behalf of my own generation." Ten days later, when he was visiting Cromwell's first farm at St. Ives, some fifty "tall robust figures... of honest countenance, many of them thoughtful or even intelligent men," sitting upon wooden benches behind the railings that encircled a work-house, looked up at him with a grief and shame that reminded him of Dante's Hell. Where Cromwell had begun his career of public service by championing his poor neighbors victimized in the draining of the Fens, there was need of another powerful friend of the people.

In October Carlyle, having become interested in the old abbey of St. Edmund's by visiting the Buller country house near it, began to read Jocelin of Brakelond's Latin chronicle of its affairs in the twelfth century. This chanced to give a picture of efficient rule rivalling Cromwell's in its contrast with the drifting England of the moment. Before the middle of December, he laid aside his history in order to write a book enforcing this contrast. He refused to join the Anti-Corn-Law League, saying, "I am already engaged for a far bigger League (that of the oppressed Poor against the idle Rich)." He understood his strategic position "among the meanest of men and yet withal among the high and highest" that gave him the ear of the rich without lessening his understanding of the poor. He read the autobiography of the silk-weaver Samuel Bamford, who had been at Peterloo, and wrote to Thomas Ballantyne, editor of a labor newspaper at Liverpool, for information concerning this and other labor struggles. He also pored over reports of Parliamentary investigations into factories, mines, and the administration of the Poor Law, and Dr. W. P. Alison's *Observations of the Management of the Poor in Scotland;* terrible documents of human woe, squalor, and crime which were to be summarized in that appalling book, Friedrich Engels's *Condition of the Working Class in England in 1844.*

Written with the speed that came of long meditation, *Past and Present,* three hundred and ninety-nine octavo pages, was finished in two months and published in April, 1843, by Chapman and Hall, who were to handle Carlyle's books thereafter.[44]

Friends advised against employing Robson as his printer, saying, "He is a little dearer." Carlyle, consistently hostile to the fetish of competition, replied, "Well, ought he not; being considerably *better?*" At the end of June, when *Past and Present* was a literary sensation, Alexander Carlyle, defeated in his long battle for a living in Scotland, emigrated to America, his brothers Thomas and John giving him two hundred and fifty pounds each as capital for the adventure.

Past and Present united Carlyle's salient qualities; the social sympathy and popular style of *Chartism,* the historical imagination and poetic exaltation of *The French Revolution,* the social satire of *Sartor Resartus,* and the profound philosophy of *Characteristics.* It is one of the key books for the understanding of the Victorian age and its influence on the style and content of literature. Like most of Caryle's writings, it is not logically arranged. To get at the heart of its argument, it is necessary to abandon for a moment the order in which it was presented to the reader, before returning to examine the suitability of that order to the Victorian audience.

At the source of the social decay and chaos about him, Carlyle saw his old enemy, mechanistic science. This was the parent of deism, which banished the Creator from interference with the affairs of the world after the act of creation, and even of scepticism, which considered the world "a great unintelligible PERHAPS." Deism, confident that the world-mechanism would function automatically for social good without man's intervention, begot "Donothing Governments," *laissez-faire* economics, and their corollary, democracy. Scepticism brought the moral decay that condoned adulteration, mendacious advertising, and "buccaneering" business ethics: "The Universe *being* intrinsically a Perhaps, being too probably an 'infinite Humbug,' why should any minor Humbug astonish us?" Belief that man need not be responsible for his fellow-man produced the superstition of a "sacred right" of private property divorced from social duties. The age boasted of peace and liberty, when peace was "a perpetual life-in-death" amid "devil-take-the-hindmost" competition, and liberty meant only "liberty to starve to death."

From such evils the twelfth-century England of Jocelin's chronicle was remarkably free. Then society was unified by belief in a Divine plan and government of the world, that gave meaning to strange customs like trial by combat. One-fifth of the land was in the hands of monasteries and churches for spiritual and educational uses. Tenure of land in secular hands was contingent upon military protection of the serfs, who had permanent right to work and food. Thus the inefficient and foolish could not long retain feudal lordship or kingship. Even in the period when Richard was on the Crusades and John plotted against him at home, Jocelin's chronicle showed the rise of the Monk Samson, who had first learned to obey, to be a remarkable reforming abbot at St. Edmund's; another hero to vindicate the great man against the belittling of democrats. The gist of the contrast between the past and the present Carlyle put into two significant paragraphs:

"Gurth, born thrall of Cedric the Saxon, has been greatly pitied by Dryasdust and others. Gurth, with the brass collar round his neck, tending Cedric's pigs in the glades of the wood, is not what I call an exemplar of human felicity: but Gurth, with the sky above him, with the free air and tinted boscage and umbrage round him, and in him at least the certainty of supper and social lodgings when he came home; Gurth to me seems happy, in comparison with many a Lancashire and Buckingham-shire man of these days, not born thrall of anybody! Cedric *deserved* to be his master. The pigs were Cedric's, but Gurth too would get his parings of them. Gurth had the inexpressible satis-faction of feeling himself related indissolubly, though in a rude brass-collar way, to his fellow-mortals in this Earth. He had superiors, inferiors, equals.—Gurth is now 'emancipated' long since; has what we call 'Liberty.' Liberty, I am told, is a divine thing. Liberty when it becomes the 'Liberty to die by starvation' is not so divine!

"Liberty? The true liberty of a man, you would say, con-sisted in his finding out, or being forced to find out the right path, and to walk thereon. To learn, or to be taught, what work he actually was able for; and then by permission, persuasion, and even compulsion, to set about doing the same! That is his true blessedness, honor, 'liberty,' and maximum of wellbeing: if liberty be not that, I for one have small care about liberty. You do not allow a palpable madman to leap over precipices; you violate his liberty, you that are wise; and keep him, were it in strait-waistcoats, away from the precipices! Every stupid, every cowardly and foolish man is but a less palpable madman: his true liberty were that a wiser man, that any and every wiser man, could, by brass collars, or in whatever milder or sharper way, lay hold of him when he was going wrong, and order or compel him to go a little righter. O, if thou really art my *Senior, Seigneur,* my *Elder,* Presbyter or Priest,—if thou art in very deed my *Wiser,* may a beneficent instinct lead and compel thee to 'conquer' me, to command me! If thou do know better than I what is good and right, I conjure thee in the name of God, force me to do it; were it by never such brass collars, whips, and handcuffs, leave me not to walk over precipices! That I have been called, by all the Newspapers, a 'free' man will avail me little, if my pilgrimage ended in death and wreck. O that all the Newspapers had called me slave, coward, fool, or what it pleased their sweet voices to name me, and I had attained not death, but life! —Liberty requires new definitions."

But Carlyle did not advocate a return to the "hard, organic, limited feudal ages." Even in Jocelin's narrative there appear symptoms of the breaking of feudal ties, for "all manner of Ideals have their fatal limits and lot; their appointed periods, of youth, of maturity or perfection, of decline, degradation, and final death and disappearance." The coming of industrialism made the old style of monk obsolete, and an age of questioning put an end to blind obedience. The world was dynamic, a Sphinx posing ever-new social problems, the failure to answer which was death. In the eighteen-forties was ripe another time of housecleaning and reconstruction, like that of Abbot Samson.

Such reconstruction could not rest upon the current compromises and makeshifts, but must be drastic, proceeding from principles. Carlyle accused his age not only of having "no religion," but "next to no reflection." It must discard the false idea of the world as a dead machine, and see it as a living organism, typified by the tree Igdrasil of Norse mythology. It must understand Nature as so constructed that good would triumph, though the triumph were long delayed. It must acknowledge the brotherhood of man, a responsibility beyond cash nexus.

In the application of these principles contemporary society must learn much from the Middle Ages. England having subordinated agriculture to industrialism, "captains of industry" should succeed to the responsibility and chivalrous code of the lord of the manor. These captains of industry must not only accept the welfare legislation initiated by the factory acts, but must make permanent contracts with their workingmen, assuming responsibility for their maintenance during so-called "overproduction" crises. If workers were thus given an assured economic status, they would themselves shatter the illusion of "overproduction" by becoming an insatiable home market for the goods they produced. Assuming the ethics of chivalry instead of the ethics of buccaneers, manufacturers should coöperate to abolish poverty, admitting workers to profit sharing, if that were found not to interfere with necessary subordination. Landlords should realize that property in land was not absolute, but contingent upon its wise use and the care of its tillers; instead of wasteful "dilettantes" they should be real aristocrats with social conscience, like the living Lord Ashley. The spiritual direction of society should return to clergy that ceased to fight with "extinct Satans," and applied the ethics of Jesus to up-to-date social problems, and to men of letters who made literature no idle amusement or pandering to popularity, but the expression of their profoundest thought for the guidance of mankind.

The function of the central government would be that of keeping the ruling classes true to their ideals. It should enforce welfare legislation improving conditions of factory and agricultural labor, directing education and emigration, and organizing colonial markets for British goods. These activities would give ample outlet to restless energies that had hitherto gone into war:

"O Heavens, if we saw an army ninety-thousand strong, maintained and fully equipt, in continual action and battle against Human Starvation, against Chaos, Necessity, Stupidity, and our real 'natural enemies' what a business were it! Fighting and molesting not 'the French,' who, poor men, have a hard enough battle of their own in the like kind, and need no additional molesting from us." The government should give free education to all, not only because, as Chadwick's reports showed, it increased capacity to perform complicated industrial processes, but especially because, in a period of complex problems, intelligence in all classes must contribute to social efficiency. Whether government could be safely democratized was the problem of the future: "How, in conjunction with inevitable Democracy, indispensable Sovereignty is to exist: certainly it is the hugest question ever heretofore propounded to Mankind!"

Such is the bare outline of Carlyle's argument, which he presented in a form better adapted to reach and to influence his immediate readers. A short introductory Book states with unforgettable concrete detail the magnitude and the menace of the social problem. The current shibboleths that have brought on the crisis are placed in sharp relief against a background of moral axioms to which a professedly Christian society did lipservice: "Am I my Brother's Keeper?"; "A man's life consisteth not in the abundance of things which he possesseth"; "Ye have forgotten God." Book Second presents the twelfth century, in which these axioms were really believed and acted upon. By an amazing feat of historical imagination Carlyle restores the feudal past with a breadth, an impartiality, and a convincingness unequalled in nineteenth-century English literature. We see the functioning of feudalism in the daily life of all ranks, and pass from old women menacing a tax-gatherer to the supreme disappointment of Richard Cœur-de-Lion before the walls of Jerusalem. In the manner of his *French Revolution* Carlyle keeps up a running comment as to the lessons to be drawn by his contemporaries; but so real and solid is his revival of mediaeval society, that we oscillate between past and present without jar, even at the final moment when magical evocation drops with daring abruptness into humorous matter-of-fact: "The magnanimous Abbot makes preparation for departure; departs,—and Jocelin's Boswellian narrative, suddenly shorn-through by the scissors of Destiny, *ends*. There are no words more; but a black line, and leaves of blank paper. Irremediable: the miraculous hand, that held all this theatric-machinery, suddenly quits hold; impenetrable Time-curtains rush down; in the mind's eye all is again dark, void; with loud dinning in the mind's ear, our real-phantasmagory of St. Edmundsbury plunges into the bosom of the twelfth century again, and all is over. Monks, Abbot, Hero-worship, Government, Obedience, Cœur-de-Lion and St. Edmund's Shrine, vanish like Mirza's Vision; and there is nothing left but a mutilated black Ruin amid green botanic expanses, and oxen, sheep and dilettanti pasturing in their places."

The third and fourth Books mark the maturity of the popular style begun in *Chartism*. In his zeal to move readers to action by direct application of the historical lessons of Book Second and the moral axioms of Book First, Carlyle disregards literary convention and purist vocabulary, and employs the methods of the Evangelical preacher, the stump orator, the advertising man, and the sensational journalist. From his ministerial training come Biblical texts, catechismal affirmations, sermon tags like "the potter's wheel" and "Mammonism," theological doctrines like "the Maker's first plan of the world," moral dogmatism, the prophetic fervor of perorations, the tone of prayer. Hence also the constant repetitions and rhetorical questions, to awake the hardened or indifferent, to instruct the ignorant or stupid. Closely allied are habits of the lecture platform, methods of oratory. It is a spoken style, loud-voiced, with an overemphasis aided by Carlyle's old habits of rhetorical punctuation and capitalization. Emerson had caught its possibilities five years before: "I think he [Carlyle] has seen, as no other in our time, how inexhaustible is the language of Conversation. He does not use the written dialect of the time, in which scholars, pamphleteers and the clergy write, nor the Parliamentary dialect, in which the lawyer, the statesman, and the better newspapers write, but draws strength and mother-wit out of a poetic use of the spoken vocabulary, so that his paragraphs are a sort of splendid conversation." [45]

The current of the harangue follows an emotional order; chapter-headings are poor guides to content, for Carlyle's mind flits tangentially. Pulpit and lecture platform alike contributed to the cocksureness of manner; there is no hint that Utilitarians or dilettante aristocracy may have some right on their side. Although despising sensational journalism and advertising, Carlyle could not resist enlisting their methods in a good cause. His generic pictures of social types: of Bobus Higgins the ancestor of George F. Babbitt, of Plugson of Undershot the prototype of Mr. Ford, and of Sir Jabesh Windbag, the politician without a policy, have the effectiveness of cartoons and billboard illustrations. Like newspaper headlines and advertising slogans are a multitude of up-to-the-minute catch-phrases: "Morrison's Pill," "Man as patent-Digester," "Captains of Industry," "devil-take-the-hindmost," which, paralleling Theodore Roosevelt's "big stick," "muck-raker," and "Ananias Club," exhibit grasp of the methods whereby the man in the street is ruled. Carlyle points his ideas with a variety of devices: antithesis, paradox, irony, contrasts of broad and subtle humor, of loud and obvious declamation with sardonic restraint and purple patches of Romantic prose. Behind these devices is a quality infrequent in rhetoricians—sincere and noble indignation. The seriousness and importance of his message give frequent grandeur to a style that sometimes falls into rant, but is more often an authentic poetry at emotional heights.

Past and Present, with its bold satire on contemporary England and Englishmen, like the merciless scene in which Mr. Shaw exhibited Lord Asquith and Mr. Lloyd George in *Back to Methuselah,* could not be received with indifference. Two numbers of the *Athenaeum* read Carlyle a lecture, in the superior manner of Macaulay, on the unreason of his attacks on the dogma of progress: "Any schoolboy would muster fact enough to show the infinite superiority of modern times in every particular, both moral and physical.... Is it philosophy to idly invoke an irrevocable past? ... We say it is childishness and absurdity." Although unable to resist commendation of the satire on democracy, especially the brilliant passage on liberty requiring new definitions, the Tory *Blackwood's* likewise dismissed Carlyle in the tone of a later generation that would profess not to take Mr. Shaw seriously: "We should hardly think of entering with Mr. Carlyle into a controversy on the corn laws, or schemes of emigration, or any disputed point of political economy. He brings to bear on these certain primitive moral views which are but very remotely applicable in the solution of these weighty problems.... If we could surmise that this piece of extravagant and one-sided invective were meant to be seriously taken, as embodying Mr. Carlyle's social and political creed, we should scarcely find words strong enough to reprobate its false and mischievous tendency." Lockhart acknowledged a presentation copy by stating candidly his disagreement with all of Carlyle's conclusions save one, "that we are all wrong and likely to be damned." The amiable Monkton Milnes, touched to the quick in his triple capacity of capitalist, aristocrat, and politician, exploded privately: "It would be very dangerous if turned into the vernacular and generally read. It is most unjust and insulting to all but the utterly ignorant and helpless, calling Peel 'Sir Jabesh Windbag,' and every attempt at legislation or good of any kind a Morrison's Pill." Emerson saw clearly why outraged officialdom had no legal redress: "Here is a book as full of treason as a nut is full of meat, and every lord and lordship and high form and ceremony of English conservatism tossed like a football into the air, and yet not a word in the book is punishable by statute. The wit has eluded all official zeal, and yet these dire jokes, these cunning thrusts,—this flaming sword of cherubim waved high in the air illuminates the whole horizon and shows to the eyes of the universe every wound it inflicts.... What a man's book is that. No prudences, no compromises, but a thorough independence."

Although failing to convert captains of industry, who were scarcely touched until the eighteen-eighties (when Mrs. Beatrice

Potter Webb describes her father, the railway magnate, turning to Carlyle for enlightenment "with a puzzled expression"),[46] *Past and Present* went into familiar quotation and aroused thought and action to an extent unparalleled by books of the time. Thomas Huxley, assistant to a physician in the slums about the London Docks, found in Carlyle a champion of the poor whose misery daily rent his heart. The young engineer John Tyndall, engaged in ordnance survey near the factory town of Preston, admired the courageous plain-speaking which he and Huxley were later to carry into the dissemination of scientific discovery. These examples are typical of a widespread influence which the *North British Review* (Edinburgh Evangelical) described in 1846: "While other authors may be, in a looser sense, more popular, and more rapidly and eagerly read, we doubt if there is any one, whose works have gone more deeply to the springs of character and action, especially throughout the middle classes." This influence went into three main channels: political, religious, literary.

The political importance of *Past and Present* was partly accidental, the result of coincidence with the great stream of reaction against modern tendencies and toward the Middle Ages, of which Scott's novels and the Oxford Movement in the Church of England begun in 1833 by Newman, Pusey, Keble and others formed part. The method of contrasting the present with the past had already been employed by Southey in his *Colloquies on Society* (1829) that resurrected Sir Thomas More to castigate the degeneration of England under industrialism; by the Catholic architect Welby Pugin,[47] in a book of drawings called *Contrasts; or a Parallel between the Noble Edifices of the Middle Ages and the Corresponding Buildings of the Present Time* (1836, 1840); and by Tennyson, whose "Morte d'Arthur" (1842) was placed in a framework, "The Epic," as an apologue illustrating the disadvantages of "the decay of faith Right thro' the world." Disraeli, endeavoring to capitalize this reaction by forming a Young England group of Tories for the restoration to power of a paternalistic landed aristocracy, found *Past and Present* a convenient quarry for his propaganda. Supported by the London *Times,* Young England alarmed the Whigs considerably, especially when Disraeli recaptured the Tory party for the agricultural interest by his famous revolt against Peel's repeal of the Corn Laws in 1846. Its policy, outlined in Disraeli's novel *Sybil* (1845), was partially realized in the "Tory socialism" of the welfare legislation of his Premiership, which came tardily in the eighteen-seventies.

Past and Present was welcomed by the opposite poles of religious thought, by the Roman Catholics of the *Dublin Review,* and by the Broad Church Anglicans. The sympathetic picture of Abbot Samson and his faith awakened in the *Dublin Review* the hope of seeing Carlyle a convert, which was rudely shattered by the Protestant partisanship of his succeeding book on Cromwell. The Coleridgeans F. D. Maurice and Charles Kingsley accepted Carlyle's taunts about "extinct Satans" as a stimulus to make the Church of England a force for social service. Their program of "Christian Socialism" launched in 1848 marks the beginning of the welfare activities of present-day Anglicanism.

Emerson immediately grasped the significance of *Past and Present* in literary history: "It is a brave grappling with the problem of the times, no luxurious holding off, as is the custom of men of letters, who are usually bachelors and not husbands in the state; but Literature has here thrown off his gown and descended into the open lists." Carlyle turned the novel of humanitarian propaganda already popularized by Dickens to the consideration of the problems of industrialism. His influence can be seen in Disraeli's *Sybil* (1845), one of the first novels to touch factory life, in Kingsley's *Alton Locke* (1850), a portrayal of the horrors of London sweatshops in which Carlyle was adumbrated in the character of Sandy Mackaye, and in the better informed and balanced *Mary Barton* (1848) and *North and South* (1855) of Mrs. Gaskell, and *Shirley* (1849) of Charlotte Brontë.[48] In poetry Carlyle's social gospel was preached by the young Clough's "Bothie of Tober-na-Vuoloch" (1848) and by Tennyson in the opening sections of "Maud" (1855). *Past and Present* and Carlyle's personality were among the chief forces that diverted John Ruskin from art criticism to the propaganda against *laissez-faire* economics first manifested in *Stones of Venice* (1851-53).[49] Ruskin's *Unto this Last* (1860) was an early example of the essay of social preachment, of which *Chartism* and *Past and Present* established the genre, and into which desire to get at closer grips with contemporary realities drew the poets Matthew Arnold and William Morris. *Sartor Resartus* and *Past and Present* mark the turning of English Romanticism from the problems of the individual to the problems of society.

Relieved of an intolerable weight of responsibility for his fellow men, Carlyle could return to the arduous work of interpreting Cromwell. In *Past and Present* he had indicated the Restoration of the Stuarts as the point at which England had strayed into the compromise and insincerity that had brought her to evil days. Now he made use of the career of Cromwell, as he had used the French Revolution and Jocelin's chronicle, to show his generation the error of its ways. He made this purpose explicit by running comment on Cromwell's letters and speeches, joined by luminous narrative of the circumstances of their writing and delivery.

The subject was ideally suited to Carlyle's abilities and sympathies. Although he had outgrown the seventeenth-century Puritan faith in which he had been reared, he retained a lively memory of the sincerity of the Biblical phraseology that seemed to most cultivated Englishmen the language of cant. He was thus able to remove from Cromwell's utterances the aspersion of hypocrisy that had long lain upon them, and make impressive the great army prayer meetings that preceded momentous decisions like the seizure of Charles I. He also found in Cromwell a hero he thoroughly approved, unlike the somewhat tarnished heroes of the French Revolution. Cromwell's peculiar combination of emotionalism and political practicality was very like his own, and he shared his attitude toward royalty, parliaments, lawyers, the common people, and his policy of organized imperialism. The time was auspicious for writing on the Commonwealth, whose anticipation of so many nineteenth-century political aspirations and reforms had aroused an interest in Whigs and Radicals. Macaulay had championed Cromwell in his essay on *Milton* (1825), and John Robertson had written a spirited vindication of his career in the *London and Westminster* in 1839. There lay at Carlyle's disposal the unrivalled King's Collection of documents in the British Museum, and his friend John Forster's *Statesmen of the Commonwealth* (1840), which he considered "a vigorous tearing-up of all the old hypotheses on the subject, and an opening of the general mind for new." The most recent authoritative comment, the Preface to *A Bibliography of Oliver Cromwell* (1929) by Professor Wilbur Cortez Abbott, calls Carlyle's book "the chief landmark thus far.... In it was summed up all, or nearly all, of the development of Cromwellian historiography. It was, and it remains, the greatest literary monument to the Protector's memory. Carlyle's chief contribution was the assembling of the material in convenient order and his vigorous plea for his hero; and no one familiar with the period but must conceive that his actual additions to knowledge yield in importance to the emotional stimulus of his 'appreciation' of the subject; for virtually all the documents he published were already in print."

As in *The French Revolution,* his methods were less those of the research worker than of the artist. We see him covering the margins of an unsatisfactory source book "with notes and contradictions, with references, deductions, rectifications, execrations." He found virtue in his inability to use any system of cataloguing notes: "Only what you at last *have living* in your memory and heart is worth putting down to be printed; this alone has much chance to get into the living heart and memory of other men." The result was a resurrection of Cromwell's flashes of insight and of anger, his heart-searchings, and the atmosphere and spirit of the battle scenes such as Dunbar. Carlyle's final words emphasized his didactic purpose: "The Voices of our Fathers, with thousand-fold stern monition to one and all, bid us awake."

§ 5

"MAY it prosper with a few serious readers!" was his hope as *Oliver Cromwell's Letters and Speeches* appeared in three volumes in 1845. To his surprise they sold widely, going into a second edition in 1846, to which he added many new letters. A chief reason for this large audience was the belief of Dissenters and Evangelicals that Carlyle was one of them, notwithstanding his explicit statement that "Puritanism was *not* the Complete Theory of this immense universe." Evangelicals and Dissenters, numbering considerably above half of the church-goers in that earnestly religious Early Victorian era, much more than offset the loss of the Roman Catholics, incensed at the justification of Cromwell's ruthless Irish policy, and of democrats like Mill, shocked at the defence of the turning out of the Long Parliament by military force. Carlyle's literary income jumped to £700 in 1845, and to £800 in 1847. His gloom as to literature being "ground down to penny journals" was lightened by this evidence of a market for solid books. "You get an audience at last," he admitted. But he had waited until his fiftieth birthday.

He was too well aware of the fluctuations of literary taste to increase his scale of living. Thackeray said in 1848: "Tom Carlyle lives in perfect dignity in a little £40 house at Chelsea, with a snuffy Scotch maid to open the door, and the best company of England ringing at it. It is only the second or third chop great folk who care about show." The previous year Carlyle had confessed to his youngest sister: "Really one feels, with one's head grey, and one's heart long tempered in the Stygian waters, very independent indeed; and quite as a kind of secret emperor among these beggarly populations, all hunting like ravens, all hungry as ravens, tho' with heaps of ill-smelling carrion already piled round them!" A white hat, broad-brimmed like a Quaker's, was a symbol of his defiance of conventional dress; the suits and shoes he ordered from Dumfries satisfied his requirements of comfort and durability.

He continued to work with the terrible conscientiousness described by his wife: "Oh dear me, if all book writers took up the business as he does, fidgeting and flurrying about all the while like a hen in the distraction of laying its first egg, and writing down every word as with his heart's blood; what a world of printed nonsense would be spared to a long-suffering public!" By three o'clock the two main meals of the household were over; a substantial breakfast and the heavy early-afternoon dinner of those days. Oatmeal porridge, meat, bread and potatoes, with few other vegetables and no fruit, washed down by immoderate tea or coffee, was precisely the diet to aggravate the biliousness of both Carlyles. Two hours of daily walking or riding saved Thomas from the full effect of combining the food of a manual laborer with sedentary occupation. He returned to light reading or to the visitors who usually dropped in after five. Callers were offered no entertainment but conversation, or Scottish ballads sung by Jane. At seven they joined in "high tea," with bread and butter, crackers, and jam. Conversation continued until ten, Thomas and the males obeying the drawing-room ban on smoking by escape to the study or the garden. Then he was off for a brisk walk "to purchase a sleep," which was often jeopardized by the return to a bowl of porridge and writing in his Journal. His waking hours were ceaselessly active. If he read, it was pencil in hand to annotate with lively comment. If there were no callers, he communed with absent friends by letter, or with himself in his Journal, in which he continued the confessional habits of the clergyman and the Romanticist. His sleep was disturbed by dreams and by noises; he awoke haggard to meet the irritation of piano practice of neighboring young ladies, and of the street noises that became steadily worse as Chelsea was swallowed up by London.

Like most modern intellectual workers, he was satisfied with neither city nor country. He wrote anent a visit to Annandale: "The clear brooks ran each with the beauty of an Eurotas or Siloa for me; on the other hand, the stupidity of fools was enough to drive me *mad*. Alas, there is no health in London, for the body or the mind. It is a fever-dream there of double and treble feverishness; a mad dream, from which one awakes in Eternity! Unhappy that the tools for your work; that the free heart of your fellow man, opened fearlessly to you fearless, were it only once in the thousand trials, is nowhere else to be met with. One must take the evil and the good." What reconciled many to London, the amusements and the artistic opportunities, meant little to Carlyle. He disliked the theatre and the opera, and indeed had no taste for music except Chopin and Jane's ballads, or for painting except portraits.

This unvaried routine lived with such a dynamo of energy as her husband became increasingly difficult for Jane when her always uncertain health declined with advancing years. Her encouragement and good sense had been invaluable to him in his years of struggle, but now there was nothing she could do but keep him comfortable and undisturbed at his work, and entertain his friends and admirers. Childlessness, which had helped preserve the independence of his pen from financial temptations, now increased the void Jane must fill in. Her tenderness, like that of many another woman, was expended on a succession of pet dogs. Her husband had saved her from the frivolities of her sex, but had not succeeded in putting an absorbing interest in their place. She had no independent concern for large intellectual and social problems, upon which she usually accepted her husband's opinions. She read in the desultory fashion of her youth, chiefly novels, including George Sand and other French advocates of unrestrained passion whom Carlyle abominated. He encouraged her to write, but her literary temperament and talent were unaccompanied by the ruthless urge, the constructive power of the creative artist. They found outlet only in voluminous letters, among the best in English, graceful, humorous, satiric, but expended on trifles: the trials and adventures of housekeeping, her husband's eccentricities and her own, gossip about acquaintances. She had a reputation among women for retailing domestic scandals of literary folk. On one occasion, when Mrs. Oliphant interposed the comment that "Mr. Carlyle seemed to be the only virtuous philosopher," Jane retorted gaily, "My dear, if Mr. Carlyle's digestion had been stronger, there is no saying what he might have been." Scorning the taboos that bound her sex, she rode on the tops of omnibuses and dined alone in restaurants. If a man misinterpreted her unaccompanied state in the streets, she said "Idiot!" and passed on unperturbed. Americans visiting Cheyne Row were shocked by her mild profanity and indulgence in puffs of her husband's pipes—possibly among them the Americans whom Carlyle described as spitting his fire out with their tobacco.

Uncomfortable between a man's world and a woman's, she often felt that she had made a "mess" of her life. Sometimes she took out her dissatisfaction on her husband, who annoyed her with his absorption in work, his clumsiness, his loud denunciations and lamentations over men and affairs and equally loud complaints of his health and of domestic accidents like the mislaying of a book, "one of those books seen for a moment, laid out of his hand, and then swept *irrevocably* into the general chaos of this house!" His gloom, his pity and indignation laid too great a strain on her frayed nerves and frail body. With her passionate love of London society, she could never learn to take calmly his periodic threats to remove to the country, of which she had had more than enough in the Craigenputtock years. Since she had condescended socially in marrying him, it was a bitter experience to shine chiefly in his reflected glory, to entertain the wives and bores while he retired to smoke with celebrities. She described the companion best suited to his days of fame: "C. should have had a 'strong-minded woman' for wife, with a perfectly sound liver, plenty of *solid fat* and mirth and good humor without end.....*I* am too like himself in some things—especially as to the state of our livers, and so we aggravate one another's tendencies to despair!" Each also encouraged the other's harsh judgment of people and things, which obscured the sympathetic side of their natures as they grew old. But their correspondence shows the deep affection of early years persisting beneath surface bickerings. Their bold sallies at each other before company could

never have been endured by a couple on the verge of estrangement, as they sometimes seemed to observers expecting the conventional Victorian married relation.[50]

They coöperated ideally as hosts, each excelling as a conver-
sationalist in a very different way. Carlyle was a spectacular
monologuist when monologuists like Coleridge and Macaulay
were in fashion. He discussed men and issues with the earnestness, vigor, vividness, and humor with which he wrote. Although
his Annandale pronunciation was unaffected by years in London,
his vocabulary was English; his voice rose and fell with a lilt or
chant more English than Scottish, but his careful enunciation
contrasted with English slurring. He looked his hearer straight
in the eye, and spoke loudly, with vehement gestures. Glances
of his deep violet eyes recognized contradictions, but he was impatient of interruption except by his equals. He liked to tell the
story of a journalist's complaint to Crabb Robinson of an evening's buffeting: "Why, I couldn't have been always in the
wrong!" He paid for early popularity in the United States by
hosts of American visitors, bringing banal questions on religion
and philosophy. For them he prepared a wild diatribe they
learned to expect; holding them with a glittering eye, he denounced all American prejudices. With his intimates and equals,
however, conversation was give and take, or silences of sympathetic understanding, as with Tennyson over pipes in the kitchen.

Jane, with great sad eyes and delicate features, talked in
quiet mocking tones. She delighted to cut into her husband's
over-earnest harangues with "Don't be angry with Mr. Espinasse,
he's not to blame," or "My dear, your tea is getting quite cold;
that is the way with reformers." He looked on benignantly
while she developed some exaggerated account of his absent-
mindedness or told an anecdote with neat piquancy. Men found
her a fascinating and resourceful hostess. One evening, Tennyson,
notoriously shy with women, called with his publisher Moxon
and found Carlyle out. Assuming her husband's rôle, Jane
brought out pipes, tobacco, and brandy. Thus put at his ease,
Tennyson talked without the usual condescension to female in-

telligence. Carlyle, returning too late, was astonished to find her *"alone* in an atmosphere of tobacco so thick that you might have cut it with a knife."

With the exception of Dickens, Carlyle had the advantage of knowing the chief Victorian authors, Tennyson, Browning, Thackeray, before the days of their fame. His favorite was Tennyson, "a most useful, brotherly, solid-hearted man," whose voice was "like the sound of a pine-wood." He found the novelists, even with *Vanity Fair* and *Dombey and Son,* insufficiently propagandist, but later was satisfied by *Hard Times* and *A Tale of Two Cities,* whose lesson was drawn from his own *French Revolution.* He preached to the poets his favorite doctrine that they should abandon verse in order to get closer to the problems of the day; advice fortunately disregarded. When Tennyson chanted to him his stirring ballad of *The Revenge* (1878), the aged Carlyle said half to himself: "I knew that Alfred would treat that episode in a masterful manner, and he'd not allude to Elizabeth's starving the poor sailors." But in 1844, when a bad investment swept away most of Tennyson's inheritance, and he had as yet little income from his verse, it was Carlyle who prevailed upon Monkton Milnes to secure him a government pension of a hundred and fifty pounds. Of Scottish writers, the snobbish Lockhart, curiously enough, was most congenial. Jane remarked that her husband always returned from his house "full of too piquant anecdotes (a thing rare with him), chiefly of Edinburgh"; among them doubtless broad stories with which Scott had made a convivial Abbotsford table roar.

The Carlyles, especially Jane, enjoyed informal gatherings of literary folk, of which a party just before Christmas, 1843, at the home of the actor-manager Macready is typical. Jane described the delight of the children at Dickens's conjuring tricks, and "then the dancing—old Major Burns with his one eye—old Jerdan of the *Literary Gazette,* . . . the gigantic Thackeray, etc., etc., all capering like Maenides!! Dickens did all but go down on his knees to make me—waltz with him! But I thought I did my part well enough in talking the maddest nonsense with him,

Forster, Thackeray, and Maclise.... After all the pleasantest company, as Burns thought, *are* the blackguards!—that is; those who have just a sufficient dash of blackguardism in them to make them snap their fingers at ceremony and 'all that sort of thing.' I question if there was so much witty speech uttered in all the aristocratic conventional drawing-rooms thro'out London that night as among us little knot of blackguardist literary people who felt ourselves above all rules and independent of the Universe!" [61] Into formal dinners Carlyle did not fit so well. His seriousness led him to denunciation of men and institutions which even Thackeray, with all his persiflage, could not divert into lighter channels. So inveterate was the earnestness deriving from his family background that he never realized that people might advance for conversational purposes opinions which they did not believe. This foible the mischievous "Dicky" Milnes exploited by provoking his pet prejudices and listening to him growl.

The forthrightness of Carlyle's moral judgments attracted liberal clergymen. Charles Kingsley found his writings more effective than Evangelical and High Church sermons: "He finds fault in tangible original language—they speak evil of everyone but their own party, but in such conventional language that no ear is shocked by the oft-repeated formulae of 'original sin' and 'unconverted hearts' and so on; and the man who would be furious if Carlyle classed him among the 'valets,' bears with perfect equanimity the information of Mr. B.... that he is a 'vessel of wrath' or of Dr. P. that he has put himself beyond the pale of Christ's atonement by sin after baptism!!" F. D. Maurice defended Carlyle against an attack by the *Christian Remembrancer* (High Church) in 1843 "because he abuses the clergy, which is the very best thing (and the friendliest thing) for us." Their group of Coleridgeans welcomed Carlyle's revival of the social ethics of Jesus, which Milnes dismissed as "naïve" and the *Quarterly Review* as "primitive" when applied to the official mysteries of politics and political economy. To Maurice, Carlyle was "the beginner of a restoration in history, for he believes in a God who lived till the death of Oliver Cromwell." But he deplored Carlyle's "wild pantheistic rant" and could not refrain from pressing upon him the necessity of belief in a personal God. Carlyle avoided committing himself, for entire frankness would have involved his asking why a clergyman who had outgrown the literal interpretation of the Scriptures did not follow the logical course of leaving the Church altogether. He preferred the simple faith of the wives of the Coleridgeans, "beautiful religious women (true *schöne Seelen,* many of them)" to the self-deluding rationalizing of their husbands.

Maurice suspected that Carlyle thought him a "sham," and their unspoken disagreement became an open contest over Maurice's brother-in-law, John Sterling, whom Carlyle gradually influenced to the loss of Christian faith. Maurice was distressed over the views expressed in Sterling's article on Carlyle's works in 1839, seeing "a friend go back to a stage he had fancied he had passed through long ago." As Sterling's tubercular condition, which Carlyle described as "a burning of him up with his own fire," became hopeless, the struggle took on tragic significance. It was with Carlyle's eyes that Sterling faced death: "I tread the common road into the great darkness, without any thought of fear, and with very much of hope. Certainty indeed I have none." To which Carlyle replied in a farewell letter of brotherly affection: "We are journeying toward the Grand Silence; what lies beyond it earthly man has never known, nor will know, but all brave men have known that it was Godlike, that it was right Good—that the name of it was God." A few days later, on September 18, 1844, Sterling was dead.

Interest in German higher criticism was a common ground with Connop Thirwall, Julius Hare's tutor at Cambridge, whose elevation to the Bishopric of St. David's after the outcry against his translation of Schleiermacher's *Critical Essay on Luke* (1825) Carlyle called the only good deed Brougham had ever done. Both enjoyed the anomaly of Carlyle's visit to the Bishop's Palace in 1843. "I have very little doubt," Thirwall wrote Milnes, "that the people here will believe Carlyle to be the celebrated atheist [Richard Carlile], which he will probably confirm by his demeanor." Carlyle wrote Jane: "With the Bishop himself, I, keeping a strict guard on my mode of utterance, not mode of thinking, get on extremely well." Jane was amused at the thin ice on which the Unitarian James Martineau, brother of their friend Harriet, was skating; he seemed so "very near kicking his foot through." In 1856 Martineau wrote a discerning article for the *National Review* on "Personal Influences on our Present Day Theology: Newman—Coleridge—Carlyle." As Sterling had slipped away to him from Coleridge, so in 1849 Carlyle received a deserter from the camp of Newman, James Anthony Froude, who, having acquired historic doubts in the course of writing the life of Saint Neot, had recently turned his back on Christianity in his *Nemesis of Faith*. In 1872 Carlyle was to introduce Froude, his future biographer, to Emerson as "the valuablest Friend I now have in England."

Carlyle was not satisfied with shaping public opinion through men of letters and clergymen, nor, like John Mill, since the breakup of the Radical party and the abandonment of the *London and Westminster Review,* through the educative effect of his writings. Tortured by widespread misery and neglected legislative opportunities, he sought direct contact with the aristocratic and plutocratic families who governed England through the votes of the admiring middle class put in nominal power by the Reform Act. The opportunity to reach this inner circle came through acquaintance with Bingham Baring and his wife, Lady Harriet. Baring was heir to one of the greatest fortunes in England, yielding £60,000 a year, amassed chiefly by his grandfather, knighted in 1793 while Chairman of the East India Company, and by his father, Alexander Baring, created Lord Ashburton in 1835 in recognition of his service as President of the Board of Trade in Peel's first ministry. The Barings were international bankers, with large American interests. Alexander Baring, who married a daughter of Senator Bingham of Pennsylvania, had transacted the sale of Louisiana to the United States, and in 1842 negotiated the Webster-Ashburton Treaty settling the long-disputed boundary between Maine and Canada.

The rise of the Barings, descended from a Lutheran pastor who emigrated from Germany in the early eighteenth century, through cloth manufacture, foreign trade, and banking into large landowning and the peerage, was typical of the manner in which the aristocracy was constantly invigorated by plutocratic blood. Lady Harriet wittily remarked of her husband's family: "They are everywhere, they get everything. The only check on them is, that they are all members of the Church of England; otherwise there is no saying what they would do." The half-American Bingham Baring had married into the hereditary landed aristocracy. Lady Harriet, daughter of the sixth Earl of Sandwich, was of the old family of Montagu. Clever and imperious, she was endeavoring to advance the political fortunes of her husband, Secretary of the Board of Control in the second Peel ministry, by holding a salon in which she mingled politicians, like Buller and Milnes, with authors, like Mill and Thackeray, who might be useful as well as entertaining.

Early in 1839 Bingham Baring invited Carlyle, whom he knew through Sterling, to meet the German ambassador, Baron Bunsen, and other distinguished guests at Bath House, his father's imposing London residence. Lady Harriet found him so interesting that she talked with him for an hour, while he considered her "the most like a dame of quality I have yet seen." Although not handsome, she was impressive in figure and carriage, and her sprightly conversation, flavored with wide social experience, had a substratum of hard common sense.[52] Carlyle also liked her husband, who had been awakened by study in the University of Geneva to the disgraceful backwardness of England in education. He was unassuming and straightforward, with "an almost pedantry of veracity" and a sense of responsibility for the country. Through the Barings Carlyle was introduced into the country house parties at which so much of the business of government was transacted informally. In 1844 he had a glimpse of the class solidarity that cut across party lines by meeting at the Tory Barings' two influential Whigs, Lord Howick, son of Earl Grey of the Reform Bill, and Lady Holland, whose house had been Whig headquarters since the days of Fox. Later in the year he was guest of the head of the family, Lord Ashburton, at his country house, the Grange, with a seventeenth-century interior by Inigo Jones, where he met a various company including Charles Greville, whose then unsuspected diary was to make the details of Victorian court gossip live for our time.

In December, 1845, when both the Carlyles were at another Baring country house, enjoying idleness after the completion of the *Cromwell,* the *Times* arrived with the electrifying announcement that Peel was about to reverse the policy of his party by repealing the Corn Laws. This was also good news for Bingham Baring, whom international finance inclined toward free trade. It was the best of news for the majority of the population. The failure of the potato crop, the staple food of the peasants of greatly over-populated Ireland, coincided with a very bad English harvest, and hardship in England would be added to Irish famine unless the tariff wall could be torn down to admit foreign grain. But hope was deferred by the discovery that it was a premature announcement, which obliged Peel to resign because he could not carry his Cabinet with him.

In this crisis, the Whigs revealed that they preferred the interests of the landlords to that of the bulk of the population by refusing to take office and sponsor the legislation for which they had agitated while in Opposition. Faced with the choice between his duty to Queen and country and his sympathy with the landed aristocracy, the old soldier Wellington decided to aid Peel, whose manufacturing interests had already led to minor reductions of tariff somewhat alleviating the sufferings of the *Past and Present* period, to take office again pledged to the perilous step of repeal. Carlyle, impressed by Peel's sacrifice of political expediency to public duty, sent him a copy of his *Cromwell* as a token of his respect for the "great veracity done in Parliament" by putting the Bill through the Commons in June, 1846. Peel replied courteously on June 22. Three days later, on the every evening that it passed repeal in the House of Lords, Peel's government was defeated in the Commons by a coalition of Whigs with irreconcilable Tory squires spurred into revolt by the eloquence of Disraeli. This split put the Tories out of power for twenty years; for most of their leaders, including Gladstone, were loyal to Peel, whom the rank and file persisted in regarding a traitor to the agricultural interest. But Peel took a place beside Wellington as a national hero, who had saved England from want.

The fidelity of Wellington and Peel to the feudal tradition of responsibility, and the sight of Bingham Baring leaving luxurious surroundings for arduous duties in Parliament, encouraged Carlyle to believe that the conservative aristocracy, in face of the moral bankruptcy of the Whigs, held the best possibilities of wise leadership. Terrible events called out to them for redress. In September, 1846, Carlyle travelled for a week amid the stench of rotten potatoes in Ireland, which the Corn Law repeal had been insufficient to save from depopulation by famine and by emigration to the United States, whither the more fortunate were fleeing to nurse a hatred of England. Of the eight million Irish, over half a million perished, and a million more emigrated before 1851. As he urged subscriptions for relief of the famine, he saw the need of more drastic reforms to prevent its recurrence: "Ireland is a perpetual misery to me; lies like a nightmare on my thoughts." In the Manchester region he saw that the factory legislation needed extension and much stricter enforcement: "The mills, oh the fetid, fuzzy, ill-ventilated mills! And in Sharp's Cyclopean smithy ... the poor grinders sitting underground in a damp dark place, some dozen of them, over their screeching stone cylinders, from every cylinder a sheet of yellow fire issuing, the principal light of the place! And the men, I was told, and they themselves knew it, and 'did not mind it,' were all or mostly all *killed* before their time, their lungs being ruined by the metal and stone dust! Those poor fellows, in their paper caps with their roaring grindstones and their yellow *oriflammes* of fire, all grinding themselves so quietly to death, will never go out of my memory."

For the hope of persuading the powerful to redress these monstrous evils, he clung to his friendship with the Barings when

Jane passionately tried to detach him. Contrary to the habit of most literary men of the time, Carlyle expected his wife to be received everywhere he went. So Jane had met the Barings, and for a while had been charmed by Lady Harriet. But the arrival of her climacteric prematurely in 1846 had awakened latent jealousy of a woman whose qualities were very like her own. Lady Harriet also shone in male society, "making high comedy of daily life" and indulging in "burlesque and caricature" to the extent of "satirical injustice." She had wider experience and a higher social station than Jane, whose husband was obviously flattered by the attention of so great a lady. There lay the rub. Driven to morphia by pain, Jane was in no mood to be reasoned with. But by temporizing, tact, and tenacity Carlyle managed to retain an intimacy which meant much to him. He moved with easy naturalness amid luxury and notabilities, while Lady Harriet said: "Coming back to Carlyle after the dons at Oxford is like the return from some conventional world to the human race." In his Journal for February 9, 1848, Carlyle summarized his impressions of the aristocratic society which he had been observing with the curious eyes of an historian: "Have seen a good deal of the higher ranks—plenty of lords, politicians, fine ladies, etc. Certainly a new *top-dressing* for me that, nor attainable either without peril. Let me see if any growth will come of it, and what. The most striking conclusion to me is, how like all men of all ranks in England (and doubtless in every land) intrinsically are to one another. Our aristocracy, I rather take it, are the best, or as good as any class we have; but their position is fatally awry. Their whole breeding and way of life is to go 'gracefully idle'—most tragically so, and which of them can mend it?"

§6

As Carlyle pondered upon the problem of making aristocratic rule efficient, events obliged him to consider the rising tide of democracy more thoroughly than in *Chartism* and *Past and*

Present. In late February, 1848, Parisian workingmen, made desperate by an industrial depression, began a revolt against the limited monarchy sustained by the commercial and industrial *bourgeoisie;* the aged King Louis Philippe fled to England as "Mr. Smith." This third French Revolution fanned into flame the long smoldering popular hatred of absolute monarchy in Austria and Prussia, which, with the support of Russian autocracy, had dominated the Continent since the overthrow of Napoleon. The King of Prussia was forced to grant a Constitution, and the flight of the Austrian Emperor and his great reactionary Minister, Metternich, left Vienna in the hands of a Committee of Publi- Safety. Under the pressure of nationalist uprisings in Hungary and Italy the Diet of the conglomerate Empire of Austria released the peasants from feudal obligations.

The news from France seemed confirmation of Carlyle's theory of history: "All the people are in a sort of joydom over the new French Republic, which has descended suddenly (or shall we say, ascended, alas!) out of the Immensities upon us; showing once again that the righteous Gods do yet live and reign! It is long years since I have felt such deep-seated joyous satisfaction at a public event." As revolution spread to other countries in that memorable spring, and sent "kings running about like a gang of coiners when the police had come upon them," he broke his habit of not reading newspapers regularly by subscribing to the London *Times* and the Paris *National,* "the world's history ... getting into such a gallop everywhere, one can hardly keep pace with it." Of special interest was the experiment of national workshops for the unemployed made by the Provisional Government at Paris. Carlyle was in touch with public men who regarded the revolutions variously; dining on March 14 with the American ambassador and fellow-historian George Bancroft, who thought the moment had come for the spread of democracy through Europe, and on March 24 sitting at a Baring dinner beside Sir Robert Peel, who believed that his prompt action on the Corn Laws had saved England from the fate of France. This meeting with Peel was impressed on his memory by the discovery that while they had been dining "the streets of Berlin were all blazing with grapeshot and the war of enraged men." Two days later Mazzini called for a farewell at Cheyne Row as he hurried to join the uprising in Italy which he had devoted his life to prepare.

When revolution threatened to spread to London with a Chartist uprising scheduled for April 10, and there was an exodus of prominent people while Wellington stood on guard with 170,000 special constables, Carlyle remained to see the anti-climax of its peaceable dispersion. In September, when he was visiting at the Grange with Bingham Baring, who had just succeeded to the title of Lord Ashburton, he was deeply concerned with a more serious rebellion against English misrule in Ireland. The companions of his Irish tour in 1846, John Mitchell and Gavan Duffy, had been apprehended for treason, and he was appealing to the Lord Lieutenant for clemency. He pressed upon his fellow guest, Charles Buller, who occupied the strategic post of Chief Commissioner of the Poor Law, to take drastic measures to remove the causes of Irish discontent. Buller, who shared many of his former tutor's ideas, might have done something. His sudden death in December was a great blow to Carlyle. He pulled strings to be appointed Buller's successor, but the Whigs were inveterately hostile. The desire to examine Irish conditions at first hand led him to a second tour in July and August, 1849, with the Nationalist leader Duffy, just released from prison, once more his guide.

An ironic thought came to Carlyle in his pity and horror at the overwhelming Irish wretchedness: " 'Blacklead these two million idle beggars,' I sometimes advised, 'and sell them in Brazil as Niggers—perhaps Parliament, on sweet constraint, will allow you to advance them to be Niggers!' " Using for the identical purpose the method of Swift's *Modest Proposal,* he tried to shock the English into attention by a sinister parable on *The Negro Question,* published in *Fraser's* for December, 1849. Carlyle heightened the contrast of Parliament's solicitude for the Negro with its callousness toward the Irish, by pointing to the English colony of Jamaica, where Negroes had been freed in the general emancipation of 1833. The freed slaves refused to work on sugar plantations as long as tropical fruits and vegetables would maintain them in idleness, while the wage slaves of the British Isles had no choice but overwork or starvation. Economists were advocating the importation of more free Negroes to remedy the ensuing shortage of labor in Jamaica. This, Carlyle showed, would be effective only when the population became too dense for subsistence on tropical foods; that is, when Jamaica would be a horrible "Black Ireland." Such was the dilemma into which sugar planters had been thrown by what Carlyle, with his phrasemaking genius, now dubbed unforgettably the "dismal science" of political economy.

But the dilemma could be avoided by abandoning the sham of "free labor" and returning to a system of slavery shorn of its abuses, approximating the mediaeval serfdom described in *Past and Present*. This would ensure the Negro the benefit of "permanence of contract" with subsistence in periods of unemployment, while forcing him to productive labor. Industrious and intelligent Negroes could buy freedom at a fixed sum; the rest needed to remain in tutelage. To anticipate the cry of horror sure to greet this proposal, Carlyle pointed out that there were already worse slaveries in the British Empire: "The slavery of the Wise to the Foolish," and the wage slavery of the superior White while the inferior Black lounged "up to the ears in pumpkin." He interpreted his meaning to Emerson: "An able-bodied starving beggar is and remains (whatever Exeter Hall may say to it) a Slave destitute of a Master."

Carlyle had gauged the romanticizing of the Negro, made into the image of the noble savage created by the imaginations of eighteenth-century humanitarians and Evangelicals, by such books as Harriet Martineau's *Toussaint L'Ouverture*: "How she has made such a beautiful 'Black Washington' or 'Washington-Christ-Macready,' as I have heard some call it, of a rough-handed, hard-headed, semi-articulate gabbling Negro; and of the horriblest phasis that 'Sansculottism,' can exhibit, of a Black Sansculottism, a Musical Opera or Oratorio in pink stockings!" He was not surprised when philanthropists and economists united in a storm of protest. The memory of their former intimacy could not restrain John Mill from retorting hotly in an open letter published in the next number of *Fraser's*. He was especially irritated by Carlyle's assumption of innate superiority of Whites over Blacks, and by the arrogance of his tone: "The author issues his opinions, or rather ordinances, under imposing auspices; no less than these—'the Immortal Gods,' 'the Powers,' 'the Destinies' announce through him, not only what will be, but what *shall* be done; what they 'have decided upon; passed their eternal Act of Parliament for.' This is speaking as one having authority, but authority from whom? If by the quality of the message we may judge of those who sent it, not from any powers to whom just or good men acknowledge obedience." The close of the letter rose to the pitch of denouncing the article as "a true work of the devil," inasmuch as it would encourage supporters of slavery in the United States.

Such a response showed that Carlyle had over-reached himself in the effort to drive his meaning into dull ears, destroying the nice equilibrium of content and manner achieved in *Past and Present*. His dictatorial tone and paradoxical choice of illustration repelled sincere humanitarians, no longer accustomed to eighteenth-century satire, before they could perceive his foresight of the disasters involved in giving the Negro the illusory freedom of the competitive labor market, and before they could understand the parable as to "free" labor in England.

Carlyle had been irritated into overstatement by what he considered the fatally mistaken liberalism of friends such as Hunt, Mill, Mazzini, and Emerson. Their varieties of liberalism stemmed from the conception of man as naturally good, and hence perfectible, either by liberation of his instincts, as with Hunt, by rational training, as with Mill, or by some mystic or divine process, as with Emerson and Mazzini. Carlyle, reared in a village, had no illusions as to human nature. Hunt seemed to him sentimental, Mill misled by a false psychology, and Mazzini unwilling to face facts contradicting his belief that the voice of the people would be the voice of God. Of Emerson's shrewdness he had expected better things. But wearied of the crassness of American materialism described in his classic lines

> "Things are in the saddle
> And ride mankind,"

Emerson had sought repose in cloudlands of German Transcendentalism and Oriental mysticism. Carlyle, who had used the Transcendentalism of Kant as a means of escape from the machine universe without lingering long in the philosophic idealism of his followers, had shaken his head when in 1840 he heard of his American friend "taking it upon him...to deny that poor old External Nature existed at all, 'otherwise than relatively';—a most questionable state in these times in these latitudes!" Two years later he spoke out against the unsubstantial speculations of the *Dial:* "Surely I could wish you *returned* into your own poor nineteenth century.... A man has no right to say to his own generation, turning quite away from it, 'Be damned.' It is the whole Past and the whole Future, this same cotton-spinning, dollar-hunting, canting and shrieking, very wretched generation of ours. Come back into it, I tell you." When Margaret Fuller brought a letter of introduction from Emerson in 1846, Carlyle apprised him of the broadside with which her brand of liberalism was greeted: "It could not be concealed, least of all from the sharp female intellect, that this Carlyle was a dreadfully heterodox, not to say a dreadfully savage fellow; believing no syllable of that Gospel of Fraternity, Benevolence, and New Heaven-on-Earth preached forth by all manner of 'advanced' creatures, from George Sand to Elihu Burritt, in these days; that in fact the said Carlyle not only disbelieved all that, but treated it as poisonous cant,—sweetness of sugar-of-lead,—a detestable phosphorescence from the dead body of a Christianity that would not admit itself to be dead, and lie buried with all its unspeakable putrescences, as a venerable dead one ought!"

The next year Emerson had come to England. One night in October, 1847, he called at Cheyne Row: "The door was opened by Jane Carlyle, and the man himself was behind her with a lamp in the hall. They were little changed from their old selves of fourteen years ago (in August), when I left them in Craigenputtock. 'Well,' said Carlyle, 'here we are shovelled together again.' The floodgates of his talk are quickly opened and the river is a plentiful stream." A few months later these floodgates were loosed against Emerson, after he had delivered lectures that seemed to his friend mere "intellectual sonatas." Emerson proclaimed his belief in an irresistible tendency of good to triumph over evil, that could best be accelerated by allowing every man freedom to follow his instincts. He preached a doctrine of universal love, tolerance, non-resistance. Carlyle attacked this limitless *laissez faire* with the vehemence of which his reception of Margaret Fuller had given a foretaste, insisting that it would logically "prevent a man from so much as rooting out a thistle." Emerson took the assault amiably, though depressed by Carlyle's saying that he looked upon mankind with "abhorrence mingled with pity," and that the sight of a vast crowd made him fancy "the earth was some great cheese and these were the mites." He saw the congruity of the opinions with the man: "Carlyle has a hairy strength which makes his literary vocation a mere chance, and what seems very contemptible to him. I could only think of an enormous trip-hammer with an Aeolian attachment. . . . He is not mainly a scholar, like most of my acquaintances, but a very practical Scotchman, such as you would find in any saddler's or iron dealer's shop." Carlyle could not help smiling at Emerson's procedure with his naughty son: "I will love the devil out of him." He commented in his Journal on his friend's return to America in July, 1848: "Gave Emerson a 'Wood's Athenae,' parted from him in peace. A spiritual son of mine? Yes, in a good degree, but gone into philanthropy and other moonshine."

1849 saw a sudden collapse of European liberalism that confirmed Carlyle's conviction of its essential flimsiness. In June, Louis Napoleon, elected President of France the previous December, made a bid for Catholic support by restoring the Pope to Rome, whence he had been driven since February by Mazzini's Young Italy. Mazzini, who had had his heart's desire by ruling in the Eternal City for four months, was once more forced backward toward his London exile. Russian interference helped Austria reabsorb Hungary and Italy. Prussia crushed democracy in small German states. The *coup d'état* whereby Louis Napoleon in 1851 made himself Emperor of the French was to wipe out the last vestige of republicanism in large European states.

The inadequacy of liberal nostrums to the stern realities of human existence, Carlyle urged in a series of eight *Latter-Day Pamphlets,* issued monthly from February to August, 1850. In these his political thinking reached its most brilliant development, anticipating twentieth-century events and currents of opinion. Believing the suppression of popular aspirations to be only temporary, he warned the younger generation, if it were to avoid anarchy, to prepare for the reconstruction of society upon sounder principles: "All so-called reforms hitherto are grounded either on openly admitted egoism (cheap bread to the cotton spinner, voting to those who have no vote, and the like) which does not point towards very celestial developments of the Reform Movement; or else upon this of remedying social injustices by indiscriminate contributions of philanthropy, a method surely still more unpromising. Such contributions, being indiscriminate, are but a new injustice."

From the former prescription for reform was derived the superstition that universal suffrage would elicit collective wisdom equal to any emergency with which society would be faced; a superstition which Carlyle challenged with a celebrated simile: "Unanimity of voting,—that will do nothing for us if *so.* Your ship cannot double Cape Horn by its excellent plans of voting. The ship may vote this and that, above deck, and below, in the most harmonious exquisitely constitutional manner: the ship, to get around Cape Horn, will find a set of conditions already voted for, and fixed with adamantine rigor by the Ancient Elemental Powers, who are entirely careless how you vote." The apparent success of democracy in the United States was no guarantee of its future: "Americans sit idly *caucusing,* and ballot-boxing on the graves of their heroic ancestors, saying, 'It is well, it is well!' ... America's battle is yet to fight." Carlyle likewise saw clearly the disastrous future of the false conception of liberty current in England: "For British Liberty, it seems, the people cannot be taught to read. British Liberty, shuddering to interfere with the rights of Capital, takes six or eight millions of money annually to feed the idle laborer whom it dare not employ. For British Liberty we live over poisonous cesspools, gully drains, and detestable abominations; and omnipotent London cannot sweep the dirt out of itself.... And if the Peers become mere Big Capitalists, Railway Directors, Gigantic Hucksters, Kings of Scrip, *without* lordly quality or other virtue except cash; and the Mitred Abbots change to mere Able-Editors, Masters of Parliamentary Eloquence, Doctors of Political Economy, and such like; and all have to be elected by a universal-suffrage ballot-box,—I do not see how the English Parliament itself will long continue sea-worthy!"

The mistake of the other program of indiscriminate philanthropy Carlyle illustrated by an account of the model prison he had visited; a prison in which scoundrels had better food and lodgings than honest men in the slums who were, by an added injustice, taxed indirectly for the support of the prison. Why should "rose-pink sentimentalism" try to reform scoundrels before it had done its best for honest men? Carlyle waved aside the reply that Christianity prescribed this course: "Does the Christian or any religion prescribe love of scoundrels then? I hope it prescribes a healthy hatred of scoundrels;—otherwise what am I, in Heaven's name, to make of it?" In holding consistently to a scoundrel theory as the antipodes of his hero theory, Carlyle broke with Christian morals. This cavalier attitude toward religion, as well as a caricature of John Howard, the eighteenth-century prison reformer, and an advocacy of the tread-wheel for unruly convicts, prejudiced his case with many readers.

From such iconoclasm, Carlyle turned to outline a course of wise social reconstruction. Retaining what was good in the original democratic impulse, "the career open to the talents," he urged that rulers be sought from the wisest among the British population, without regard for social class, political party, or even ability to get elected. These should form an executive cabinet under the leadership of a dictator, who would brush aside Parliament when necessary, and deal drastically with national problems. A Minister of Works should rescue the army from "strenuously organized idleness" to form the nucleus of "industrial regiments" of the unemployed, disciplined to do useful public works and sanitary offices, and the navy to carry unusable population to the empire overseas. These reforms, together with universal education, should be the first duties of an unselfish, far-sighted dictator; possibly Sir Robert Peel, one of the few honest men with political experience.

On June 30, Carlyle and Thackeray, riding out to Addiscombe for a Sunday evening with the Ashburtons, found them alarmed by the report that Peel had had a serious fall from his horse. For the next two days there were uncertain rumors of his condition. Carlyle could learn nothing by calling at Peel's London house, but he clung to "an obstinate hope." On Wednesday morning Lady Ashburton came to Cheyne Row to say that Peel was dead. She had been deeply attached to him, and they shared their grief. Jane observed that "Mr. C. is mourning over him as I never saw him mourn before—went to-day to look at the house where he lies dead."

The full extent of his despair he confided to his Journal: "I now have no definite hope of peaceable improvement for this country;...the one statesman we had, or the least similitude of a statesman as far as I can know or guess, is suddenly snatched away from us.... In the meantime the wrigglings and strugglings in Parliament, how they now do, or what they now do there, have become a mere zero to me, tedious as a tale that has been told." Carlyle had reached the dregs of the cup of political wisdom. "The world is a poor slave," he said with sad finality, "and will always be governed in a low way." [53]

CHAPTER VI

DESPAIR

━━»» ««━━

§ 1

SEVEN weeks after Peel's death Carlyle, having written the last of the *Latter-Day Pamphlets,* took a summer holiday in Wales. In its largest city, Merthyr Tydvil, he found confirmation of his fears as to the future of England, if it continued on the path of *laissez faire.* With his customary contrast of past and present, he explained to Jane: "In 1755 Merthyr Tydvil was a mountain hamlet of five or six houses, stagnant and silent as it had been ever since Tydvil, the king's or laird's daughter, was martyred here, say 1300 years before. About that time (1755) a certain Mr. Bacon, a cunning Yorkshireman, passing that way, discovered that there was iron in the ground—iron and coal. He took a ninety-nine year lease in consequence, and—in brief, there are now about 50,000 grimy mortals, black and clammy with soot and sweat, screwing out a livelihood for themselves in that spot of the Taff Valley. Such a set of unguided, hard-worked, fierce, and miserable-looking sons of Adam I never saw before. Ah me! It is like a vision of Hell, and will never leave me, that of these poor creatures broiling, all in sweat and dirt, amid their furnaces, pits, and rolling mills. For here is absolutely 'no' aristocracy or guiding class; nothing but one or two huge iron-masters; and the rest are operatives, petty shop-keepers, Scotch hawkers, etc." He later elaborated his comment, calling

234

DESPAIR

235

the city the *"non-plus-ultra* of Industrialism, wholly Mammon-
ish, given over to shopkeeper supply and demand;—presided over
by sooty Darkness, physical and spiritual, by Beer, Methodism,
and the Devil, to a lamentable and supreme extent."

Carlyle returned to find London humming with preparations
for an International Exhibition of the industrial arts under the
patronage of Prince Albert, to be held in Hyde Park in 1851.
England had passed out of the "hungry 'forties" into a period
in which she had no fear of the industrial rivals whom she was
inviting to compete at this parent of all world's fairs. Prosperity
had come partly from the opening of foreign markets and partly
from the welfare legislation Carlyle had supported. Shut out of
Europe by high tariffs, she had doubled her exports of plain
cotton goods between 1839 and 1849 by selling shirts to brown
men, yellow men, and black men. India and the Turkish Empire
had doubled their orders, Hong Kong had opened a large Chi-
nese market, and the emancipated Negroes of the West Indies
needed cheap clothing. The invention of cotton and wool mix-
tures suited to its climate created a great customer in the United
States, which also bought three-fifths of England's rapidly increasing exports of iron in 1849. Europe dared not shut out British
coal, which was necessary for her manufactures. In consequence
of this industrial expansion, the census of 1851 was to show over
half of the population of England and Wales living in cities;
something probably unprecedented in so large a country in the
world's history.

England had been helped to undersell her competitors by
the circumstance that the efficiency and standard of living of her
industrial population had been raised without a corresponding
increase of wages. The repeal of the Corn Laws and other tariff
measures had reduced the cost of living for the common man
about thirty percent between 1840 and 1850.[54] The manufacturers
who had fought the Factory Act of 1847 establishing a ten-hour
working day, found to their surprise that it did not diminish
output, since less fatigued labor produced more per hour. With
steadier employment, the workingmen indulged in the unwonted

luxuries of soap and glass windows. The manufacturer saw the condition of his workers improved without any change in his relation with them, while the landlord, who thought Corn-Law repeal meant the ruin of agriculture, discovered a good market for his produce in the growing cities, where foreign foodstuffs could not seriously compete. These triumphs of free trade made the public indifferent to the thunders of the *Latter-Day Pamphlets,* which did not sell well. But Carlyle believed that the necessity for fundamental reconstruction was only postponed. The lack of any constructive policy among the manufacturers he had observed at a meeting of the Anti-Corn-Law League in 1842: "If their Corn-Law Repeal were granted them, they would go on just as they had done; amassing money, fulfilling their appetites and whims; living without God in the world; therefore without sympathy for man in the world." Merthyr Tydvil, profiting from free trade and outside the scope of the Factory Acts, showed the hideous problems still to be grappled with. So he mocked at the "gigantic birdcage" of the Crystal Palace built to house the great Exhibition, and bided the time when the 6,000,000 enthusiasts visiting it would awake to find the boasted modern "progress" an illusion.

§ 2

HE could disregard the Exhibition furore the more easily because duty called him to revive memories of past struggles and friendships just as he was entering the long autumn of his days. Shortly before his death, John Sterling had left his scant literary output in the hands of Carlyle and Julius Hare, with the option to collect it in a volume. Carlyle, busied with Cromwell, devolved the entire responsibility upon Hare. In a short biographical introduction to the writings, published in 1848, Hare emphasized the portion of Sterling's life that interested him most; the eight months spent as his curate at Hurstmonceaux. Unfortunately the religious press seized the occasion to denounce the heterodox views which caused withdrawal from the Church. Sterling's family, grieved by the unpleasant notoriety, appealed to his non-clerical friends to produce a biography showing his religious activity as a mere incident in a full and varied life chiefly devoted to secular affairs. Carlyle tried to persuade Emerson, whose ministerial career had terminated similarly, to undertake it. Emerson declining, he thought it his duty to save his friend from being remembered as "a pale sickly shadow in a torn surplice." From February to April, 1851, he wrote the mellowest of his books, *The Life of John Sterling.*

He took the opportunity to defend the man whom, along with Irving and Mill, he had loved most, and also by analogy his own course in turning from the Church and the other established professions to the doubtful profession of authorship. Sterling's numerous false starts were typical of honest and eager youth in an age in which institutions had lost their vitality, and literature offered a "chaotic haven of so many frustrate activities." His religious experience was a crucial test of character: "This battle, universal in our sad epoch of 'all old things passing away' against 'all things becoming new,' has its summary and animating heart in that of Radicalism against the Church; there as in its flaming core, and point of focal splendour, does the heroic worth that lies on each side of the quarrel most clearly disclose itself."

Here lay the ground of Carlyle's distrust of Coleridge, whose influence had drawn Sterling into the Church. Carlyle charged Coleridge with cowardice; with developing a sophistical legerdemain whereby he could believe and disbelieve at the same time. Juggling the Kantian distinction between the Reason and the Understanding, Coleridge attempted to prove that his own beliefs, abreast with nineteenth-century thought, were still contained in the Thirty-nine Articles of the Anglican Church formulated in the sixteenth century. Carlyle, who had used this distinction to justify a complete psychological, instead of a narrowly intellectual, response to questions of belief, condemned the other use as a perversion, obliterating the line between truth and falsehood: "What the light of your mind, which is the direct inspiration of the Almighty, pronounces incredible,—that, in God's name, leave uncredited; at your peril do not try believing that. No subtlest hocus-pocus of 'reason' *versus* 'understanding' will avail for that feat; and it is terribly perilous to try it in these provinces." The Broad Church position was a snare for young men, giving them "an eye to discern the divineness of Heaven's splendors and lightnings, the insatiable wish to revel in their godlike radiances and brilliances; but no heart to front the scathing terrors of them, which is the first condition of your conquering an abiding place there." It was the logical antecedent and impulse toward "spectral Puseyisms"; that is, toward the High Church interpretation of the same Thirty-nine Articles in a contrary and traditional sense (Newman's Tract XC (1839) had shown them capable of a Catholic meaning). Carlyle maintained that Coleridgean liberalism led to reaction in religion, just as in *Latter-Day Pamphlets* he had shown political liberalism and indiscriminate philanthropy leading to injustice and economic exploitation.

Viewed in this light, Sterling's heterodoxy was not abnormal or reprehensible, but a sign of normal intellectual and spiritual growth. Carlyle boldly revealed the fact that most intelligent men had ceased to believe in the popular religion of Heaven and Hell and were not depressed thereby, but delighted at release from superstitious chains. Sterling's was not a negative nature, but on the contrary one prone to "too hasty and headlong belief," which plunged him into legal studies, into Benthamism and revolutionary liberalism, into the Church and out again into the literary fad of writing poetry when his talent was for prose. At the close of his short life of thirty-eight years, his mind was maturing and broadening into economic and social criticism, into interest in science and historical Biblical scholarship.

Carlyle maintained toward his friend a remarkable balance of sympathy and detachment. He portrayed him as what to-day's language calls an extravert. Sterling's versatility and restless activity were encouraged by a youth spent in several countries, an irregular education, and the omnivorous superficiality of a journalist's household. Carlyle hinted the crucial weakness of his character by saying that he "lacked persistence"; Jane said bluntly in private: "Sterling had no backbone." His entrance into the Church Carlyle convincingly attributed to remorse over the Torrijos tragedy; he interpreted this psychological crisis, followed by the slow awakening of doubts, as skillfully as he had his own crisis in *Sartor Resartus*. Ill health was not Sterling's real reason for resigning the Hurstmonceaux curacy. The same excuse had already been used to explain his not joining the Spanish expedition, when he had been ashamed to plead his engagement to be married; and was to be repeated later when he left Bordeaux, ostensibly to avoid the cholera, but actually to escape boredom. Carlyle's analysis was subtle: "I take it, in this as in other cases known to me, ill-health was not the primary cause but rather the ultimate one, the summing-up of innumerable far deeper and unconscious causes,—the cause which could boldly show itself on the surface, and give the casting vote. Such was often Sterling's way, as one could observe in such cases; though the most guileless, undeceptive and transparent of men, he had a noticeable, almost childlike faculty of self-deception, and usually substituted for the primarily determining motive and set of motives, some ultimate ostensible one, and gave that out to himself and others as the ruling impulse for important changes in life. As is the way with much more ponderous and deliberate men; as is the way, in a degree, with all men." With modern terminology at his disposal, he would have called it a case of rationalization. His lack of our glib vocabulary should not conceal the fact that no later biographer has had a better psychological equipment than Carlyle.

Sterling's chaotic career gave Carlyle scope to unite with his interest in personality his interest in social history. He exposed brilliantly the humbug of the English educational system, of the professions of law and the Church, of journalism, of literary fads. He brought vividly to life the stir of political liberalism around 1830 and the concomitant growth of religious radicalism encouraged by German Biblical scholarship popularized by Strauss's

Life of Jesus, as well as by the impact of *Lyell's Principles of Geology* upon the chronology of *Genesis.*

The style and arrangement of the *Life of Sterling* distinguish it sharply from Carlyle's popular writings, especially from *The Negro Question* and *Latter-Day Pamphlets,* which stand closest to it in date. For its special audience was typified by the club organized in Sterling's honor in 1838, including among its members Tennyson, Mill, Bingham Baring, Milnes, Copley Fielding the painter, Bishop Thirwall, Archdeacon Hare, and Hartley Coleridge, the poet-theologian's son. This distinguished group, cherishing the memories of Sterling and Coleridge and associated with Hare, must be convinced that Hare's biographical sketch was mistaken in its emphasis, and Coleridge's influence on Sterling unfortunate. Exaggeration, overemphasis, repetitiousness would prejudice these fastidious judges, and give Hare the opportunity to retaliate the charge of disproportion. Carlyle was obliged to present his materials quietly and in logical arrangement. His emotion can be felt, but is restrained out of regard for cultivated readers, who can take a hint and need no repetitions.

This restraint was the final touch needed to ripen Carlyle's style. The famous chapter on Coleridge is one of the high water marks of Romantic prose. Emotional surge and fecund imagery are kept in the molds of carefully designed paragraphs, which develop inevitably to emphatic closes, and are joined by clear transitions. Carlyle evolves an intricate pattern of images; the comparison of Coleridge's talk to a flood of water is carried dexterously through five paragraphs. An idea is hinted at, returned to, and finally given climactic development. Variety is achieved by passage from the abstract to the concrete, from short to polysyllabic words. Carlyle pokes mischievous fun at Coleridge after the manner of his early enthusiasm, Gibbon. He is not knocked down with a club, like adversaries in *Past and Present* or *Latter-Day Pamphlets,* but deftly dissected for the delectation of a critical audience. It was unfortunate for Carlyle's art that he seldom felt the necessity of such restraint. He recognized this in writing to Emerson in 1853: "I was much struck with Plato, last year, and his notions about democracy; mere Latter-Day Pamphlet *saxa et faces* (read *faeces* if you like) refined into empyrean radiance and lightning of the gods."

Critics of all shades of opinion were delighted by Carlyle's unexpected change of tone and manner. Even the purist *Athenaeum* was disarmed: "Our old opinion that Mr. Carlyle's turgid style was the growth of an affectation, is confirmed by the simplicity of this volume. When the heart speaks, it does not fail to speak intelligibly." Especially discerning comments came from opposite religious camps, from Marian Evans (George Eliot to be) in the rationalist *Westminster Review,* and J. B. Mozley, in the High Church *Christian Remembrancer.* Miss Evans, who had a personal interest in defending Sterling's withdrawal from the Church, saw also the originality of the biographical method: "We have often wished that genius would incline itself more frequently to the task of the biographer—that when some great or good personage dies, instead of the dreary three or five volumed compilations of letter, diary, and detail, little to the purpose, which two thirds of the reading public have not the chance, and the other third the inclination, to read, we could have a real 'Life,' setting forth briefly and vividly the man's inward and outward struggles, aims, and achievements, so as to make clear the meaning which his experience has for his fellows."

Mozley, though condemning Carlyle's attitude to Christianity, testified warmly to his moral influence: "He has certainly impressed upon us, with his sledge-hammer strokes, that the world in our day, and our own country, is very far from answering really, in any of its aspects, to those wholesale self-congratulatory and self-adulatory representations of it and its improvement, which used to be in fashion some years ago, but now would be considered rather shallow and behind the time. He has contributed powerfully, along with other influences, to disturb our ideas about the unparalleled solidity and excellence of our social and political state. He has sent a rude shock, not before it was time, against much smug, sleek, sleepy self-complacency; he has pitilessly given a bad name to the mere conventionalities of morals.

He has made us feel, that in the midst of our knowledge, our success, and our pride, we are still walking in the twilight and among snares, with the gulfs of the pit under our feet." Mozley made a penetrating explanation and defence of the vehicle of this wide influence, the popular style which critics were contrasting unfavorably with that of the *Life of Sterling:* "No Chartist demagogue, with St. Albans for his theme, no Radical alderman, declaiming about Bishops, no inventive controversialist, adapting the cry of the day to his theological necessities, ever took such a wide range, dashed at his game with such frank vigor, or brought up from all sides such perfect and unexpected adaptations of language to stamp it with appropriate symbols of infamy.... The licenses of familiar gossip, the antique roughnesses of the ballad, the grotesque vocabulary of the Puritans, and an equally quaint one of Mr. Carlyle's own...unprecedented as the mixture was...became in Mr. Carlyle's hand a homogeneous and living style."

§ 3

ALTHOUGH since 1842 Craigenputtock had been adding one hundred and fifty pounds yearly to his income, Carlyle's savings were only £2000, not a solid provision for a vigorous man of fifty-six with the prospect of longevity. There seemed need of another work of the magnitude of the *Cromwell,* whose three editions were testimony to the appetite for substantial books. Besides, activity was a necessity to him; he had written to Lady Ashburton after the completion of *Latter-Day Pamphlets:* "I must *write;* it is my one way of expressing all the imprisoned existence of me." He sought a subject which would exhibit, like the chronicle of St. Edmund's, the portrait of a real ruler to an England that tolerated the anarchy of Merthyr Tydvil and its like. He found it in Frederick the Great of Prussia: "Last of all our 'Kings,' and with some prophecy in him too of being the first of our coming Kings." With admirable penetration he had seized upon what is still the crucial problem for critics of democracy;

the causes of the downfall of monarchy and aristocratic society. But Carlyle dubitated on the brink of this vast and important enterprise: "The man looks brilliant and noble to me; but how *love* him, or the sad wreck he lived and worked in? I do not even yet *see* him clearly; and to try making others see him—?— Yet Voltaire and he *are* the celestial element of the poor Eighteenth Century; poor souls."

In September, 1852, he went to Germany for atmosphere and for portraits of Frederick and his contemporaries. Authentic portraits were a necessity for his work; he had discovered long ago that he "had rather read of Webster's cavernous eyes and arm under his coat-tail, than all the political speculation that a cut-and-dried system could suggest." This first sight of Germany was melancholy with memories of the visit he and Jane had planned a quarter of a century before. At Frankfort, "a *known* face startled me among the trees of the Square; Goethe's face, I saw well, but it was *in stone*,—in such manner had my old wishes been fulfilled for me!" The Ducal Court at Weimar, "with its silent stagnation from all real business, with its solemn inanities and dilettantism," made him sorry for the Goethe who had lived and worked there. The entire trip was disillusioning and discouraging: "Actual Germany, with its flat-soled puddlings in the slough of nonsense (quite a different kind from ours, but not a whit less genuine) has hurt poor Fritz very much in my mind; poor fellow, he too lies deep-buried in the *middens*-tank (or dunghill), even as Cromwell was; and then he is not half or tenth-part such a man as Cromwell was, that one should swim or dive for him in that manner! ... In Germany I could not even get a good portrait of him,—though they spend the year round in singing dull insincere praises to him in every key.... They have the mask of his dead face, however; a fiercely shrivelled plaster cast.... The face of a dead lion, or else partly, alas, of a ditto *cat!* The lips are thin, and closed like pincers; not the beautifullest kind of face. In fine why should I torment my domestic soul writing his foreign history?"

Nevertheless, torment it he did, in a work of even greater

difficulty and magnitude than he foresaw. Before the end of the year he had buckled down to "annihilating Rubbish ... with a New Assistant, a gentleman named Old Age, looking in upon me; courteously informing me that *he* will help, for the future, more and more." But old age did not overcome Carlyle's persistence in a heart-breaking task of thirteen years.

The approach to sixty showed itself in a morbid sensitivity to noises that obliged the construction of the celebrated soundproof attic study in 1853, and in eyes that needed spectacles for reading. The familiar physical woes remained with him: "'I dream horribly—the fruit of incurable biliousness; waste scenes of solitary desolation, gathered from Craigenputtock." The daily stint of writing was four hours, as compared with six when he worked in his prime on *The French Revolution*. A touch of venerableness was added by the beard Jane and Lord Ashburton persuaded him to grow in the new fashion of 1854, which makes us think of him and his contemporaries as having been always bearded. But underlying boyishness came out in pranks, such as tying a can to the tail of Jane's poodle Nero and enjoying his distracted yelpings about the house, and hale vigor in strenuous vacations, with long walks and violent gallopings about Scotland and bathing in the icy waters of the North Sea and the Baltic. An Annandale boy watched him going for a plunge in the Solway when he was sixty. Carlyle was "quite erect and moved about rapidly with an air of great decision. He stepped high and had a faraway look, just like many of the farmers, and so was his way of opening his mouth at times to breathe; but what was odd was that he seemed the embodiment of will."

This indomitable will was needed to battle with the uncongenial past of Frederick's century, which "did nothing I approve except *cut its own throat,* in the French Revolution," and in the equally uncongenial present, that rejoiced in "its Crystal Palaces, its Turkish Wars, etc." By Turkish Wars was meant the Crimean War (1854-56), fought, Carlyle believed, "at the command of the newspapers," another sinister influence in modern life. The national complacency displayed in the 1851 Exhibition was confirmed by the doubling of the real value of British exports in the decade of the 'fifties, and its almost redoubling in the 'sixties. England was the world's factory, the world's money market, and the world's carrier, while her rivals were handicapped by fighting among themselves in a period of national consolidation. In 1859 France helped Italy free herself from Austria; in 1861-65 Civil War decided national unity in America; Prussia's victories over Austria in 1866 and over France in 1870 resulted in the establishment of the German Empire. The Reciprocity Treaty with France in 1860 was a victory for free trade, whose disastrous effect on British agriculture did not disclose itself until about 1870, when improved Atlantic transport brought cheap wheat from the new and broader lands of the United States.

Carlyle wrote of the changed Britain to his brother Alick, for many years established as a farmer in Canada: "Dumfriesshire and all places are what they call 'prospering' at present: many circumstances (perhaps the California Gold, I privately reckon, most of all) have given such an explosive impulse to 'trade,' all corners of this country are testifying it. To me it is by no means exclusively beautiful, this enormous effulgence of wealth, and with it luxury and gaudery and folly, on the part not of the wise men of the community (for it is not they that the 'wealth' mostly falls on): it is on the contrary inexpressibly ugly to me when I reflect on it.... However, that is the course at present; all things rising in price; all manner of gamblers getting 'fortunes,' etc., etc.; and by and by there will be a very burbly account to settle indeed!" His conversation went to denunciations and lamentations which most of his visitors regarded as mere picturesque eccentricity. We see him one evening at Cheyne Row, "on a footstool by the fire, smoking, and looking in his long brown kind of great-coat, as he was bewailing the pass men and things had come to, and as he thought of it hardly caring to live,—like a veritable Prophet, mourning in sackcloth and ashes the sins of the world." On a vacation journey in Scotland he poured himself out to the poet Dobell, unconscious of his surroundings: "You should have seen the looks of the people in the train as he rolled forth (swaying to and fro the while, with the restlessness of some wild creature), denunciations of railways, nineteenth centuries, steam-engines, cheap literature, 'clever' people, and civilization generally. Tho of course they had no notion who he was, he gradually got them into a sort of mesmeric possession that stilled every voice but his own and stretched every eye. In the midst of all this thunderous lava he was very kind and sweet."

As to remedies for these ills, he had lost the confidence of his earlier years. A critical intellect, taught by experience, checked his burning desires. His old acquaintance Sir Henry Taylor noticed how "his opinions darted about like the monsters of the solar microscope, perpetually devouring one another." But in one reform his faith remained unshaken; in free education, not mere reading and writing, that produced glib salesmen, but manual training, that might restore honest craftsmanship and non-parasitic activities. The endowment of such training he urged upon Lord Ashburton, who approved but did nothing of consequence. The bad materials and workmanship of his supposedly soundproof study were favorite illustrations of the "age of shoddy" England had entered, for which Carlyle saw no remedy but "a thorough revolution; not a revolution after the French model— a quiet, peaceable, sensible revolution." "But I see no help for these times—" he continued on another occasion, "they must go to perdition their own way, and then—" "And then?" echoed a visitor. "And then," Carlyle said sorrowfully, "revolutions and misgovernment in cycles—in eternal cycles as far as I can see."

Despair grew with his advancing years, to the regret of his old friends, especially the optimistic Browning, who finally was moved to a protest after Carlyle's death in his *Parleying* with Bernard de Mandeville.[55] Tennyson was less congenial after fame and the Laureateship came with *In Memoriam* in 1850; he courted popular approval, and the Carlyles read his *Idylls of the King* "with profound recognition of the finely elaborated execution, and also of the inward perfection of *vacancy,*—and to say truth, with considerable impatience at being treated so very like infants, though the lollipops were so superlative." Thackeray could not renounce the vanities he satirized, and Dickens, turning popular entertainer, hastened his death in 1870 by exhausting public readings from his novels. The Coleridgeans were alienated, partly by the *Life of Sterling,* partly by their satisfaction with the superficial prosperity of the times. "The long and short of it is," said Kingsley in 1856, "I am becoming an optimist." In 1862 Maurice called at Cheyne Row "with some reluctance and much fear," but a long conversation with Carlyle revealed that "the terrible contradictions in his thoughts," involving "oscillation between democracy and absolutism, ... cannot be resolved ... into the mere worship of Might. That comes uppermost at times. Often he recoils from it with the intensest horror, and affirms and feels Justice to be the one ruler in heaven and earth. The infinite wail for a real and not a nominal father, for a real and not imaginary King, comes out in Carlyle more than in any man I know, and I am shocked at myself when I feel how I have been refusing to hear it, and only interpreting it by the devil's cry, 'What have I to do with thee?' which mingles with it." Emerson, likewise distressed, became once more Carlyle's most penetrating and sympathetic critic when he gave *Latter-Day Pamphlets* a second reading in 1854; they then seemed "enunciating with brilliant malice what shall be the universal opinion of the next edition of mankind. And the sanity was so manifest, that I felt that the over-gods had cleared their skirts also to this generation, though without this single voice perhaps I should not acquit them. Also I pardon the world that reads the book as if it read it not, when I see your inveterated humors. It required courage and required conditions that feuilletonists are not the persons to name or qualify, this writing Rabelais in 1850."

Carlyle's chief support came from a younger generation, men almost twenty-five years his juniors, like Ruskin and Froude. Ruskin continued his war against political economy with acuter destructive analysis and greater historic grasp, but less common sense. Froude followed the method and shared the point of view of his histories; his epic of the triumph of Protestantism in sixteenth-century Engand (1856-70) had its inception in Carlyle's suggestion that Henry the Eighth deserved the rescue from obloquy which he had given Cromwell. There was also the satisfaction of the great body of earnest readers described by an unsympathetic reviewer: "The influence of Mr. Carlyle's writings, and especially of his *Sartor Resartus,* has been primarily exerted on classes of men most exposed to temptations of egotism and petulance, and least subjected to anything above them,—academics, artists, littérateurs, 'strong-minded' women, 'debating' youths, Scotchmen of the phrenological grade, and Irishmen of the Young Ireland school." Deeply sympathetic with strugglers in need of guidance, Carlyle cheerfully assumed the drudgery of writing in reply to their requests for advice; and very sensible advice he gave.

Thoroughness in going back to the historic dawns of Prussia and its ruling houses added to the difficulty of the *Frederick.* Carlyle's Journal and letters are filled with groans over masses of dullness. The loss in 1854 of his mother, who had called forth the depths of his tenderness, was the more felt because Jane's climacteric, prolonged over ten years, still cast gloom over his domestic life. Visits to Bath House for the distraction of a lively and urbane society were paid for by discord at home. The crisis of Jane's jealousy appears in painful entries in her diary from October, 1855, to April, 1856. Thereafter returning health began to drive away suspicion, which was removed by the death of Lady Ashburton in April, 1857.

Carlyle's sorrow over this loss was compensated by the return of the Jane of Craigenputtock days, revealed in her comment on the proof-sheets of the first two volumes of the *Frederick* in August of that year: "Oh, my dear! what a magnificent book this is going to be! The best of all your books. I say so, who never flatter, as you are too well aware; and who am 'the only person I always know that is in the right'!" These volumes, a lengthy introduction to the main work leaving Frederick at the outset of his kingship, were a financial success beyond all previous works, bringing their author £2600. "The British public, having tried in vain to starve me into compliance or death, now renounces the attempt and says, 'Live!'—Now when one is so near done with it, at any rate!" Carlyle explained his good fortune: "I suppose there is a new set of men coming forward now." Although disgusted at the whitewashing of Frederick's impossible father, reviewers were enthusiastic over the history as a work of art, covering a vast panorama with swift compression, striking portraiture, humor, and satire.

Carlyle spent an interval of rest in a tour of Germany to study Frederick's battlefields, in the course of which he caught a chill from bathing in the Baltic. The day after his return to Chelsea he resumed the task on which he had already spent five years. Now there were more groans than ever, for the Frederick of fact was hard to reconcile with the model ruler whom the purpose of the history demanded. Disgust at dubious conduct and indecent speech and writings found outlet in pencilled annotations of source books and in complaints that made Jane wish that Frederick "had died when a baby." But having set his hand to the task, Carlyle kept stubbornly on: "Shall we be beaten in our old days, then?" In the middle of one of a series of sleepless nights in 1860 he got out of bed and "huddled in rugs, dressing gown and cape," began smoking up the chimney, convinced that Frederick would finish him before he finished Frederick. A trip to Scotland restored his courage, but he vowed that he would never return until his book was completed. He kept the vow, though it exiled him from his native countryside for five years.

Foreign and domestic events deepened the gloom of this final period of effort. Civil War in America saddened Carlyle as the tragedy of good Anglo-Saxons killing each other in a "Nigger-agony" to decide what was the best method of hiring servants. In *Macmillan's Magazine* for August, 1863, appeared his brief but notorious *Ilias (Americana) in Nuce,* which he summarized even more effectively in conversation: "The South says to the Naygur, God bless you, and be a slave! The North says, God damn you, and be free!" This attitude deeply pained many of his American admirers, including Emerson, who had forgotten his non-resistance theories in fervid advocacy of the Northern cause. But in 1866 Emerson confessed to Carlyle his disillusionment: "Peace came, and every one ran back to his shop again, and can hardly be won to patriotism more, even to the point of chasing away the thieves that are stealing not only the public gold, but the newly won rights of the slave, and the new muzzles we had contrived to keep the planter from seeking his blood." Carlyle in his turn admitted that there might have been more at issue than slavery.

A month after the publication of the *Ilias,* Jane, avoiding a cab that dashed in between her and an omnibus she was about to enter, fell heavily on her side. Neuralgia confined her to bed for months. She terrified her husband by twice requiring his solemn promise not to put her in a madhouse if she lost her mind, and by giving detailed directions for her burial at Haddington. He deadened his anxiety by intensive work on the *Frederick,* which perceptibly neared completion. In January, 1864, he added to a business note to Joseph Neuberg, one of his volunteer helpers with research: "We are in profound misery here; I cannot for my life *understand* in what degree of *danger;*—but the suffering itself is heartbreaking." Two months later the death of Lord Ashburton increased his load of sorrow. In July, Jane asked to be taken to the home of her old family physician at Thornhill, near Templand, and there her condition turned for the better. By October she was back in Chelsea. Her husband welcomed "the beginning, as of a second youth (almost of a second childhood with the wisdom and graces of old age)." She remained very feeble, but her mind burned as brightly as ever. Something she concealed from her husband reveals how deeply the anxious poverty of the *French Revolution* period had eaten into her spirit, probably to be a cause of the nervous illnesses of her later years. This winter of 1864-65 she privately instructed a servant: "When I am dead, go upstairs into the closet of the spare room. There you'll find two wax candles wrapped in paper. I want you to light and burn them beside me. Once when I was giving a party after I came to live in London, my mother, who was here and wanted everything very nice, went out and bought candles and confectionery. She set out a table and lighted the room splendidly, and then called to me to come and see. I was angry, saying that people would say I was extravagant and would ruin my husband, and I took away two of the candles and some of the cakes. My mother was hurt and began to cry; and that hurt me, and I repented and tried to comfort her and was dreadfully sorry. The two candles I had taken away are those you'll find."

In January, 1865, when Carlyle was in his seventieth year, appeared the last two volumes of *The History of Frederick, Called the Great*. Borne on the momentum of his reputation, plaudits were more nearly unanimous than ever. But his right arm had been shaking for two years, and he felt he could never write another book.

The monumental work gives no hint of age in its unflagging high spirits, even to burlesque, its battle scenes, its trick of disguising exposition as lively narrative. Its "spiritual hero" Voltaire, aging, irritable, shady in minor moralities but indomitable in single-handed battle against the major evils of his time, is a masterpiece of sympathetic portraiture. The history covers magnificently a vast panorama of world affairs. Yet it is a failure; for its main purpose is unachieved. In the long battle between Carlyle's desires and his critical intellect, this time the desires won. As Emerson had flown from intolerable realities to the cloud-lands of mysticism, so Carlyle, who must have a hero for the instruction of his countrymen, made of the Cynic-Stoic Frederick what Professor Saintsbury has aptly called "a kind of abstraction of the Ruler, a personified and incarnate Government." There was self-deception, but no deliberate dishonesty, for Carlyle printed enough documents to permit his readers to form a very different judgment of his practical hero. He does succeed in showing that Frederick's political chicanery was no worse than what he had to meet in his opponents; yet to show that one king is somewhat better than another is hardly worth thirteen years' labor. Carlyle's display of the general weakening of moral fibre in the governing classes of Europe is unaccompanied by the analysis of its causes helpful to those who, like himself, would renew some sort of aristocracy. Battle scenes lured him away from the study of internal administration and other applications of his ideal of the business of the historian. Thus the *Frederick*, though entertaining, is conventional, throwing little light upon the great problems it touches. The justification of the *Real-Politik* of the Hohenzollerns was to have an unfortunate effect upon Carlyle's reputation.

§ 4

EVEN more satisfying to Jane Carlyle than the successful completion of the six-volume history was her husband's election, by double the vote of his rival, Disraeli, to the honorary post of Lord Rector of Edinburgh University. She had married him against the advice of her relatives, and had seen Edinburgh hold out longer than London against recognition of his merit. In 1841, when Carlyle had discouraged an effort of Edinburgh University students to have him appointed to the chair of Civil History, Jane had written to her mother, who naturally wished her near: "No, no, we are done with Edinburgh. It is only now when London and the world have discovered his talent that they are fain to admit it. As for me, I would as soon go back to Craigenputtock as to that poor, proud, formal, 'highly respectable' city." When the occasion of triumphal return came with Carlyle's installation in 1866, she was too feeble to accompany him. She filled her small flask with brandy, and asked him to take inspiration from it and her before he began his address.

Standing with her back to the living-room door, she kissed him twice goodby, as Professor Tyndall took her place as his travelling companion. Professor Huxley, who was also receiving an honorary degree, joined them on the way, and John and James Carlyle met their brother in Edinburgh. The proud city thronged to hear him. His voice was weak, but his words had their old pungency and humor.

He spoke extemporaneously, pouring out the thoughts that filled his mind at the sight of eager youths preparing for life as he had done on the same spot over fifty years before. Could he spare them his errors by giving them the benefit of his long experience and his meditations on the theme of education, that had always been close to his heart? The recent wave of university reform, touching even Oxford, offered a convenient point of departure. Carlyle was glad to know that the Edinburgh University library had been reformed, but supposed there was still room for improvement. A library was the most important part of an institution of learning, for the invention of printing had made lectures obsolete. Professors were still needed to show "how to read" and what to read, but the wisdom of the ages was best expressed through the printed page. Good libraries should be not only in every college, but also "in every county town, for the benefit of those who could read well, and might if permitted." But education was not wholly, or even chiefly, a matter of books and speaking. Training for useful work of every sort was more important. A youth needed vocational instruction and guidance, even if the work for which he was best suited proved to be "the breaking of colts." Carlyle concluded with a warning against his own errors. Students should not endanger their health in the pursuit of knowledge, should avoid the literary profession as a general rule, and should never suspect a conspiracy to block their paths, when the world was merely "travelling in a different way," quite indifferent to them. Finally the melancholy sage of Chelsea bade his youthful hearers "work and despair not."

They burst into rounds of applause, and followed him with hurrahs to his lodgings. He wrote to Jane: "You never saw such a tempest of enthusiastic excitation as that among the student people," and added that he had thought of her as he drank from her travelling flask. Tyndall had telegraphed her: "A perfect triumph." Dined and fêted for four days, Carlyle sought a rest before meeting similar felicitations in London. His brother James and his sister Mary took him to Scotsbrig, where a sprained ankle prolonged his stay to three weeks. On April 21, two days before his planned return, he was visiting his youngest sister Jean at Dumfries, when a telegram announced Jane's death. Shocked by an accident to her pet dog, she had passed away quietly in her carriage in Hyde Park.

It was Saturday night, and the Scottish Sabbath made his railway journey to London impossible until Monday. His over-charged heart could find no relief in tears, even though on Sunday evening there came into his hands a cheerful letter Jane had written the day of her death. John accompanied him to Cheyne Row, where the brothers looked on her dead face "beautiful as Eternity, soft as an Angel's or a babe's." Carlyle tried to comfort himself by remembering that her death had been without struggle, and her last days "the happiest she had had for many years." Queen Victoria sent a message of condolence, tactfully mentioning her own recent bereavement. Jane was laid beside her beloved father in the ruined choir of the beautiful thirteenth-century Gothic church of St. Mary's, Haddington.

John, a widower for over ten years, hoped to remain as his brother's companion to the end of their days. He had early retired from medical practice, but of his literary ambitions nothing had come but a mediocre prose translation of Dante's *Inferno*. After John's wife had left him a comfortable fortune, Thomas had written to Alick: "He and I never have a cross word now; for I have long since recognized that rebuking him is of no use; that Nature is stronger than any argument against Nature, and that my poor Jack is even *made* so, and might have been infinitely worse made." But living together in Cheyne Row renewed the old friction between strenuosity and indolence, and John returned to his home in Dumfries before midsummer. Thomas was left alone, looking over his wife's letters, notebooks, and diaries, exaggerating his faults toward her in the desolation of grief. With thoughts flowing toward the irrevocable past, he began writing his reminiscences of Edward Irving. In December, the second Lady Ashburton took him from the inner and outer gloom of Chelsea to the sunshine of the Riviera, where the stern son of

the North first knew the charm of Southern scenery. In smiling
Mentone he completed his reminiscences of Irving, and added
those of Jeffrey, which still kept him close to Jane. All of her
relatives having died before her, soon after his return to London
in 1867 he bequeathed Craigenputtock to Edinburgh University,
with the provision that its income be spent as "John Welsh bur-
saries" for meritorious poor students. John Carlyle made a similar
bequest for medical scholarships.

In London the political situation, of which disquieting echoes
had reached Mentone, broke insistently upon Carlyle's communion with the past. Since the death of Lord Palmerston in
1865, the old Whig ascendancy was over, and the party had become Liberal in fact as in name. Gladstone and Bright gave heed
to the demand of the industrial workers for the vote, which had
been in abeyance since the collapse of Chartism in 1848. John
Mill was drawn from the retirement in southern France which
had been almost continuous since Mrs. Taylor had been free to
marry him in 1851, in order to enter Parliament as advocate of
an extension of the suffrage to women as well as to workingmen,
to be counterbalanced by plural votes for persons of superior
education and by proportional representation for the protection of
minorities. These safeguards he saw swept aside by a series of
surprising political manoeuvres; the defeat of a Liberal Reform
Bill by the die-hard Whig minority, a change of front on the part
of the Tories counselled by Disraeli, and the liberalizing of the
Bill they in turn introduced by amendments pressed by Gladstone and the Opposition. Mill's advocacy of women's suffrage
was laughed at, but the Reform Act of 1867 put an end to middle-
class dominance by granting the vote to industrial workers. Only
miners and agricultural workers remained to be enfranchised.
England had committed herself to the principle that political
wisdom could be derived from the majority, and the aristocracy
of talent Mill and Carlyle had dreamed of was further off than
ever.

Carlyle was enraged by what he considered the betrayal of

the duty of government by the Tories under the evil guidance of Disraeli. His feelings found vent in *Shooting Niagara: and After?,* published in *Macmillan's Magazine* for August, 1867, when the House of Lords was passing the second Reform Bill. This Constitutional change by "traitorous politicians, grasping at votes, even votes of the rabble," he saw ushering in a society ruled by "Count of Heads" and given over, with the weakening of religious and moral restraint, to "Free Trade, in all senses and to all lengths." He reviewed the means he had proposed to prevent such a decline of civilization. Priesthood of men of letters—actual men of letters flattered the mob or retired into the regions of Art, leaving unattempted their task of finding "new definitions of LIBERTY." Captains of industry—goods of British manufacture, once known throughout the world for high quality, were now justly reputed "cheap and nasty"; a house had become "a congeries of plastered bandboxes, shambling askew at all joints and corners"; a description only too familiar to the city-dweller of to-day. A rejuvenated aristocracy—the actual aristocracy idled away time in hunting, shooting, and the social round; having abdicated its function of ruling, it awaited destruction by the forces of democracy it was unloosing. Alas, a candid examination revealed no signs anywhere of a sizable minority who, in Cromwellian phrase, "would spend their blood rather" than see England float to ruin on the Niagara rapids: "Certain it is, there is nothing but vulgarity in our People's expectations, resolutions, or desires, in this Epoch." Notwithstanding the intemperance of much of the phraseology, there was a magnificent detachment in this admission of the bankruptcy of the thought and effort of a lifetime.

This was the end; no hope remained. But Ruskin struggled on till madness came; and two years after *Shooting Niagara* the appearance of Matthew Arnold's *Culture and Anarchy* announced a new entrant upon the stony road of social reconstruction. Thus the hope of order springs eternally in the breasts of a few Englishmen, with the result that London is to-day something of a cosmos as compared to the chaos that is New York.

§ 5

CARLYLE had thirteen years to live after having arrived at this plenitude of despair. After 1870 his arm was useless for writing, its last task being the annotation of Jane's letters. Gleams of hope came only from abroad; from the development of Germany and Russia, where aristocracy survived. He had the satisfaction of swaying English opinion from intervention against those powers; by his celebrated letter to the *Times* for November 18, 1870, defending the historic justice of Germany's exaction of Alsace-Lorraine from defeated France, and by a short note to the same newspaper in 1872 denouncing a suspected design of Disraeli to involve England again in defence of Turkey against Russia. Otherwise, England advanced steadily on her chosen road, guided chiefly by Gladstone, whom Carlyle called contemptuously "People's William." The new biological science conspired with democracy to banish the sense of the heroic. How could man feel responsibility and aspire to dignity, if he believed, with the Darwinians, that he was a cousin of that disgusting animal, the monkey, and ultimately descended from a bit of protoplasm that had become animated by accident? Carlyle's Journal and conversation were full of anger and sorrow at the spread of this new science, which he did not understand, but which seemed to involve worse consequences than the mechanistic physics against which his youth had revolted.

As a consequence of the Companies Act of 1862 legalizing limited liability for investors in joint-stock companies, his mail was flooded with circulars, often cleverly disguised, advertising a thousand and one enterprises which he detested as gambling. The postman told him that a promoter had mailed 28,000 circulars in one day. On July 12, 1872, Carlyle called his niece Jane Carlyle Aitken, his housekeeper from 1868 until his death, and dictated short essays on *Promoterism, Trades Unions,* and *Signs of the Times,* that were a melancholy commentary on *Past and Present:* "What a frightful bend-sinister (or abysmal gash-sinister) in our poor Prophecy of Industrialism marching irresistibly towards government by the noblest! Has come upon us by surprise even; no such anticipation until in such form the weird Thing (blowing by the 28,000?) is here. (Put Capital into the hands of Government—Alas, what is 'Government'?—General reformation of ourselves,—which nobody will believe in.)" These, published posthumously, were Carlyle's last words on the social question, that had engaged his best energies.

Upon his disillusioned, solitary age, the world showered the money and honors that once would have meant much to him and Jane. The despised and rejected *Sartor Resartus* sold 20,000 copies in ᴢ shilling edition, and the People's Edition of his Collected Works, priced cheaply at two shillings the volume by his request, had a circulation of 50,000. Six volumes of selected writings had been published in Germany as early as 1855-56, and French translation had begun appropriately with the *French Revolution* in 1865-67. There were also translations into Dutch, Hungarian, and Russian. In 1869 Queen Victoria honored him with an audience along with Browning and Grote. In 1872 the recently crowned Empress of Germany called at the modest Chelsea house. In 1874 Carlyle accepted the Prussian Order of Merit established by the great Frederick. But in the same year he gratefully but firmly declined an English baronetcy, with the Grand Cross of Bath and a pension, writing to Disraeli, who had magnanimously made the offer: "Titles of honor are, in all degrees of them, out of keeping with the tenor of my poor existence hitherto in this epoch of the world, and would be an encumbrance, not a furtherance, to me; ... as to money, it has, after long years of rigorous and frugal, but also (thank God, and those are gone before me) not degrading poverty, become in this latter time amply abundant, even superabundant." His eightieth birth year in 1875 showered him with honors and congratulations: an honorary degree from Harvard University, a letter from Chancellor Bismarck, gold medals from Edinburgh University and from a group of one hundred and nineteen distinguished English men and women, including Browning, Chadwick, Darwin, George Eliot, Fitzgerald, Huxley, Lecky, Harriet Martineau, Leslie Stephen, Tennyson, Morley, and Tyndall. He wrote to Alick: "Outward things go what might be called altogether prosperously with me;... but it has become of small moment, and indeed to a degree that astonishes me utterly *indifferent* in the sight of the Immensities and Eternities which I now see close ahead."

Sometimes the journey to the Immensities and Eternities seemed so slow that he wished he could end himself like a noble Roman. Then again his magnificent constitution gave "glimpses or bright remembrances of what I might in the language of flattery call *health*—very singular to me, now wearing out my eightieth year. It is strange and wonderful to feel these glowings again of intellectual and spiritual clearness, followed by base physical confusions of feeble old age." A fall from his horse had put an end to riding when he was seventy-two, but he continued to walk the London streets, a picturesque figure in his familiar wide-brimmed hat, which he always took off at the spot in Hyde Park where Jane had died. He crossed streets whenever he wished, poking his umbrella into the noses of horses that threatened to run him down. When he chanced upon a piece of bread, he put it in some conspicuous place, to be found by the poor. His one luxury was charity, into which went much of the superfluity of his income, and Lord Ashburton's entire legacy of £2,000. His chief occupation was reading, especially rereading the books that had charmed his youth, though he found it "a poor resource in comparison with writing." He was frequently a guest at the country houses of the aristocracy, and his visits have left their record in charmingly urbane notes.

The brilliant society of his happier days came seldom or never to Chelsea: Tennyson and Browning were absorbed in circles of their admirers; Dickens, Thackeray, and John Mill were dead. But callers of younger generations were numerous; Tyndall, Lecky, Ruskin, and the always attentive Froude, though now and then an inopportune visitor chanced upon a reception similar to that of the poet Allingham in 1865: "Call at Carlyle's. When the door opens, see him in the passage; he says in an

angry voice—'Go away, sir! I can do nothing with you.' I go
away, with reflections many and black." He had to be humored
at times, but even the young men who did not share his opinions
enjoyed his company. Leslie Stephen wrote to James Russell
Lowell, who had attacked Carlyle in *My Study Windows:* "I
don't think that you or any other Yankee can find it in your
hearts to be quite just to Carlyle.... Perhaps it is proper to feel
more strongly than I can do about his political delinquencies; but
I can't help loving the old fellow; and amongst other reasons
for this that of all us literary professionals in London he is in his
life the manliest and simplest. It is a pleasure to see anybody who
has the courage to live so little spoilt by the flattery which might
have choked him and made him into a windbag." In congenial
society his conversation was charming, full of recollections of
people and books, flashing into quaint turns of humor, as when
he asked Darwin if there were any chance of men turning back
into monkeys. Coming away from a luncheon at the age of
eighty-two, he patted one of his nieces on the shoulder, saying,
"Well, Mary, we've had a pleasant visit, but we're both rather
drunk." The proper Scotch maiden protested in vain that she had
touched only water. The old vehemence also remained. In 1874
he was astonished at the moderate tone of an article of the Conservative Lord Salisbury on *Difficulties of the Liberal Party:* "I
thought with shame how impossible it would have been for me
to avoid bursting out in the most violent language."

In 1876 Alick died in Canada, whence he had never returned.
The death of John in 1879 broke Thomas's last hold on life. He
became slowly feebler. Ruskin, shattered by a mental breakdown, called at Cheyne Row: "They greeted each other affec-
tionately, and Ruskin knelt on the floor, bending over Carlyle as
they talked." In January, 1881, when Carlyle was in his eighty-
sixth year, Froude found his mind wandering: "Is it not strange
that these people should have chosen the very oldest man in all
Britain to make suffer in this way?" Newspaper reporters, symbols of the blatant spirit of an age he despised, kept ringing at

the street door for news of his condition, until bulletins pinned up outside abated the nuisance.

On February fifth, all was over. Allingham, one of the first to look on his dead face, wrote in his diary: "The large beautiful eyelids were closed forever on a pair of eyes that, for carrying messages inwards or outwards, had scarcely met their equals on the earth, or left such behind."

Dean Stanley offered Westminster Abbey, but Carlyle had left directions for his burial without religious services, beside his parents at Ecclefechan. The place and day were not announced. But a crowd of curious villagers had gathered in the churchyard when a funeral procession of a dozen carriages arrived from the railway station about noon of a dreary day. Froude, Lecky, and Tyndall, representing the great world in which an Ecclefechan boy had found his true place, stood with the inevitable newspaper-men in the thawing snow beside his brother James and three sisters, as Thomas Carlyle, after a long and strange pilgrimage, returned to the earth which had first nourished him.

CHAPTER VII

FIFTY YEARS AFTER

⇛ ⇚

§ 1

"AFTER forming the literary taste of England to an extent which no contemporary (unless, possibly, one of a very different class, Macaulay) has approached, he has become, while yet alive and at work among us, something of a classic," was the verdict of the authoritative *Quarterly Review* when Carlyle had fifteen years to enjoy his fame. The dedications of the Chartist Thomas Cooper's *Purgatory of Suicides* (1845), Charles Kingsley's *Alton Locke* (1850), Charles Dickens's *Hard Times* (1854), G. H. Lewes's *Life of Goethe* (1855), John Ruskin's *Munera Pulveris* (1871), and Robert Browning's *Agamemnon* (1877) were among the many testimonies of respect and affection from his fellow-craftsmen. During the last seven years of his life, his disciple Froude was preparing a biography that would reveal his personality fully to the world; over a month before his death Froude had set printers to work on his *Reminiscences*.

Hardly had the world's regret at Carlyle's passing begun to get itself uttered, when the *Reminiscences,* appearing early in March, 1881, caused a sharp revulsion of feeling by their strictures on men of letters whose memory was revered. Swinburne wrote indignant sonnets in championship of Coleridge, Lamb, and Wordsworth, and the occasion awakened the political animosities of the *Edinburgh, Athenaeum,* and *Quarterly*. Popular resentment interfered seriously with subscriptions for a Carlyle memorial, which finally took the form of the familiar statue facing the Thames at the foot of Cheyne Row. The failure to delete personal attacks, from which Carlyle's writings were conspicuously free even in the years when journalism was savage, was Froude's mistake. He had disregarded Carlyle's appended prohibition of publication without editing, alleging verbal permission given later, when Carlyle had probably forgotten what he had written for his own eyes in the period of depression after his bereavement.

Worse errors followed. In two installments (1882, 1884) appeared the exceedingly frank biography, which Froude had tried to write in the spirit of Carlyle's objurgation in the essay on Scott: "How delicate, decent is English Biography, bless its mealy mouth!" He brought to the task honesty and brilliant literary gifts, but too little humor to interpret the sharp banter and unceremoniousness of the Carlyles toward each other or to allow for the habitual exaggeration of their speech, and too much imagination to present the romance of their marriage without embroidery. Chivalrous devotion to Mrs. Carlyle made him her champion in their points of difference, especially in regard to Lady Ashburton. An unconventional married relation, easily understandable to-day, shocked his Victorian sense of the proprieties, and he uttered his disapproval without forethought of the damage which its reverberations among respectability might do to the reputation of the great man he admired so sincerely. The concomitant publication of *Letters and Memorials of Jane Welsh Carlyle* (1883) dealt a further blow by Froude's representation of the exaggerated self-accusations of a grief-stricken old man as the penance of a repentant sinner. He had produced one of the most dramatic and vital of biographies, but over-emphasis of shadows fixed in the popular mind the image of Carlyle as a dyspeptic, wife-baiting misanthrope.

A discerning few rushed to Carlyle's defence; notably George Meredith, who had experienced the peculiar difficulties of the mating of artists. In 1882 he wrote to André Raffalovitch: "Your article on Th. Carlyle's 'Reminiscences' was prompted, I think, rather by enthusiasm for the lady who stands close and in contrast with him than by an accurate knowledge of his works, nature, and teaching. Our people over here have been equally unjust, with less excuse. You speak of vanity, as a charge against him. He has little, though he certainly does not err on the side of modesty;—he knew his powers. The harsh judgment he passed upon the greater number of his contemporaries came from a very accurate perception of them, as they were perused by the intense light of the man's personal sincereness. He was one of those who stood constantly in the presence of those 'Eternal Verities' of which he speaks. For the shallow man of mere literary aptitude he had perforce contempt.—Between him and his wife the case is quite simple. She was a woman of peculiar conversational sprightliness, and such a woman longs for society. To him, bearing that fire of sincereness, ... society was unendurable. All coming near him, except those who could bear the trial, were scorched, and he was as much hurt as they by the action rousing the flames in him. Moreover, like all truthful souls, he was an artist in his work. The efforts after verification of matters of fact, and to present things distinctly in language, were incessant; they cost him his health, they swallowed up his leisure. Such a man could hardly be an agreeable husband for a woman of the liveliest vivacity. But that is not a reason for your passing condemnation on him. . . . I knew them both. She did me the honor to read my books, and make him listen to extracts, and he was good enough to repeat that 'the writer thereof was no fool'—high praise from him. They snapped one another, and yet the basis of affection was mutually firm. She admired, he respected, and each knew the other to be honest." [56]

All the new evidence, from Charles Eliot Norton's edition of Carlyle letters in 1886 to the most recent summaries of each side of the controversy, has not exceeded the insight of this judgment. Perhaps the most unfortunate result of the long controversy [57] has been distraction of attention from the writings to the man. Most of the matters in dispute, including sexual impotence, are irrelevant to an evaluation of Carlyle's works. They have made Carlyle, in Professor Saintsbury's phrase, "the stumbling block of fools."

§2

CARLYLE's writings declined in estimation shortly after his death; to some extent because of an unpleasant conception of his personality, but chiefly because of an unfavorable social and literary environment. The triumphant advance of capitalistic industry, science, and democracy since the day of the Crystal Palace discredited him to the extent that H. D. Traill, in editing the Centenary Edition of his works (1896-97), could say: "His boding prophecies ... are marred for us to-day by an ever-present consciousness of their subsequent falsification." The strong American disapproval of his heterodoxies, inflamed by his pronouncements on the Civil War, was represented by W. C. Brownell in *Victorian Prose Masters* (1901); Walt Whitman was almost alone in admitting, "I doubt if he ever thought or said half as bad words about us as we deserve." Classical economists continued to brush aside his criticisms as unscientific, and the same damning charge was made against his histories by Professor J. R. Seeley and other specialists. The rising men of letters, such as Pater, Wilde, and Stevenson, were in revolt against the didactic tone of the earlier Victorians, so conspicuous in Carlyle. The vogue of French prose models, with their purism, coherence, symmetry, and distaste for the mixing of *genres,* made it easy to follow Matthew Arnold's advice to "flee Carlylese as you would the Devil." Carlyle's staunch admirer, Professor Saintsbury, noted in 1895 his unpopularity with "a considerable literary class that takes very little interest in politics, a good deal in art (for which Carlyle cared absolutely nothing) and most of all in mere literature (which he always attempted to scorn and snub)." But a great British and American public, unaffected by literary fashions, continued to read him for moral and intellectual stimulation. Germany's interest in the champion of her literature and institutions was expressed in a steady demand for his works, especially the *Frederick,* and in much scholarly investigation and critical comment, notably by Schulze-Gavaernitz in 1893. His works also found their way into Spanish, Italian, Polish, Swedish, and Serbian.

Notwithstanding the reopening of the biographical controversy by Froude's posthumous self-defence in *My Relations with Carlyle* (1903), the early twentieth century was a more favorable atmosphere because of the beginning of disillusion with science and the spread of socialistic ideas. In England a new group of prophets arose in Mr. Shaw, Mr. Wells, and Mr. Galsworthy; the ironic close of *John Bull's Other Island* (1904) makes explicit the spiritual kinship of Mr. Shaw's mouthpiece, Father Keenan, with Ruskin and Carlyle. The changing social attitude, that denied the classicality of political economy in the light of better knowledge of economic history, was reflected in the United States by Miss Vida Scudder's treatment of Carlyle in *Social Ideals in English Letters,* and in France, hitherto uncongenial ground for so Teutonic an author, by the remarkable monograph of Professor Louis Cazamian. In 1899 Professor G. M. Trevelyan, at the outset of his distinguished career, rebelled against the exclusive pretensions of the scientific school of historians with a spirited defence of the imaginative penetration and artistic finish of Carlyle's histories, which have since held their ground against Dryasdust.

The World War brought a sudden change of values. Carlyle's championship of the Germany of the past, notorious in the *Frederick,* counted heavily against him in England, especially since it was easy to find in so paradoxical a writer apparent advocacy of the un-moral use of force. After the Peace were raised the voices of indignant young men, blaming the Victorians somewhat indiscriminately for the complacency that had drifted into the catastrophe of 1914-18. Froude had saved Carlyle from the deflation to which whitewashing biographers had exposed most of his contemporaries, including Tennyson; but he could not escape the inevitable reaction against the nineteenth century in favor of the eighteenth led by Mr. Lytton Strachey. Similarly John Sterling, representative of the sophisticated London literary set of 1839, had scorned "that flat and meagre English eighteenth century which produced the houses, the furniture, the thoughts, the people, that we are most accustomed to consider decayed and out of date." [58] Carlyle also lost hold on the average reader, who no longer lived in the Victorian atmosphere.

That he spoke so directly and compellingly to his own time, is the chief obstacle to his communication with posterity. His various styles, encrusted with Romantic eccentricity, with pulpit and stump oratory, puzzle or repel those who pick him up casually. His ideas also are swathed in the "time-vesture" of the nineteenth century; "Morrison's Pills," "Joe Mantonism," and "Paralytic Radicalism" require a glossary such as the Englishman needs for *Babbitt*. The bulk and solidity of his output are formidable; he makes no concessions to weak intelligences in weighty subjects, and deals in parable and paradox. For the American there is an additional obstacle. What school, church, and political platform have implanted in him as axioms, Carlyle challenges; he must listen to a case argued passionately against him, and test dogmas by facts. Thus the general reader knows only the Carlyle nearest his experience and stylistic tradition; the struggles of the self-made man in the essays on Burns and Johnson, the spiritual crisis of *Sartor Resartus,* the lecture tone of *Heroes and Hero-Worship,* the drama of the *French Revolution,* and possibly the Victorian panorama of the *Life of Sterling*. But matchless phrases from unexplored regions of Carlyle pass into familiar quotation through steady currency in newspapers and periodicals.

For a minority with sturdy intelligence and historical imagination, he remains one of the most fascinating of British authors. He lies square across the path of those who would understand the Victorian age as the best representative of its thought and feeling, the chief influence on its gifted youth. "He was the greatest of the Britons of his time," said George Meredith, "—and after the British fashion of not coming near perfection; Titanic, not Olympian; a heaver of rocks, not a shaper." He perceived in their obscure beginnings social phenomena whose importance is now writ large. He turned the current of English literature from individualism to consideration of social welfare. His life and works form a splendid bridge from decaying feudalism to the inchoate something we call the modern world. He likewise has continued appeal to those sensitive to literary art. As Emerson perceived, *Past and Present* was "the first domestication of the modern system, with its infinity of details, into style"; it stands as a model to writers striving to make literature an adequate reflection of the bewildering complexity of the present scene. Of the very different craft of interpreting and expressing individual feeling, Carlyle is also among the masters. The flexibility and subtlety of the *Life of Sterling* is but the best known example of the biographical genius scattering itself throughout his writings in marvellously compressed miniatures that reveal the inmost of men. Everywhere is the impress of his protean personality, most intimate in his Journal and letters with their lordship of language adequate to every passing mood; grandiose, heroic, satiric, irritable, pathetic, plaintive.

The present writing is in the midst of post-war turmoil such as provoked Carlyle's social criticisms. England, the birthplace of machine industry, may become its victim, as everywhere production outstrips distribution and consumption, with unemployment on a scale that threatens a world-wide breakdown of capitalism. Thoughtful men question the wisdom of seeking further command over nature until means have been devised to prevent fools and knaves from misusing in war and peace the terrifying powers already unloosed by science. The cry is for strong government. Growing doubt of the capacity of the average man to rule himself through his representatives is driving a desperate world to the experiments of Fascism and Communism. In the crisis he foresaw, Carlyle is being remembered. Editions of translated excerpts from his writings in 1920, 1921, and 1922 accompanied the rise of Fascism to power in Italy. Mr. Shaw's *Apple Cart* has preached to England, in the manner of *Frederick the Great,* the parable of a patriot king striving to protect the people from their elected rulers, who will not turn the powers of science and industry to their welfare. Germany, under the frightful strain of war ruin, reparation payments, and economic and political instability, is imbibing courage from selections from Carlyle that have sold to the extent of 300,000 copies since 1926.

Will the author of *Past and Present* be read so widely in England and America? The chastened mood of the moment is auspicious. The dogmas of democracy and *laissez faire* are shaken. Science, especially the physics that tried Carlyle's faith, no longer speaks the language of crass materialism. Moral responsibility, lately out of fashion, begins to be perceived as the indispensable cement of a fast disintegrating society. The great public is listening to writers who say incompletely and imperfectly what Carlyle said with unparalleled brilliance and cogency. If Victorian clouds do not shroud his lightnings, it may next turn to him. In our partially aroused state we have need of his obstinate faith that the modern world contains resources for its own salvation. The stupendous scale of the contemporary scene dwarfs our thinkers. We must await men of Carlyle's range and stature for the achievement of a social synthesis, if procrastination has not already put it beyond human capacity. Until Titans arise, we will look with envy and regret at the lost opportunity of a generation that had a Carlyle.

INTRODUCTORY BIBLIOGRAPHY

※ ⋘

BIOGRAPHIES OF CARLYLE

THE standard Life of Carlyle is by James Anthony Froude, 1882, 1884. It should be supplemented and corrected by reference to the recent biography by David Alec Wilson, (*Carlyle Till Marriage*, 1923, etc.), of which five out of six volumes have appeared.

AUTOBIOGRAPHICAL MATERIALS

Froude, James Anthony, edit., *Reminiscences*, by Thomas Carlyle, 1881.

Norton, Charles Eliot, edit., *Early Letters of Thomas Carlyle (1814-1826)*, 1886.

——, *Letters of Thomas Carlyle (1826-1836)*, 2 vol., 1888.

Carlyle, Alexander, edit., *New Letters of Thomas Carlyle* (1836 to his latest years), 2 vol., 1904.

——, *The Love Letters of Thomas Carlyle and Jane Welsh*, 2 vol., 1909.

CARLYLE'S WORKS AND CARLYLE CRITICISM

Dyer, I. W., *A Bibliography of Carlyle's Writings and Ana*, 1928. The standard text of Carlyle's works is published by Chapman and Hall, London.

CARLYLE AND HIS CIRCLE

Allingham, H., and Redford, D., edit., *William Allingham: A Diary*, 1907.

Carlyle, Alexander, edit., *Letters of Thomas Carlyle to John Stuart Mill, John Sterling, and Robert Browning,* 1923.
Drew, Elizabeth, *Jane Welsh and Jane Carlyle,* 1928.
Espinasse, Francis, *Literary Recollections and Sketches,* 1893.
Neff, Emery, *Carlyle and Mill,* 1926.
Norton, Charles Eliot, edit., *The Correspondence of Thomas Carlyle and Ralph Waldo Emerson,* 2 vol., 1883.
Roe, F. W., *The Social Philosophy of Carlyle and Ruskin,* 1921.

THE SCOTCH BACKGROUND

Mathieson, W. L., *The Awakening of Scotland (1747-1797),* 1910.
——, *Church and Reform in Scotland (1797-1843),* 1916.
Cockburn, Henry, *Memorials of his Time,* 1874.
——, *The Life of Lord Jeffrey,* 1852.
Masson, David, *Edinburgh Sketches and Memories,* 1892.

THE ENGLISH BACKGROUND

Trevelyan, G. M., *British History in the Nineteenth Century,* 1925.
Halévy, Élie, *A History of the English People in 1815.* Translated from the French by Watkin, E. I., and Barker, D. A., 1924.

ECONOMIC BACKGROUND

Hammond, J. L. and Barbara, *The Rise of Modern Industry,* 1926.
Clapham, J. H., *An Economic History of Modern Britain,* Volume I, 1926.
Thorp, W. L., and Mitchell, W. C., *Business Annals,* 1926.

LITERARY BACKGROUND

Thorndike, Ashley H., *Literature in a Changing Age,* 1920.
Collins, A. S., *The Profession of Letters (1780-1832),* 1928.
Walker, Hugh, *The Literature of the Victorian Era,* 1910.

NOTES

※》《

THE *notes refer chiefly to unpublished material, controversial matters, and fuller treatments of important topics.*

1. (To page 14). W. L. Mathieson, *The Awakening of Scotland*, Glasgow, 1910, p. 286. J. H. Clapham, *An Economic History of Modern Britain*, Cambridge, 1926, I, pp. 188-89.
2. (To p. 17). For elementary and secondary education in Scotland and England, see Élie Halévy, *A History of the English People in 1815*, translated by E. I. Watkin, New York, 1924, pp. 458-69.
3. (To p. 20). See Henry W. Meikle, *Scotland and the French Revolution*, Glasgow, 1912.
4. (To p. 23). For a comparison of English and Scotch universities, see Élie Halévy, *A History of the English People in 1815*, pp. 469-80.
5. (To p. 25). David Masson, *Edinburgh Sketches and Memories*, London, 1892, p. 230 ff.
6. (To p. 33). J. H. Clapham, *An Economic History of Modern Britain*, I, pp. 139-42.
7. (To p. 37). The 1805-6 version of Wordsworth's *Prelude*, edited by Ernest de Selincourt, Oxford, 1926, p. 412, lines 904-5.
8. (To p. 40). MS. letter of Alexander Carlyle, Mainhill, 14th November, 1818. Pierpont Morgan Library. New York.
9. (To p. 42). Élie Halévy, *A History of the English People, 1815-1830*, tr. by E. I. Watkin, New York, 1928, p. 64 and note 1.
10. (To p. 45). MS. letter of James Carlyle, Mainhill, 9th March, 1820. Pierpont Morgan Library.
11. (To p. 46). MS. letter of Alexander Carlyle, Mainhill, 10th February, 1820. Pierpont Morgan Library.
12. (To p. 47). MS. letter of Alexander Carlyle, Mainhill, 25th March, 1820. Pierpont Morgan Library.
13. (To p. 47). Compare W. L. Mathieson, *Church and Reform in Scotland*, Glasgow, 1916, pp. 157-60, with the letter of Thomas Carlyle to Alexander Carlyle, Edinburgh, 19 April, 1820 (*Early Letters of Thomas Carlyle*, edited by Charles Eliot Norton, London, 1886, pp. 138-39).

14. (To p. 51). Carlyle's essay, "Characteristics," *Edinburgh Review*, December, 1831.

15. (To p. 53). David Alec Wilson, *Carlyle Till Marriage*, London, 1923, p. 208 and note 1. Carlyle's Diary for December 7, 1826. J. A. Froude (*Thomas Carlyle: The First Forty Years*, New York, 1910, I, p. 302) shows the passage quoted to be a translation from Tieck.

16. (To p. 61). *Sartor Resartus*, Book II, Chapter VII.

17. (To p. 64). A. S. Collins, *The Profession of Letters (1780-1832)*, London, 1928, p. 132.

18. (To p. 71). Cited by Edmund Blunden, *Leigh Hunt and His Circle*, London, 1930, p. 212.

19. (To p. 73). V. Stockley, *German Literature as Known in England (1750-1830)*, London, 1929, p. 144.

20. (To p. 82). Edith J. Morley, "Carlyle in the Diary, Reminiscences, and Correspondence of Henry Crabb Robinson," *London Mercury*, October, 1922, Vol. 6, p. 617.

21. (To p. 82). V. Stockley, *German Literature as Known in England (1750-1832)*, p. 258. See also Jean Marie Carré, *Goethe en Angleterre*, Paris, 1920.

22. (To p. 93). See note 20, above.

23. (To p. 113). J. H. Clapham, *An Economic History of Modern Britain*, I, p. 602.

24. (To p. 114). For a fuller treatment of the agricultural laborers' revolt in 1830, see J. L. Hammond and Barbara Hammond, *The Village Laborer*, London, 1911, Chs. XI, XII.

25. (To p. 116). MS. letter of John Carlyle, London, November 15, 1830. Pierpont Morgan Library.

26. (To p. 117). For a fuller account of the Saint-Simonians and their influence on Carlyle, see Emery Neff, *Carlyle and Mill*, New York, 1926, Ch. V, pp. 208-21.

27. (To p. 120). MS. letter of John Carlyle, London, November 15, 1830. Pierpont Morgan Library.

28. (To p. 122). MS. letter of John Carlyle, London, postmarked June 9, 1831. Pierpont Morgan Library.

29. (To p. 128). For a full account of the vogue of the novel of fashionable life and of Carlyle's satire directed against it, see Michael Sadleir, *Bulwer: a Panorama*, I, pp. 97-118, 168-91, 221-224. The attribution to Carlyle of the articles in *Fraser's Magazine*, "Dominie's Legacy; Fashionable Novels," and "Mr. Edward Lytton Bulwer's Novels," of which Mr. Sadleir is sceptical, is very probably incorrect. (See the evidence adduced by Miss Miriam M. Thrall, "Two Articles Attributed to Carlyle," *Modern Language Notes*, Baltimore, May, 1931, pp. 316-32.)

30. (To p. 131). On the subject of puffery, see also: *Biographical Memoir* prefixed to Vol. I of *Papers of a Critic: Selected from the Writings of Charles Wentworth Dilke*, by Sir Charles Wentworth Dilke, London, 1875; *The Literary Profession*, by A. S. Collins, Ch. II and Epilogue; *Introductory Note* to *John Francis: A Literary Chronicle of Half a Century*, by John C. Francis, London, 1888; *Selections from the Correspondence of MacVey Napier*, by his

son, MacVey Napier, London, 1879, p. 110; *The Autobiography of William Jerdan*, London, 1853, Vol. 4, pp. 21-22, 68-70; *The John Bull Magazine*, London, 1824, Vol. I, p. 76.

31. (To p. 136). For an extended account of the relations of Carlyle and John Stuart Mill, see Emery Neff, *Carlyle and Mill*.

32. (To p. 143). For Carlyle's dealings with Napier, editor of the *Edinburgh Review*, see *Selections from the Correspondence of MacVey Napier*, by MacVey Napier.

33. (To p. 145). Carlyle's article on "Corn Law Rhymes," *Edinburgh Review*, July, 1832.

34. (To p. 148). The correspondence of Carlyle and Mill has been published in *Letters of Thomas Carlyle to John Stuart Mill, etc.*, edited by Alexander Carlyle, New York, 1923, and *The Letters of John Stuart Mill*, edited by Hugh S. R. Elliott, London, 1910.

35. (To p. 161). Cited by Edmund Blunden, *Leigh Hunt and His Circle*, London, 1930, p. 225.

36. (To p. 163). For W. J. Fox and his circle, see Graham Wallas, *William Johnson Fox*, London, 1924, and Richard Garnett, *The Life of W. J. Fox*, London, 1910.

37. (To p. 165). MS. letter of John Carlyle, Munich, November 12, 1835. Pierpont Morgan Library.

38. (To p. 176). Carlyle's article, "Sir Walter Scott," *Edinburgh Review*, January, 1838.

39. (To p. 178). MS. letter of John Carlyle, Albano, July 23, 1837. Pierpont Morgan Library.

40. (To p. 182). For a defence of Scott against Carlyle's strictures, see H. J. C. Grierson, "Scott and Carlyle," in *Essays and Studies by Members of the English Association*, Oxford, 1928, Vol. XIII, pp. 88-111.

41. (To p. 185). J. H. Clapham, *An Economic History of Modern Britain*, I, pp. 601-2.

42. (To p. 189). For conjectures as to the causes of the estrangement of Carlyle and J. S. Mill, see D. A. Wilson, *Carlyle on Cromwell and Others*, London, 1925, pp. 171-74.

43. (To p. 193). *Carlyle's Theory of the Hero*, by B. H. Lehman, Duke University Press, 1928, is a thorough investigation of the sources and development of this widespread nineteenth-century idea.

44. (To p. 193). James Fraser died on October 2, 1841, from a lingering illness said by the newspapers to have been the result of a brutal beating in 1836 by Grantley Berkeley, whose historical romance, *Berkeley Castle*, had been reviewed by *Fraser's Magazine* in its usual slashing manner. Carlyle's relations with his new publishers have been touched upon by Arthur Waugh in *A Hundred Years of Publishing, Being the Story of Chapman and Hall, Ltd.*, London, 1930, pp. 74-77 and elsewhere.

45. (To p. 205). Emerson's Journals, which contain the best contemporary criticism of Carlyle, have been conveniently abridged by Bliss Perry, *The Heart of Emerson's Journals*, Boston, 1926.

46. (To p. 207). Beatrice Webb, *My Apprenticeship*, London, 1926, p. 175.

47. (To p. 207). Kenneth Clark, in *The Gothic Revival*, New York, 1929, pp.

152-91, gives an account of Pugin's ideas, which offer striking parallels to *Past and Present*.

48. (To p. 208). *Le Roman Social*, by Louis Cazamian, Paris, 1904, is the best account of the novel of industrial life in the Victorian era.

49. (To p. 209). For Ruskin's relations with Carlyle, see F. W. Roe, *The Social Philosophy of Carlyle and Ruskin*, New York, 1921.

50. (To p. 215). The best study of Jane Welsh Carlyle is by Elizabeth Drew: *Jane Welsh and Jane Carlyle*, New York, 1928.

51. (To p. 217). *Jane Welsh Carlyle, Letters to Her Family*, edited by Leonard Huxley, London, 1924, pp. 170-71. To Jeannie Welsh, 23 Dec. 1843.

52. (To p. 220). In *Monographs*, London, 1873, Lord Houghton (Monkton Milnes) gives an intimate sketch of Lady Ashburton.

53. (To p. 233). Francis Espinasse, *Literary Recollections and Sketches*, New York, 1893, p. 182.

54. (To p. 235). J. H. Clapham, *An Economic History of Modern Britain*, I, p. 466 and note 2.

55. (To p. 246). For evidence that the *Parleying* with Mandeville was directed against Carlyle's position, see W. C. DeVane, *Browning's Parleyings*, New Haven, 1927, Ch. I.

56. (To p. 264). *The Letters of George Meredith*, edited by his son (William Maxse Meredith), London, 1912, II, p. 332-33.

57. (To p. 264). The Froude-Carlyle controversy has recently been reviewed, with conclusions favorable to Froude, by Waldo Dunn in *Froude and Carlyle*, New York, 1930. Carlyle is defended by D. A. Wilson in his current biography (*Carlyle Till Marriage*, London, 1923, etc.), and in *The Truth about Carlyle*, London, 1903. See also *The Nemesis of Froude*, by Sir James Crichton-Browne and Alexander Carlyle, London, 1903. A much less favorable estimate of Carlyle as a man and a writer than that of the present volume has been made by Norwood Young, *Carlyle; His Rise and Fall*, London and New York, 1928.

58. (To p. 267). "Carlyle's Works," by £ (John Sterling), *London and Westminster Review*, October, 1839, Vol. 33, p. 35.

INDEX

➤➤➤ ◄◄◄